Through the Lens of Dharma-Ethics

Through the Lens of Dharma-Ethics

Indrani Sanyal

Suryodaya Books

Cataloging in Publication Data — DK
[Courtesy: D.K. Agencies (P) Ltd. <docinfo@dkagencies.com>]

Sanyal, Indrani, author.
Through the lens of Dharma-ethics / Indrani Sanyal.
pages cm
ISBN 9788192611426

1. Dharma. 2. Hindu ethics. I. Jadavpur University. Department of Philosophy.publisher. II. Title. III. Title: Dharma-ethics.

B132.D5S26 2015 DDC 294.548 23

ISBN 978-81-926114-2-6
First published in India in 2016

Published by:
Department of Philosophy
Jadavpur University
Kolkata - 700 032

and

Suryodaya Books
"Suryodaya", D-36A/1, Mohan Garden
Najafgarh Road, New Delhi - 110 059
Phone: (011) 2535 3435

Distributed by:
D.K. Printworld (P) Ltd.
Regd. Office: "Vedaśrī", F-395, Sudarshan Park
(Metro Station: Ramesh Nagar), New Delhi - 110 015
Phones: (011) 2545 3975, 2546 6019
e-mail: indology@dkprintworld.com
Website: www.dkprintworld.com

Printed by: Suryodaya Books, New Delhi

To

Aindri, Oishi, Saibal and ***Saumi***

my sources of constant inspiration

and respectfully to the memory of my late husband,

Shyamal Kanti Sanyal

kurvanneveha karmāṇi jijīviṣet śatam samāḥ ।
evam tvayi nānyatheto 'sti na karma lipyate nare ॥

— *Īsa Upaniṣad* 2

Doing verily works in this world one should wish to live a hundred years. Thus it is in thee and not otherwise than this; action cleaves not to a man.

— Aurobindo 2004a: 5

Preface

Through the Lens of Dharma-Ethics is the fruit of many years labour. Nearly thirty years back when I joined Jadavpur University as a lecturer in philosophy, among other subjects I was also entrusted with the task of teaching the postgraduate course on Hindu Ethics. Initially I was not quite happy with that particular subject allotment, for as a student I had not developed much liking for the course on Hindu Ethics. Out of utter naïveté and ignorance, I was then nourishing the idea that Hindu Ethics is very doctrinal and it dogmatically seeks individual's actions to comply with the prescribed schedule of *dharma* (duties). But at the same time I knew being a juniormost faculty and an entrant to the Department I have no option but to bear the burden of responsibility. So my journey begun with *The Ethics of the Hindus* by Susil Kumar Maitra, University of Calcutta Publication (1963) and I most gratefully acknowledge my indebtedness to the author of this text, for without the guidance of this particular text it would never have been possible for me to enter into the vastness and intricacies of this kaleidoscopic discourse of Hindu Ethics.

In this volume I have made a modest attempt to express some aspects of the Vaidika Dharma-Ethics without being guided by any preconceived belief or bias. In all cases I have tried to follow some texts to bring out the main contentions of major contributors to this domain. The materials collated, explained and analysed in this volume however are not claimed to be an outcome of exhaustive reflection on the subject matter. This volume *Through the Lens of Dharma-Ethics* itself may be considered as a preface to the whole discourse of Vaidika Dharma-Ethics. I have realized how difficult it is to paint a complete picture of this prototype of

Dharma-Ethics; of whatever infinitesimal I am convinced to be the genuine spirit of Dharma-Ethics, I tried my best to impart to the readers. None the less, my limitations in all respects – in matter of competence on the subject, in selection of texts, in command over language, in skilful construal of arguments and counter-arguments, in communication skill to reach the readers – need to be excused.

I very sincerely remember all my research scholars who did MPhil dissertations or PhD dissertations on areas of ethics especially Hindu ethics under my supervision for giving me ample opportunities to sharpen my understanding of the subject. I express my gratitude to Ms Rama Mondal, Ms Barnita Bandyopadhyaya, Dr Aparajita Mukhopadhyay, Ms Mandira Pal, Ms Susmita Saha, Ms Doyel Mukherjee, Ms Sucharita Mitra, Ms Tamalika Pal, Mr Balaram Karan, Dr Aditi Patra, Dr Meena Arora Nayak and Dr Tamasa Chattopadhyay. I would also like to put on record my indebtedness to my present research scholars namely Ms Gargi Goswami, Ms Susmita Saha and Ms Doyel Mukherjee for academic benefits accrued to me through my regular interactions with them in course of ongoing PhD research supervisions. My thanks are also due to those MPhil scholars who opted for MPhil classes on optional courses offered by me on the Ethics of the Hindus and the Nyāya Philosophy of Morals during different phases of my career.

I have already some publications in anthologies, both in Bengali and in English on the discourse of Vaidika Dharma-Ethics. The following are to name a few: "Vidhir Artha Viṣaye Anunaitika Paryalocanā" in *Bhāratīya Dharmanīti* (ed. Amita Chatterjee, Allied Publishers, Calcutta and Jadavpur University, Calcutta, 1998), "The Just War or the Dharmayuddha", in *Ethics: An Anthology* (ed. Madhumita Chattopadhyay and Tirthanath Bandyopadhyay, Jadavpur University, Kolkata and Allied Publishers, Kolkata, 2002), "The Nature of Human Motivation", in *On Mind and Consciousness: Selected Papers from the MiCon 2002 Conference* (ed. Chhanda Chakraborti, Manas K. Mandal and Rimi B. Chatterjee, Indian

Institute of Advanced Study, Shimla and Department of Humanities and Social Sciences, IIT, Kharagpur, 2003), "Mahābhārata Abalambane Dharmayuddhatattva", in *War: A Threat to Civilisation and Human Progress*, Proceedings of the UGC Sponsored State Level Seminar (Basirhat College, 2005), "Prābhākara Mīmāṁsā sammata Niyoger Dhāraṇā" in *Dharmanīti O Śruti* (ed. Indrani Sanyal and Ratna Dutta Sharma, Jadavpur University, Kolkata and Mahabodhi Book Agency, Kolkata, 2009), "Varṇa and Jāti", in *Ethics and Culture* (ed. Indrani Sanyal and Sashinungla, Jadavpur University, Kolkata and Decent Books, New Delhi, 2010). In the preparation of the present volume, the ideas expressed through these articles have recurred in some cases with additions, alterations and revisions as deemed necessary. Chapter 5 entitled "The Fourfold Scheme of Puruṣārthas" has grown out of the keynote address delivered by me on the occasion of the seminar entitled "Bhāratīya Darśane Puruṣārtha" organized by the Radhakrishnan Study Centre, Department of Philosophy, Rabindra Bharati University in 2012. I express my thanks to the Radhakrishnan Study Centre, Rabindra Bharati University and specially to Dr Sarbani Banerjee, the co-ordinator of the Centre for giving me an opportunity to share my ideas with the august gathering.

I express my deep gratitude to the Department of Philosophy, Jadavpur University, which also happens to be the Centre of Advanced Study in Philosophy, Phase IV, for giving me this opportunity to publish this volume. Without the active encouragement of my friends and colleagues, I would not have dared to publish this volume. I sincerely acknowledge my gratefulness to Professor Gangadhar Kar, present Head of the Department and to my colleagues Professor Sadhan Chakraborty, Professor Madhumita Chattopadhyaya, Professor Saumitra Basu, Dr Aparajita Mukhopadhyay and to my friend-cum-colleague Professor Ratna Datta Sharma for their active encouragement and inspiration. I am indebted to Ms Srabani Biswas and Ms Sucharita Dutta Mitra, two of the most sincere and diligent project fellows attached to the Centre for Sri Aurobindo Studies, Department of Philosophy for their assistance in the preparation of the manuscript of the present volume. My thanks are also due to the respected referees of this book-project, Dr Roma Chakraborty, Former Professor of Philosophy, University of Calcutta, and Dr. Nirmalya Narayan Chakraborty, Professor of Rabindra Bharati University, Kolkata. I acknowledge my gratitude to the University Grants Commission, New Delhi for financial assistance and to Jadavpur University for all sorts of administrative assistance. My special thanks are due to Mr Susheel Mittal for without his cooperation and always ready-to-help attitude this publication would not have materialized. My thanks are also due to Mr Rajendra Agarwal, Suryodaya Books, New Delhi for carrying on the whole process of publication meticulously with utmost dedication. Finally, there are many people who helped me in one way or other, whom I do not mention by their names; to all of them I express my gratitude.

7 January 2015 **Indrani Sanyal**

Contents

Introduction

Through the Lens of Dharma-Ethics offers reflections upon the vast and enigmatic Dharma-Ethics discourse exemplified in the Vaidika Dharma-Ethics, one of its prototypes. The present Dharma-Ethics study delineates a philosophical way of thinking upon the Vaidika scheme of morality. Characteristically, this meta-ethical approach to Vaidika Dharma-morality as distinguished from normative ethical approach does not seek to weigh up pros and cons of actions in terms of their goodness or badness. Ethics is the branch of philosophy that informs us about what is right, what is good or what is duty. Indian philosophical texts and literatures are also engaged with such concepts as duty, right and good. These discussions would indeed provide the basis for furnishing the details about the salient features of morality from the perspective of Indian philosophy. Unlike a normative moral theory focusing upon what is right or what is wrong, the present meta-ethical approach chooses to focus upon what this Vaidika Dharma-morality is all about. This is a second-order approach to morality through constructive imagination based upon some first-order beliefs about *dharma*-morality. As a meta-ethical approach to morality, this book, in its attempt to understand Vaidika Dharma-morality, finds it impossible not to respond to the metaphysical, epistemological, semantic and psychological presuppositions and commitments of such moral thought and practice. With a view to decipher its essential meta-ethical features the present philosophical and conceptual account of Dharma-Ethics proposes to be prudent in its exploration. The Dharma-Ethics covers, broadly speaking, three major ethical traditions of India, namely the Vaidika Ethics, the Buddhist ethics and the Jaina ethics under its fold. The title "Dharma-Ethics", yet not a trendy terminology for the discourse under consideration, was introduced by Bimal Krishna Matilal in the recent past, has captured my imagination as one of the best coinages for conveying the spirit of the subject matter. *Dharma* is an essentially debated concept with enormous complexity and diversity, but the idea remains persistently ingrained within the vast portions of Indian culture. But the very question of ethics or moral philosophy in India has given rise to suspicion from different quarters. The grounds on which such doubts and suspicion have crept up are not same in all cases. There are various reasons that give rise to disappointment and in some quarters lead to malign the prospect of Dharma-Ethics. The major difficulty with Dharma-Ethics is the problem of identifying any one particular literary source or any particular author or at least few authors dealing exclusively with this ethical discourse.

In Indian texts all deliberations relating to morality are found as inalienable part of philosophical discussions. Any search into the source materials of Dharma-Ethics is hardly separable from the source materials of all schools of *darśana* excepting the Cārvākas. It is a Herculean task indeed to identify and enumerate the huge corpus of knowledge spanning over many thousand years which are sources of Dharma-Ethics. In this volume, as it has already been pointed out, an attempt has been made to concentrate upon only the Vaidika Dharma-Ethics, concerning which literary materials lie scattered in different texts of different periods covering a period of at least 4,000 years. The Vedas and Upaniṣads provide a strong foundation to the Hindu view of life. The Vedas are the earliest available records of Indian literatures, which comprise of four sections, Saṁhitā, Brāhmaṇa, Āraṇyaka and Upaniṣad. Of which the Saṁhitās are dated back to 1700–1100 BCE. The texts designated "Vedic" in the sense of subsidiaries of the Vedas is less clearly defined and may include numerous post-Vedic texts such as the later Upaniṣads, all total comprising of 1,180 branches[1] and various other Śruti literatures. Texts which are not considered to be Śruti are known as Smṛti or texts of remembered traditions. Schools of Indian philosophy which cite the Vedas as their scriptural authority are classified as "orthodox" (*āstika*). In *Yājñavalkyasmṛti* 1.3 fourteen sources of knowledge (*vidyāsthānas*) have been enumerated. Madhusudan Sarasvati in his *Prasthānabheda* cited eighteen subjects as comprising of the total scheme of Śāstra, including four Vedas, four Upavedas (subsidiary Vedas), six Vedāṅgas (accessories to Vedas) and four Upāṅgas (sub-accessories to Vedas). The four Upāṅgas include Purāṇas, Nyāya-Vaiśeṣika Darśana, Mīmāṁsā Darśana including both (Karma-Mīmāṁsā and Brahma-Mīmāṁsā), and the whole compendium of Dharmaśāstras including Smṛti literatures, *Mahābhārata*, *Rāmāyaṇa*, Sāṁkhya Darśana, Pātañjala Darśana, Pāśupata Darśana, Vaiṣṇava Darśana and others. The sources of moral knowledge has been summed up by Manu, according to whom Vedas, Smṛtis, principles exemplified in the behaviour of the moral exemplars (*mahājanas*) and one's own conscience (*ātmatuṣṭi*) are generally regarded as the sources of morality.

Though no attempt has been made to cover other exemplars of Dharma-Ethics in this volume, I would also like to draw attention to the vastness and intricacies of literary materials of each of these exemplars. According to the available historical evidences, two other indigenous sources of religious traditions prior to the Vedas and independent of the Vedas in the sense of not owing any allegiance to the Vedas, are the heterodox systems (*nāstika*) namely, Ājīvakas and the Jainas. The Jaina Dharma-Ethics is also another important component of Dharma-Ethical studies. The expression "Jaina" is derived from the Sanskrit term *jina* (conqueror). The Jaina tradition always upholds its principle of *ahiṁsā* (non-violence) as the basic principle of morality and also of

---

[1] Tarkabhusan Pramathanath and Laksana Sastri Dravid, 1843 (Śakābada), *Vedantadarsanam*, p. 218. A detailed chart of Vedic Śāstras has been included in Chap. 1 of this volume.

metaphysics. The *jina* from the Jaina perspective is a special human being who has been able to conquer the bonds of passion through strict observance of different vows or practices, which come closer to what we call nowadays as moral practices, from the bondage of worldly life and values. Jainism though predates the Vedas, scholars ascribe historicity to Mahāvīra, the last twenty-fourth *jina*, a contemporary of Gautama Buddha, sometimes between the sixth century and fourth century BCE, and to his predecessor Pārśva, whose period has been calculated to be at least 250 years before Mahāvīra. Umāsvāti (Umāsvāmi) deserves the credit for being the first to try to systematize basics of Jainism through his text *Tattvārthasūtra* (also known as *Tattvārthādhigamasūtra*). In Prākr̥t language, attempts to deal with Jaina philosophy were done by Kundakunda and Siddhasena Divākara. The conclusive dates of these thinkers are not available though Siddhasena Divākara is presumed to belong to fifth or sixth century CE. Another Jaina philosopher Pūjyapāda, who made commentaries entitled *Sarvārthasiddhi* on Umāsvāti's *Tattvārthasūtra*, belonged to the Digambara tradition. Umāsvāti was held with respect by both the Digambara and Śvetāmbara sects of Jainism. In the tradition of the Jainas and the Ājīvakas the emphasis is upon purification of the soul and for attaining such purification they duly prescribe certain practices, called moral practices.

The Buddhist Dharma-Ethics is another important domain to be incorporated in Dharma-ethical study. It is not possible to trace original teachings of Buddha with certainty for all we derive are records of memorized versions of his close disciples. The source materials for Buddhist Dharma-Ethics are also quite stupendous; the Theravāda scriptures organized into three collections known as *Tipiṭaka* consisting of *Vinaya, Sutta* and *Abhidhamma. Vinaya* of the Sarvāstivādins is preserved in Chinese and Tibetan versions. Each of these Theravādin Piṭakas is further subdivided into Nikāyas and corresponding to these Nikāyas are texts known as Āgamas in the Sarvāstivādin tradition. Because of the spread of Buddhism its literatures have also taken diverse modifications and were written in different languages. The Mahāyāna school of

Buddhism had its origin during this phase. Original Theravādin literatures and Sarvāstivādin literatures may be taken to represent the first stage of development of Buddhism. With the appearance of a large number of commentaries and sub-commentaries on the original *Tipiṭaka* and spread of Buddhism to Sri Lanka and writing of commentaries expounding the texts of *Tipiṭaka* with interpretations, additions and alterations by later scholars modified the doctrines found in the Theravāda texts. Hence source materials for Buddhism in general and Buddhist Dharma-Ethics in particular are huge and complex. In none of these cases of Dharma-Ethics, it is possible to pinpoint few texts or authors as exclusively concentrating on matters concerning morals. No attempt has been made to merge together these three major sub-systems of Dharma-Ethics for it may not be reasonable and practicable too, to subsume all the basic niceties of each of the prototypes under the cover of a single volume. The present study concerning one of the prototypes of Dharma-Ethics consists of this introductory chapter and divides into additional eight more chapters which are briefly stated here.

Chapter 1: What Is Dharma-Ethics and Why It Has Been Entitled Dharma-Ethics

The first source of disappointment about Dharma-Ethics comes from the difficulty in determining the semantics of the expression *dharma*. *Dharma* is used in so many different senses that it has been found difficult to provide any definition of *dharma*. Second, it is very much clear that Indian philosophers have never provided any clear-cut and neatly delineated theories as ethical theories. The professional Indian philosophical texts very seldom contain discussions in the manner of a what we call "moral philosophy" today. Third, Dharma-Ethics has been accused of denying all value to life. The first source of apprehension and scepticism regarding the viability of Dharma-Ethics has been sought to be dispelled in the third chapter of this volume. I have also tried to focus upon various instances of theory formulations and theorizations as evidenced in various texts in most of the chapters of this volume and especially in Chaps. 6 and 7. Of course, I have refrained from speculating about the sense of theory working behind such theorizations. A distinction between upholding a "soft sense" of theory and "hard sense" of theory has been introduced to throw some light on this debate. The objection against Dharma-Ethics as a discipline that demurs booming, buzzing throb of life is none the less damaging. Chaps. 4 and 5 primarily may provide some relief against the caustic remarks of the misguided critics.

Some basic metaphysical presuppositions of Dharma-Ethics have also been discussed in Chap. 2. In Dharma-Ethics the problem of freedom of will has never been elaborately discussed as a separate topic for discussion. But it is quite evident from the discussions of Indian philosophers on the nature of voluntary actions as distinguished from automatic or reflexive actions,[2] that they also recognized the importance of free will. One of the basic presuppositions of Dharma-Ethics is its commitment to the law of *karma*. Law of *karma* is a law pertaining to purposive or intentional action done with the intention to achieve some goal or end. Despite their differences, just like Vedic traditions, the śramaṇa tradition represented by the Ājīvakas, Jainas and Buddhists advocated similar ideas such as *karma* (retributive action) and *mokṣ* (liberation). The provision thus has been made for dispensing with retributive justice through *punarjanma* (rebirth) of the soul (*ātmā*) of the doer.[3] The other theoretical background for Dharma-Ethics is its belief in soul as an eternal entity which from one birth to another is connected with a body suitable to its merit or demerit.

Chapter 2: Basic Concepts of Dharma-Ethics and Their Interconnectedness

Dharma, *ṛta* and *yajña* are the three concepts that have markedly prepared the ground for the Vaidika Dharma-Ethics. The expressions, *dharma*, *ṛta* and *yajña* though not uncommon in popular

2 This has been discussed in detail in Chap. 5, "The Nature of Human Motivation and Agency".

3 Y. Krishnan, 1997, *The Doctrine of Karma*, p. 3.

usages, contain specialized senses in the context of the Vaidika Ethics. The concept of *dharma*, as has already been pointed out, is ambiguous. In fact, the attempt to disambiguate the notion of *dharma* is also not uncommon. Is it possible to conceive one core meaning among the many meanings of *dharma* as its primary meaning or we should accept all these meanings to be on a par as its basic meanings? The enquiry into the meaning of *dharma* may be carried on a three-tier order beginning with the Vedic–Upaniṣadic concept of *dharma*, the Dharmaśāstra concept of *dharma* and the concept of *dharma* as interpreted by the philosophical schools and finally showing whether these concepts of *dharma* are inclusive of one another or not. It should not be supposed that always in a clear-cut way it would be possible to demarcate even all the major senses of *dharma*. There is not much ground for over-ambitiously planning to arrange different senses of *dharma* in clear-cut compartments. Notwithstanding, the senses of the expression *dharma* overlap from one domain to another, a modest attempt is made to present broad taxonomical divisions of the usages of *dharma*.

In this brief discussion, we find that *dharma* has been a significant expression in the context of the Vedas and Upaniṣads, and is loaded with different connotations. *Dharma* as the Truth, the *Brahman*, the transcendental energy, the sustainer of everything, the prime source has been principally acclaimed. Thus understood, *dharma* as the Truth is static, foundational and metaphysical. The other important sense of *dharma* as a cosmic power is also derived from the Vedas and Upaniṣads. *Dharma* in its ethical sense and as duties to be performed by the human beings is also contained in the Vedic–Upaniṣadic texts. It has been suggested that these three senses of *dharma* are, however, not to be treated as three disjointed senses, rather these three may be understood in a holistic tie explaining the basics of the Vaidika Ethics. The Dharmaśāstra tradition puts more importance to action and this feature of Dharmaśāstra led some interpreter to comment, "More important in fact than the actor is the action. One's primary concern should be the propriety of the act."[4] The sense of *dharma,* in terms of actions or duties is not wholly unrelated to *dharma* as Truth, Goodness or Merit. *Dharma* as action is mostly empirical, consisting of physical, mental and speech actions through which an individual makes contribution to the Goodness or Merit. When we enter into the discourse of professional philosophers, we find the ambiguity still persists about the meaning of *dharma.* Different schools of philosophers offer notions of *dharma* from their respective metaphysical positions. The notion of *dharma* as righteousness as merit acquired from the right performance of duties (*karma*s) persists among philosophers. The second important concept prevalent in the Vaidika Dharma-Ethics is *ṛta* (cosmic order). The literal meaning of the word *ṛta* signifies the course of things or natural ways of the world. The expressions, i.e. *satya* (truth) and *ṛta* in the sense of the universal moral order of goodness and justice are often tied together and presented as two fundamental ideas of Indian culture. In *Muṇḍaka Upaniṣad,* it has been maintained that the truth triumphs (*satyam eva jayate*) and what is not *ṛta* does not triumph. *Yajña* is another elusive expression about which it is not uncommon to find a man in the street claiming authority whereas a specialist may shy away from making any outspoken comment about the true nature of *yajña.* This is a vast and intricate concept and not easy to explain. In this section an attempt has been made to bring out the most relevant facet of *yajña* that would apprise us about the true spirit of Dharma-Ethics. In this chapter, an attempt has also been made to establish a close interconnectedness among these three concepts.

Chapter 3: Dharma: As Duties Universal and Specific

This chapter draws attention to the interesting aspect of the Vaidika Dharma-Ethics as represented through diverse literatures unanimously accepting broadly two classes of duties known as *sādhāraṇa-dharma* (common duties) and *varṇāśrama-dharma* (specific duties relating to one's *varṇa* and *āśrama*). Praśastapāda also

---

4 Krishnan 1997, op. cit., p. 3.

classifies duties in the similar manner like that of Manu into *sāmānya-dharma*s (common duties) and *viśeṣa-dharma*s (specific duties). The duties which are recognized as standard duties (*sādharaṇa-dharma / sāmānya-dharma*) are obligatory for all men. The so-called *varṇāśrama-dharma* are also called relative duties. *Dharma* as universal duties (*sāmānya-dharma*) has also been classified into different types. Manu has enumerated following *dharma*s:

- Patience (*dhṛti*)
- Non-stealing (*cauryabhāva*)
- Wisdom (*dhī*)
- Absence of anger (*akrodha*)
- Forgiveness (*kṣamā*)
- Purity (*śauca*)
- Scholarship (*vidyā*)
- Restraint (*dama*)
- Repression of sense-organs (*indriya-nigraha*)
- Truthfulness (*satya*)

Coming to the discussion of specific duties, the Vaidika Dharma-Ethics presents before us two broad scheme of duties, in the first place, relative to the different social classes or, *varṇa*, known as *varṇa-dharma* and second, the duties relative to the different stages of life (*āśrama*), known as *āśrama-dharma*. The concepts of *varṇa-* and *āśrama-dharma* are two pivotal concepts of Hindu morality and over which lots of discussions and debates have taken place. The Vaidika Dharma-Ethics views an embodied individual also in his social setting, as a member of a society or a community. It is expected of each individual to accomplish his obligation to the society through proper performance of his duties. However, the grave repercussions of caste system in Indian society necessitate a re-look into the ideology of *varṇa-dharma*. The Vedic tradition especially is often held responsible for caste and all the issues relating to caste that we experience till today. In this study, I have specifically tried to dig out relevant sections from some literatures to see exactly what the Hindu attitudes to *varṇa-dharma* were. One thing, however, seems to be quite certain that there are also some strong literary evidences for interpreting *varṇa-dharma* in such a way so that it does not turn into a machinery of casteism and oppression. I have tried to convince that a line of clear-cut demarcation needs to be maintained between what Vaidika Ethics ought to have been and what it actually happened to be in the hands of mercenary Vedists (*vedavādaratāḥ*). None the less to arrive at a decisive conclusion either in favour of the theory supporting division of *jāti* on the basis of quality and *karma* (*guṇa-karmagata-jātivāda*) or in favour of the theory supporting division of *jāti* on the basis of heredity and birth (*janmagata-jātivāda*) is indeed a difficult task for there are many supporting or opposing Vedic and Smr̥ti statements corroborating both the viewpoints; we need to ponder basically over the possible ways of resolutions of conflicts, if possible, keeping within the framework of the Vedic tradition. To abandon a theory or to reject a theory by taking the perspective of an external critique would in no way be beneficial in the context of Dharma-Ethics. There are some interpreters for whom *varṇa* and caste are just two sides of the same coin. But persons like Ambedkar had admitted that *varṇa* and caste are not the same: according to Ambedkar the underlying principle of *varṇa* is worthy.

Two other important observations to be drawn on the basis of the discussion of this chapter are as follows:

1. In the Vaidika Dharma-Ethics tradition, emphasis on social obligation of an individual was quite obvious. The logic behind making *saṁnyāsa*, or recluse the final stage in the life cycle is to vindicate that for an embodied social being performance of social obligations is not less important than renunciation.
2. The four *āśrama*s are theoretical preconditions to the concept of *puruṣārtha*s (fourfold objectives) of human existence.[5]

---

[5] In Chap. 4 the fourfold *puruṣārtha*s are being discussed.

Chapter 4: The Fourfold Scheme of Puruṣārthas

*Puruṣārtha*s of humans as have already been pointed out are enumerated to be four and these are *dharma* (morality), *artha* (wealth), *kāma* (desire) and *mokṣa* (liberation). These four *puruṣārtha*s are closely interrelated with one another. However, questions may arise as to if the Indian theory of *puruṣārtha* is only a description of what human beings psychologically desire, and does not have any value or normative component in its meaning, how far the discussion on the theory of *puruṣārtha* would be relevant in the context of Dharma-Ethics. Does the theory of *puruṣārtha* contain an evaluative aspect as well? Does the theory of *puruṣārtha* convey anything about what a human being ought to desire or aim at as his goal? Significantly, the question may be reformulated as follows: what human values should or ought to be valued? In this connection, I have referred to the writings of some recent interpreters who analysed the concept *artha* occurring within the compound word, *puruṣārtha* as containing some in-built value component or normative component. The question, however, still remains, if the theory of *puruṣārtha* is interpreted as the theory of human values, does it necessarily convert itself to the theory of human ethical values?

One of the frequently debated issues, that in Indian culture, no importance has been assigned to human life and worldly existence, may also be considered through this discussion. We may be able to throw some light on the important role of the Vedic viewpoint in generating optimism and encouragement to human existence. It is important to deliberate on the Indian concept of man, i.e. how do Indian philosophers understand the essence of man. Without entering into any detailed discussions about the nature of man, with reference to different Indian viewpoints separately, it suffices to mention, following two central beliefs in general, of *āstika*-minded Indian philosophers: one is man's aspect of spiritual immortality and the other is his aspect of mortality, struggling with daily chores of human existence. Of the four objectives of human life (*puruṣārtha*s) recognized by the Hindu belief system, three objectives, viz. *dharma, artha* and *kāma* mainly cater to this worldly existence; on the other hand, the last one, *mokṣa* is indicative of transcendence. *Dharma, artha* and *kāma* are regarded as three *varga*s, but these are not of equal importance in the scheme of *puruṣārtha*. We have already seen that the regulation of *artha* and *kāma* by *dharma* has been given much importance. To attain goals of *artha* and *kāma*, to be worthy of their purpose, it has been advised, one must always follow moral means. The role of *dharma*, of moral value, has been essential in this fourfold scheme of *puruṣārtha*. It may be the primary reason for placing *dharma* first followed by *artha* and *kāma*. *Mokṣa* as the highest ideal has not find spontaneous support from all the interpreters of this ethics. In this chapter it has also been discussed as to why *mokṣa* as *puruṣārtha* seemed to be quite odd one among the rest of the three *varga*s. A deeper reflection upon Dharma-Ethics has been carried out to show that these objections are rather unsympathetic to the point of view of Dharma-Ethics.

Chapter 5: The Nature of Human Motivation and Agency

In this chapter, an attempt has been made to analyse and explicate the notion of conation or will (*prayatna/pravṛtti*) to find out the causes of its origination. In this connection an enquiry, mainly after *Siddhāntamuktāvalī* of Viśvanātha, has been carried out. The interesting deliberations have been offered in *Nyāyasūtra* and its other commentaries about the nature of *prayatna* marking off the Dharma-Ethics perspective as different from the perspective of the doctrine that matter is consciousness or Bhūtacaitanyavāda. The discussions about the nature of human motivation are plentiful across different philosophical and psychological traditions. The materialistic determinists assume that all thoughts, values, volitions, decisions and acts are the products of physical, chemical or physiological processes going on in the body. The Cārvākas or the Indian materialists also argue in similar vein. The Nyāya-Vaiśeṣika and Prābhākara Mīmāṁsā thinkers provided extensive discussion about the nature of human volition. In Indian philosophy, the Nyāya-Vaiśeṣika thinkers like Praśastapāda,

Viśvanātha and many others have provided elaborate account of volition. Śālikanāth Miśra in his *Prakaraṇapañcikā* elaborates the position of the Prābhākara Mīmāṁsakas about the nature of volition. The discussion about volition, as distinguished from automatic or reflex actions, will throw some light. The Naiyāyikas elaborate the following conditions to account for the desire to perform an action:

1. Consciousness of an act as fit to be performed by an agent (*kr̥tisādhyatā jñāna*).
2. Consciousness that the performance of this act is conducive to a desirable consequence (for the agent) (*iṣṭasādhanatā jñāna*).
3. Consciousness that the benefit is unaccompanied by any stronger evil (*balavadaniṣṭānanubandhitva-jñāna*).

The Prābhākara Mīmāṁsakas do not agree with the Naiyāyika's account of volition. The Prābhākara Mīmāṁsakas maintain that *svaviśeṣaṇavattāpratisandhānajanyakāryatā-jñāna* is the cause for volition. To state preliminarily, according to the Prābhākara Mīmāṁsakas, *kāryatā jñāna* is the cause for volition. Now, what actually is meant by the Sanskrit expression *kāryatā jñāna*? The two expressions, viz. *kāryatā jñāna* and *kr̥tisādhyatā jñāna* are used as synonymous expressions by some thinkers, whereas according to some these expressions are different in senses. In this chapter, the viewpoint of Naiyāyikas and why for them *kr̥tisādhyatā jñāna* and *kāryatā jñāna* are not distinct instances of knowledge have been explained. The *kr̥tisādhyatā jñāna,* i.e. "the knowledge that an act is capable of being performed" is one of the necessary conditions for volition according to the Naiyāyikas. The sense in which the Prābhākara's notion of *kāryatā jñāna* implies something more than the Nyāya conception of *kr̥tisādhyatā jñāna* has also been elaborated in this chapter.

This chapter is an important inclusion to this volume for some important reasons. In the first place, it contains an elaborate discussion about one of the basic presuppositions of Vaidika

Dharma-Ethics, for it is discussion about voluntary action. In any ethical discourse – whether Western or Indian – the explanation of the nature of moral agency rests on the assumption of autonomous agency. The minimum requirement to account for the autonomy of the agent as perceived by the Western ethical theories has been understood in terms of complete independence from any external influences. Second, we find interestingly the important role that has been attributed to cognition and affection in accounting for volition from this Dharma-Ethics perspective. Third, this discussion on the nature of volition made clear its difference from the supporters of the theory proclaiming matter is consciousness (Bhūtacaitanyavāda) and their opposition to the position proclaiming self to be eternal. It has already been pointed out that belief in eternality of the self is another metaphysical presupposition of Dharma-Ethics. Further, since these discussions are done by professional philosophers we also quite obviously discover nicety of theorization within the scope of Dharma-Ethics. That Dharma-Ethics provides far more holistic explanation about the nature of human agency is evidenced from their meticulous enquiry into the nature of *doṣa*s (faults) – *rāga* (attachment), *dveṣa* (aversion) and *moha* (indifference) as igniting voluntary actions. Some Western ethicists have very recently realized bias for rationality fails to give true picture about human decision-making. However, this is an issue to be tackled elsewhere, but not in the present volume.

Chapter 6: Decoding Prescriptions for Actions

The Indian philosophers, who owe their allegiance to the Vedas are known as the Āstika thinkers, and for them the role of Śruti is very important in their philosophical orientation. Among the Āstika thinkers, there are lots of differences of opinion as to the question whether God is the author of the Vedas or not, but each of them accept the authority of the Vedas without question. The Vedas are classified into *vidhi-mantra-nāmadheya-arthavāda-niṣedha* according to their contents. The section of Vedas that deal with *vidhivākya*s (obligatory statements) is important in the context of discussions of Dharma-Ethics. The Āstika thinkers have raised many questions about the nature, implication of *vidhivākya*s and have also tried to provide solutions to these questions from their perspectives. The meaning of *vidhi* has been variously discussed by the Indian philosophers. The *nyāyasūtrakāra* Gautama writes, *vidhirvidhāyaka*[6] (precept enjoins or prescribes to act) and the later interpreters of the text say that statements that direct or impel are *vidhi*. *Vidhi* is taken to mean *vidhivākya*s (imperative sentences) that urge or impel to perform certain actions.

In Indian philosophy different schools like the Grammarians, Naiyāyikas, Mīmāṁsakas including Bhāṭṭa Mīmāṁsakas and Prābhākara Mīmāṁsakas have elaborately discussed this issue. In this connection, a lot of differences of opinion among these schools of thinkers are observed. Indian philosophers have offered different analysis of Vedic sentences. Apparently, the discussion about the analysis of *vidhivākya*s as has been done by different Indian philosophers does not have any direct implication of their views on Dharma-Ethics. But a deeper consideration would show how intimately the issues relating to the nature of *vidhivākya*s have determined the nature of Dharma-Ethics as such. In the context of Indian philosophy, this discussion is very much relevant because of its admitting the Vedas as the source of Dharma-Ethics. Truly speaking, the Vedas are the embodiment of language, heard, spoken or written. It is utterly mysterious, what was heard, said and written in the Vedas as obligatory has been comprehended by the mundane beings to be obligated to work accordingly. The Indian schools of philosophers, who owed their allegiance to the Vedas, however, did not leave the mystery unattended through downright rejection. The domain of Dharma-Ethics is not confined only to the empirical. The Dharma-Ethics spans the complete being of the moral agent which is eternal self in its essence. Whether this sort of ethics is suitable to one's palate is not the object of present enquiry. Thus, the most difficult question is: How is such

---

[6] Phanibhusana Tarkavagisa (ed.), 1984, *Nyayasutra, Nyayadarsana*, vol. 2, p. 327.

a *codanā* (Vedic prescription) empirically known? Sushil Kumar Maitra has very succinctly formulated the question as follows: How is the authority of a scriptural imperative revealed to the moral agent?[7] Through the study of these analyses, we get different alternative interpretations about the Dharma-Ethics also.

Chapter 7: Mitigating Qualms about Dharma-Ethics

The very kernel of Dharma-Ethics that man is possessed of potentiality to attain self-elevation by treading the path of Dharma does not go unchallenged. The idea of moral elevation may be thrown away as a preposterous idea. The highest end itself towards which moral elevation is presumed to be instrumental may be considered to be farcical. Further critics may wonder as to whether Dharma-Ethics with its overwhelming religious tone has any chance to sustain itself without invoking God's intervention. In this chapter, I would like to make some remarks keeping in view some such suspicions directed against the Vaidika Dharma-Ethics. To respond to the skeptics and critics, the discussion has been arranged centering three basic questions that are quite relevant from the context of the Vaidika Dharma-Ethics. These questions are as follows:

1. How may an individual attain moral elevation or acclivity?
2. Why does an individual need to attain moral growth?
3. Does God intervene into the domain of morality?

In framing answers to these questions which are very much relevant for any serious Dharma-Ethics study, I have made use of some insightful discussions from Gautama's *Nyāyasūtra*. In the context of Dharma-Ethics in general and the Vaidika ethics in particular the idea of gaining moral maturity or elevation is not a petty, insubstantial idea. This idea has been elaborated and explained in many philosophical texts of the orthodox (*āstika*) schools of thinkers and also by the heterodox (*nāstika*) schools of thinkers like the Buddhists and the Jainas.

[7] Sushil Kumar Maitra, 1963, *The Ethics of the Hindus*, p. 112.

Chapter 8: Conclusion

The Vaidika Dharma-Ethics – a proto-type of Dharma-Ethics – has been elaborated and explained taking into consideration its generic aspect and its specific aspect in the present volume. It is an endeavour to unearth history of an ideology of a continuing tradition through its various periods of ups and downs. *Through the Lens of Dharma-Ethics,* makes us observe the holistic perspective of the Vaidika Dharma-Ethics. Dharma-Ethics is the representative of an ethical ideology and ethical practices making it a unique model by itself. From our discussion it has been clear that there are three major perspectives, namely the Vaidika, Jaina and Buddhist, that are all accommodated within the fold of Dharma-Ethics. Dharma-Ethics lays down most imposing graph of growth and development of an individual to the highest level of truth or *dharma,* and it is for the moral agent to implement the plan to its detail for elevation through the performance of *dharma* and avoidance of *adharma*. In the process of elevation, the individual does hope for *abhyudaya* (well-being), aspire for *niḥśreyas* (liberation). In Sri Aurobindo's idiom the ideology of *divine life* is in a sense wonderful homogenization of *abhyudaya, niḥśreyas* and something else. Of the various interpretations of the Vaidika Dharma-Ethics, the most sublime is the one that does not demean it with an exclusivist perception.

1

What Is Dharma-Ethics and Why It Has Been Entitled Dharma-Ethics

DHARMA-Ethics is delineated by the discourse centring the concept of *dharma*. It has nearly 4,000 years old history of "obstinate" survival in the soil of India without yielding to the plentiful of other theories and conjectures pouring in, and fading out and replenishing the older visions and versions by the new. The objective of the present study is not to advance any prescriptions of dos and don'ts from Dharma-Ethics for anybody; rather, it is an attempt to offer reflections upon Dharma-Ethics as such and that explains, as has been discussed in the Introduction, the meta-ethical approach of the present study. The present approach may be marked as conservative in its attitude, not in the sense of being old-fashioned, but because of its intention to conserve the essential values of Dharma-Ethics. The present approach as a philosophical and conceptual account of Dharma-Ethics[1] proposes to be reconstructive, that is to be critical, evaluative but not to be destructively critical. The expression Dharma-Ethics is a new coinage, the source of which may be traced back to one of the essays of Bimal Krishna Matilal.[2] I owe some explanation for my use of the title Dharma-Ethics for the subject matter to be offered for deliberation in the present volume. In spite of there being many nomenclatures current in ordinary usages to name the subject chosen for deliberation, the question may be raised about my choice of this particular title. In the first place, I avoided the use

1 Prasad 2008a, "Theorizing in Ethics: The Indian Way", pp. 18-19.

2 Jonardan Ganeri (ed.), 2002, "Elusiveness and Ambiguity in Dharma-Ethics", in *Ethics and Epics*, p. 36.

of the expression "Indian ethics" on the ground that this expression is much wider in scope than the domain of the discourse I would like to consider. India is a country with many religions, beliefs and ideologies with their profound ethical implications and to talk under the title Indian ethics only about the views of major *āstika* (orthodox) thinkers and *nāstika* (heterodox) thinkers like the Buddhists and Jainas would be doing great injustice to the viewpoints that would be excluded from such consideration. There are Christians, Muslims, Zoroastrians and many not-yet-brought into the mainstream world-views — each of which are Indians and they have their ethical values and norms. If any discourse is projected as Indian ethics then all these viewpoints need to be accommodated as well. The other frequently used expression is Hindu ethics, but that expression has not been used quite conscientiously. There are two main reasons for the avoidance of the expression "Hindu" as mentioned above: in the first place there are lots of debates and doubts regarding both the semantics and connotation of the expression "Hindu". It is supposed that the term "Hindu" comes from a Persian word "Hind" or the Arabic "Al-hind" standing for the area of the Indus Valley. It has been presumed also the word, "Hindu" is derived from the Indo-Aryan word "Sindhu" meaning ocean or river. No early Sanskrit source for the origin of the word has been traced. The term "Hindu" has been traced much later in the fifteenth- century Kashmir when it was employed by the Śaiva historian Śrīvara to distinguish Muslims from the non-Muslims. Some have conjectured that the term "Hindu" was used in Sanskrit and Bengali Vaiṣṇava sources in the sixteenth century to demarcate those who were not *yavanas* (Muslims).[3] Towards the end of the eighteenth century the English people widely used the expressions "Hindu" or "Hindoo" to signify the people of Hindusthan, the area of north-west South Asia, who were not Muslims, Christians, Sikhs or Jainas. Some historians have traced the popular use of the term "Hindu" to the nineteenth-century India in the context of establishing a

[3] Gavin Flood (ed.), 2003, *The Blackwell Companion to Hinduism*, p. 3.

national identity to oppose colonialism. Dharma-Ethics is wider in scope for it accommodates Hindu ethics, Buddhist ethics and Jaina ethics within the fold of Dharma-Ethics, though in the present volume attention will be focused upon the Hindu ethics only as an exemplar of Dharma-Ethics. The expression Dharma-Ethics has openness for it leaves possibility for consideration of some other views under its purview. If there are any other ethics which deal with the concept of *dharma* (or allied concepts) as the focal concept may also be included within the fold of Dharma-Ethics. The other expression Vaidika Ethics[4] is not altogether unacceptable. But the scope of Vaidika Ethics is narrower compared to the scope of Dharma-Ethics because of its accepting the authority of the Vedas and thus excluding the Buddhist and Jaina ethics out of its scope.

The most important question still lies to be deciphered: what is Dharma-Ethics? The very complex phrase with the expression *dharma* hyphenated with ethics raises many questions. No doubt some uncertainty may be apprehended regarding this venture to explore Dharma-Ethics for the expression *dharma* is clouded by many shades and layers of meaning. The expression *dharma* is difficult to spell out offhand without adequate considerations because of its oblique significances. *Dharma* is an idea ingrained into the vast portions of Indian culture. The very question of ethics or moral philosophy in India has given rise to suspicion in different quarters. The grounds on which such doubts and suspicion have crept up are not the same in all cases. There are at least three broad reasons that gave rise to disappointment and in some quarters led to malign the prospect of Dharma-Ethics.

The first source of disappointment about Dharma-Ethics comes from the difficulty in determining the semantics of the expression *dharma*. *Dharma* is used in so many different senses that it has been found difficult to provide any definition of *dharma*. *Dharma* stands for, to name a few, truth, intrinsic quality, justice, merit, duty, morality, moral law. Further, different schools of Indian

[4] Sailaja Kumar Bhattacharya, 2000, *The Vaidika Ethics: An Analytical Approach.*

philosophy and religious traditions differed from one another in their use of the expression, *dharma*. This multiplicity of senses of the expression *dharma* led some to admit impossibility of defining *dharma*. This has been the reason for considering the expression *dharma* to be ubiquitous. The essay of Bimal K. Matilal[5] that inspired me to use the expression "Dharma-Ethics" is discussing "elusiveness" and "ambiguity" of the notion of *dharma*. The semantical problem of *dharma* further aggravated the problem of translatability of *dharma* in other languages. P.V. Kane writes:[6]

> *Dharma* is one of those Sanskrit words that defy all attempts at an exact rendering in English or any other tongue.

There is no single text in Indian philosophy that deals primarily with ethics or moral philosophy. It is also undeniable that professional Indian philosophers did not spare much energy in deciphering systematically issues relating to *dharma* (moral philosophy). Bimal K. Matilal writes:[7]

> Professional philosophers of India over the last two thousand years have been consistently concerned with the problems of logic and epistemology, metaphysics and soteriology, and sometimes they have made very important contributions to the global heritage of philosophy. But, except some cursory comments and some insightful observations, the professional philosophers of India have very seldom discussed what we call "moral philosophy" today. It is true that the Dharmaśāstra texts were there to supplement the Hindu discussion of ethics; classification of virtues and vices, and enumeration of duties related to the social status of the individual. But morality was never discussed as such in these texts.

J.N. Mohanty also writes:[8]

---

5 Ganeri, 2002, op. cit.

6 P.V. Kane, 1990, *History of Dharmaśāstra*, vol. 1, p. 1.

7 Bimal K. Matilal, 1992, "Moral Dilemmas: Insights from Indian Epics", in *Moral Dilemmas in the Mahābhārata*, p. 5.

8 J.N. Mohanty, 2000, "Moral Philosophy", in *Classical Indian Philosophy*.

> There are plenty of Hindu writings on virtues and duties. But in these writings there is no provision for providing any theoretical foundation whatsoever.

By drawing comparisons with Aristotle's ethics, Kantian ethics or the utilitarian ethics, it has been found discouraging to talk about Indian ethics. What is meant by theoretical foundation, however, has not at all been clarified by Mohanty. Again there are philosophers who are in favour of abandoning any project for the derivation of moral laws and principles from any theory whatsoever. From the observation of Matilal and Mohanty, it is clear that Indian philosophers have never provided any clear-cut delineated theories as ethical theories. But from the writings of Matilal and Mohanty it is quite evident that none of them would concede that morality or ethics was never a subject for discussion. It has also been observed that in many cases in discussing any moral problem, the Indian philosophers are suggesting or presupposing theories. Mohanty, however, most plausibly, I believe must have desired to provide an insightful suggestion for working out some theoretical foundation for Dharma-Ethics out of lavishly strewn and engaging philosophical, historical, Dharmaśāstra-centric literary source materials, when he writes:[9]

> Ethics is sought to be grounded:
>
> 1. In a hermeneutic of injunctive sentences,
> 2. In a psychological theory regarding how the human mind works,
> 3. In a metaphysics of the Self.

In this connection, one of the most intensely debated questions in the domain of Western ethics regarding the nature of theory in ethics can hardly be overlooked. The thinkers who seek justification for introducing specialized theory in a moral context are not less. The strong anti-theory standpoint in the domain of

---

[9] J.N. Mohanty, 2001, "Indian Thought: Between Tradition and Modernity", in *Explorations in Philosophy: Essays by J.N. Mohanty*.

ethics repudiates the move to identify ethical theory with the formulations of certain exceptionless universal moral principles. Some recent proponents of virtue ethics like Annette Baier and Bernard Williams belong to this camp. Many Western ethicists have grown suspicious about the overzealous endeavour for reinstating claims for ethical theory. In the history of Western ethics, Aristotle is one of the acclaimed ethical theorists par excellence. But it would be a too rash estimation of Aristotle to thrust upon him the tag of being the proponent of an exceptionless universal moral principle for all men. Aristotle did not propose to treat all men equally without preference, without any consideration whatsoever. The lesson to be drawn from this disclaimer is that a moral theorist may not necessarily be committed to embrace any exceptionless universal moral principle. How far recognized ethical theorists like Immanuel Kant or John Stuart Mill can be labelled as the formulator of theory, taking the notion of theory in the sense in which it is the target of disavowal of anti-theory ethicists, is indeed a debatable issue. No such discussion is outrightly available in the domain of Dharma-Ethics, but to reinstate Dharma-Ethics on a theoretical footing, astute implications of some such debates are unquestionably worthy of perusal. That the notion of theory is not an unambiguous notion is evidently shown by the stark division created between the strong protagonist of theory in moral philosophy and theorist generally spoken thereof. This division may be read as between the protagonist of moral theory, advocating a "hard" sense of theory and the recognized theorists in general of moral theory as advocating a "soft" sense of theory. Purely idiosyncratic particularistic and intuitive anti-theoretical attitude is not to be confused with the promotion of anti-theoretical perspective. No doubt, moral life, an inseparable aspect of human life as such, is too rich, too complex and too vast to be fathomable by a single theory. On the other hand, because of richness and complexity of moral life, it cannot be left to the mercy of ordinary intuition fraught with contradictions and inconsistencies. Hence the need for moral theory for systematization, of course, interpreting the expression "theory" quite broadly, cannot be said to have worn out either. In the so-called "soft" sense of theory, there is demand for theory in ethics. What is important to keep in mind is that in the case of Dharma-Ethics our objective is not to found Dharma-Ethics on certain uncompromising and invariable principles for the sake of theorization, thus taking "hard" sense of the expression "theory". The theory, understood in the "soft" sense of the term, percolates implicitly throughout the layers of Dharma-Ethics which is to be brought out. In the context of Dharma-Ethics one grand, exceptionless, uniform moral principle is a far cry.[10]

One of the very important things about Dharma-Ethics is its close association with metaphysics. In the case of Dharma-Ethics in general and in Hindu ethics particularly it is not possible to understand their moral viewpoint properly without taking into consideration basic metaphysical presuppositions behind their ethical theories and concepts. Second, some psychological considerations are also very much important. The moral agent is a psychological being and his psychological traits, desires, aversions and actions are relevant in making him a moral agent that he is. Third important aspect of Hindu Ethics is its inseparable binding with the type of philosophy of language endorsed by it. It has already been pointed out that Hindu Ethics is representative of multiplicity of viewpoints, hence we should not search for one uniform philosophy of language as a scaffolding to support Hindu Ethics. The Vedas, to the authority of which all branches of Hindu Ethics submit, are nothing but collection of sentences. In other words, rooted in the Vedas, which are the collection of sentences of Dharma-Ethics, Hindu Ethics presupposes explanation and linguistic analysis of injunctive sentences (*vidhivākya*). The quoted remark of Mohanty, from my reading of these lines, may be taken to suggest, if any systematic enquiry into Dharma-Ethics is to be undertaken, it is required to be done by attending to all these three crucial aspects of it.

---

[10] Rajendra Prasad dealt elaborately with the pros and cons of theorization in Indian ethics. R. Prasad, 2008a, "Theorizing in Ethics: The Indian Way", in *A Conceptual–Analytic Study of Classical Indian Philosophy of Morals*.

There are staunch critics who straightway reject the possibility of ethics in Indian philosophy because of its life-denial attitude. Dharma-Ethics has been accused of denying all value to life.

> It expels all volitional individuality; it preaches the unreality of the world, detachment from terrestrial interests, the unimportance of the life of the moment compared with the endless chain of past and future experiences.[11]

According to the European critic, life, the thing on which he puts an entire and unquestioning value, has been questioned in Indian philosophy. These objections, however, will be addressed in course of discussions. Keeping all these nuances in mind, I would like to proceed in this volume and whenever occasion arises I would like to suggest replies to these observations. *Dharma* is no doubt an "elusive" and "ambiguous" concept and to venture into Dharma-Ethics is not a trifling matter. Matilal perceived a "breath-taking complexity" in the very concept of *dharma*. Notwithstanding, various objections, suspicions against Dharma-Ethics, the very existential human predicament as to why should a Hindu be moral, why should a Buddhist be moral or why should a Jaina be moral turns out to be the motivating factor. What are the foundational beliefs, if any, that mould the purpose of human life? In other words, what are beliefs and how according to these beliefs life should be or ought to be directed? However, in this chapter, to determine the subject matter and range of Dharma-Ethics I would like to begin by dealing with the following:

1. Sources of moral knowledge.
2. Some basic metaphysical presuppositions of Dharma-Ethics.

The other important tasks of historical conceptual analysis of the concepts of *dharma* and explication of some other pivotal allied concepts of *dharma* are to be undertaken in the second chapter.

One thing is already clear that no single text can ever be sufficient to take stock of all the diversities and subtleties of

---

11 Sri Aurobindo, 1998, *The Foundations of Indian Culture*, p. 71.

Dharma-Ethics which is pulling through nearly 4,000 years. Hence it is very difficult to stick to any particular text as the source material for Dharma-Ethics. An impressive body of literatures dealt with the Dharma-Ethics in the tradition of the Hindus, Buddhists and Jainas. The Dharma-Ethics as an umbrella concept is flexible enough to accommodate varieties of viewpoints. But it is not possible to cover in a single volume all the shades of Dharma-Ethics, I would be mainly concentrating on the viewpoints of the Vedic–Upaniṣadic Dharma-Ethics. As prototypes of Dharma-Ethics I would concentrate on many instances on the Nyāya philosophical literatures and also to some extent on the Mīmāṁsā, and Yoga texts. Thus the overall presentation of Dharma-Ethics would be done by reference to the Vedas and Upaniṣads, second, by reference to *dharma* literatures including *Manusmṛti, Rāmāyaṇa* and *Mahābhārata*. Third, if and when necessary by reference to the philosophical literatures of different schools of philosophy, concepts and ideas would be explained.

Sources of Moral Knowledge

How do we derive knowledge of *dharma* and *adharma* is no doubt an important question. The sources of moral knowledge have been summed up by Manu. According to him Veda, Smṛti, principles exemplified in the behaviour of the moral exemplars (*mahājana*) and one's own conscience (*ātmatuṣṭi*) are generally regarded as the sources of morality. The same idea has also been conveyed through *Yājñavalkyasmṛti*, which maintains:

> *śrutiḥ smṛtiḥ sadācāraḥ svasya ca priyamātmanaḥ* |
> *śamyak saṁkalpajaḥ kāmo dharmāmūlam idaṁ smṛtam* ||[12]

Following the authors of Dharmaśāstras like Manu and Yājñavalkya, sources of moral knowledge may be traced. A descriptive account of the source materials for Dharma-Ethics is being presented in this section. To provide a scoop of Dharma-Ethics out of this vast, time-honoured and impressive source material spreading over the period of 4,000 years, if not more, is

---

12 *Yājñavalkya Saṁhitā* 1.7.

indeed a challenging task. A brief introduction is provided to give an account of each of the specific Śāstras whose influence, if not always as regards direct authorization, has been held to play a decisive role in the formation of what is today nick-named as Dharma-Ethics.

Dharma-Ethics is an inalienable part of Indian philosophy, hence one of the ways to trace the domain of Dharma-Ethics is to trace it through the periods of history of Indian philosophy, which may be divided into stages or periods as follows:

VEDIC PERIOD

The Vedic period may be divided into two:

1. *Pre-Upaniṣadic Period*: Each Veda consists of two parts, viz. the *mantra*s (metrical hymns) and the Brāhmaṇas, which are liturgical in character.
2. *Upaniṣadic Period*: Upaniṣads are the final section of the Brāhmaṇas and are considered as the fountainhead of all Indian philosophy.

POST -VEDIC PERIOD

The Post-Vedic period is divided into two:

Early Post-Vedic Period

1. The period of the *mahākāvya*s, like *Rāmāyaṇa* and *Mahābhārata*
2. *Bhagavadgītā*
3. Early Buddhism
4. Jainism.

Later Post-Vedic Period

I. The period of *Manusmṛti* and other body of vast *dharma* literatures.

II. Age of schools of philosophy:

   i. Materialism

   ii. Later Buddhist schools

iii. Nyāya-Vaiśeṣika

iv. Sāṁkhya–Yoga

v. Pūrva-Mīmāṁsā

vi. Vedānta (Advaita, Viśiṣṭādvaita).

In *Yājñavalkya Saṁhitā*, as the sources of *dharma* names of the following literatures are given: Purāṇa, Nyāya, Mīmāṁsā, Dharmaśāstra, Vedāṅga and Vedas – these are the roots of knowledge and religion.[13] We may begin by recapitulating these sources of Dharma-Ethics. Veda means knowledge. In a sense Veda is an extra-sensory (*alaukika*) means of knowledge which enables a person to attain to what is desirable and to reject what is undesirable: *Iṣṭaprāpti aniṣṭa aparihārāya alaukikamupāyam yaḥ vedyati sa vedaḥ*. It has been said that things that are not known by perception and inference are known by the Vedas and that constitute the very essence of the Vedas. The Vedas are the trustworthy assertions relating to the imperceptible (*adṛṣṭārtha*). The four Vedas (*Ṛgveda, Sāmaveda, Yajurveda* and *Atharvaveda*) are the oldest extant texts of India. The four Vedas are called Śruti, (something (revealed) heard). No exact dates of the Vedas are known. The oldest text, *Ṛgveda* has been supposed to be more or less of the period 1450–1350 BCE. The last Veda (*Atharvaveda*) is supposed to be of the period 1200–1000 BCE and the lifetime of Buddha has been calculated to be of 400 BCE, which is after almost all the Vedic texts. The Vedic texts were orally composed and transmitted without any break from the teacher to the student, which were formalized later on. The Vedas have been written down during the early second millennium CE. Their language is known as the Vaidika language, from which Sanskrit has been supposed to have derived. The collection of *mantras* is called Saṁhitā. There are four Saṁhitās – *Ṛg, Yajur, Sāma* and *Atharva*. According to one view, there were originally only three Vedas – *Ṛg, Yajur* and *Sāma* and were collectively known as *trayī* (triad)

---

[13] *purāṇanyāyamīmāṁsā dharmaśāstrāṅgamiśritāḥ* |
vedāḥ sthānani vidyānāṁ dharmasya ca caturdaśa || – 1.3

and *Atharvaveda* was a later addition. Sāyaṇācārya in his commentary on *Atharvaveda,* however, supports the view that the Vedas are four and argues for the importance of *Atharvaveda*. The Brāhmaṇas as commentaries prescribe rules and regulations for the performance of action like sacrifices, etc. All the statements of the Brāhmaṇas are divided into three classes, namely Vidhi, Arthavāda and Anuvāda. Vidhi constitutes the main subject of the Brāhmaṇas. The Vidhis are injunctions expressed as imperative statements enjoining one to perform a particular act like sacrifice to attain a specific consequence. We have already referred to that discussion about the nature of injunctions (*vidhivākyas*) as an important aspect of the Vaidika Dharma-Ethics. There are Arthavāda statements whose sole purpose is to arouse respect (*śraddhā*) among men regarding the performance of duties enjoined by the injunctions (*vidhis*). The Anuvādas are statements which repeat injunctions or directions laid down in the Vedas.

The Brāhmaṇas are divided into three sections – Brāhmaṇa, Āraṇyaka and Upaniṣad. Thus the Veda comprises of four sections, Saṁhitā, Brāhmaṇa, Āraṇyaka and Upaniṣad. The Āraṇyaka and the Upaniṣad are regarded as the fountainhead of all Indian philosophy. Each Veda is again divided into four parts:

1. Saṁhitās (collections of *mantra*),
2. Brāhmaṇas (commentaries),
3. Āraṇyakas, and
4. Upaniṣads.

Certain classes of works regarded as auxiliary to the Vedas (Vedāṅgas) and are designed to help in the correct pronunciation and interpretation of the text and the right employment of the *mantras* in ceremonies. They are six in number:

1. Śikṣā (the science of proper articulation and right pronunciation),
2. Chanda (prosody),
3. Vyākaraṇa (grammar),

4. Nirukta (etymological explanation of different Vedic words),
5. Jyotiṣa (astronomy), and
6. Kalpa (ritual or ceremonial).

Dharmasūtras are ancient Sanskrit treatises on the subject of *dharma*. Dharmasūtras are at least theoretically a part of the Vedic literature. They are subsumed under the broader category of Kalpasūtras, together with Śrautasūtras, Gṛhyasūtras and Dharmasūtras. The authority of Dharmasūtra texts is considered to be less weighty than that of the older Saṁhitās and Brāhmaṇas; the latter are Śruti, the Dharmasūtras are Smṛti (recollection).

The Dharmaśāstras are written in verses. It includes *Rāmāyaṇa, Mahābhārata,* and a vast body of Dharmaśāstra literatures. The Dharmaśāstras deal with the same subject matter as the Dharmasūtras and they are held to be more recent and no longer attached to specific Vedic schools. They are also part of Smṛti texts. Traditionally *Manusmṛti* or *Mānavadharmaśāstra* is recognized as the oldest and most important of all Dharmaśāstras. Smṛti literatures are also considered to be the important sources of morality. The Smṛti is also supposed to have divine origin. According to one belief, it has been held that the subject matter of Smṛti was communicated by the self-sprung Brahmā to Manu and he taught it to ten sages, viz. Marīci, Atri, Aṅgirā, Pulastya, Pulaha, Kratu, Pracetas, Vasiṣṭha, Bhṛgu and Nārada. The Dharmaśāstra is not a single book, but consists of Saṁhitās (a collection of texts), according to Yājñavalkya, authored by twenty sages, namely, Manu, Atri, Viṣṇu, Hārīta, Yājñavalkya, Uśanas, Aṅgirā, Yama, Āpastamba, Saṁvarta, Kātyāyana, Bṛhaspati, Parāśara, Vyāsa, Śaṅkha, Likhita, Dakṣa, Gautama, Śātātapa and Vasiṣṭha. To quote Yājñavalkya:

> *manvatriviṣṇuhārītayājñavalkyośano 'ṅgirāḥ*
> *yamāpastambasaṁvarttāḥ kātyāyanabṛhaspatī* ।
> *parāśaravyāsaśaṅkhalikhitā dakṣagotamau*
> *śātātapo vasiṣṭhaśca dharmaśāstraprayojakāḥ* ॥[14]

---

[14] *Yājñavalkya Saṁhitā* 1.4-5.

But the names of sages provided by Yājñavalkya do not always match with the names given by other authors of Dharmaśāstra. The list of names of sages derived from Yājñavalkya includes the name of the Sage Parāśara; but in the Dharmaśāstra attributed to the Sage Parāśara some of the names of sages, such as Yama, Vyāsa and Bṛhaspati as mentioned in *Yājñavalkyasmṛti*, are excluded and some new names of sages such as Kaśyapa, Gārgya and Pracetas are included. Again in *Padma Purāṇa*, altogether names of thirty-six sages have been mentioned by incorporating additional names of following sages along with the list of names of sages provided by Yājñavalkya, excepting the mention of the name of the Sage Atri as occurring in *Yājñavalkyasmṛti*: Marīci, Pulastya, Pracetas, Bhṛgu, Nārada, Kaśyapa, Viśvāmitra, Devala, Ṛṣyaśṛṅga, Gārgya, Baudhāyana, Paiṭhīnasi, Jāvāla, Samantu, Pāraskara, Logākṣi and Kauthumi.

Again in some other texts like *A Commentary on Gṛhyasūtra,* some other new names are found to occur which were not included in the earlier-mentioned texts. Some discussions are also found about the relevance of these Saṁhitās by relating them with each of the cycle (*yuga*) of the world, as believed by the Hindus. Among all these Dharmaśāstra literatures, *Manu Saṁhitā* is most widely mentioned. The later authors of Dharmaśāstra often respectfully referred to Manu as an authority. The exact date of Manu is difficult to determine. *Yājñavalkya Saṁhitā* is often regarded as second in importance to that of *Manu Saṁhitā*. In general in all these literatures, the Vedas and Purāṇas are referred to as authority, but these texts always accept the Vedas as the highest authority. There are clear instructions about how to deal with the cases of conflicts between the statements of Śruti and Smṛti:

> If there is a contradiction between the Śruti and Smṛti, the former is to be followed; but if there is no contradiction, the Smṛti should be acted upon *(Jāvāli)*.

It has also been suggested in *Yājñavalkya Saṁhitā,* "If two texts differ, practical reason must prevail". To find dates of the most classical text is a difficult task and Dharmasūtras and

Dharmaśāstras are no exception to it. The period of the principal Dharmasūtras and Dharmaśāstras may be tentatively fixed between 500 BCE and CE 500. The basic theme of *Mahābhārata* is traditionally ascribed to the Sage Vyāsa. *Mahābhārata* is said to have established the nature of *dharma* and had applied it to particular situations. *Rāmāyaṇa,* ascribed to Vālmīki, deals with the basic themes of human existence through its exploration of the meaning of *dharma*. In the Dharma-Ethics discourse without reference to these epics, much of the discussions seem insipid. The designation of *Mahābhārata* as the "fifth" Veda (*pañcama veda*) provides support to the claim about its being continuous with the Vedas.

The Purāṇas are defined by reference to five topics commonly discussed in all the Purāṇas (*pañca-lakṣaṇa*), which are as follows:[15]

1. An account of primary creation.
2. Secondary creation or the destruction and remodelling of worlds including chronology.
3. Genealogy of gods and patriarchs.
4. Reigns of Manu.
5. History.

These Purāṇas are classified on the basis of different principles. According to one viewpoint there are eighteen Purāṇas and are divided into three sorts: 1. Sāttvika Purāṇas 2. Rājasika Purāṇas, and 3. Tāmasika Purāṇas. Sāttvika Purāṇas exalting Viṣṇu are the following: (a) *Viṣṇu*, (b) *Bhāgavata*, (c) *Nāradīya*, (d) *Garuḍa*, (e) *Padma*, and (f) *Varāha*.

Rājasika Purāṇas glorifying Brahmā are the following: (a) *Brahma*, b) *Brahmāṇḍa*, (c) *Brahmavaivarta*, (d) *Mārkaṇḍeya*, (e) *Bhaviṣya,* and (f) *Vāmana*.

Tāmasika Purāṇas glorifying Śiva are the following: (a) *Śiva*, (b) *Liṅga*, (c) *Skanda*, (d) *Agni* (or in place of it *Vāyu*), (e) *Matsya*,

---

15 This translation is from H.H. Wilson, 1961, *The Vishnu Purana: A System of Hindu Mythology and Tradition*, p. iv.

and (f) *Kūrma*. But there are also other ways of classifying Purāṇas; according to some Purāṇas are divided into four and by some others into six groups.[16]

Nyāya is the system of *āstika* philosophy, the founder of which is Sage Gautama. The special feature of this philosophy is its placing great importance to reasoning. *Nyāyasūtra,* the text due to Gautama, is a collection of *sūtra*s (aphorisms) in five *adhyāya*s (chapters). The Mīmāṁsā is another school of *āstika* philosophy, the object of which is the interpretation of the Vedas. The Mīmāṁsā philosophy is divided into Karma-Mīmāṁsā and Brahma-Mīmāṁsā. According to the prevalent view Purāṇas, Nyāya, Mīmāṁsā and Dharmaśāstras are regarded as the four *upāṅga*s (subsidiary parts) of the Vedas.

About the authorship of these Śāstras and their time period there are lots of debates and controversies. Whether Vedas have authors or not, even if Vedas are admitted to have authors, who else other than God can be their author, what are the requisites for being such an author are issues to which classical Indian philosophers had no unanimous reply. Regarding the Dharmaśāstras even though there is unanimity regarding some personal authorship of those literatures, questions lark as to whether there was a single author or many authors behind their originations. Scholars still rack their brains to decisively clarify their stand in the one Manu vs. many Manus debate regarding the origination of *Manusmṛti*, which is the acknowledged citadel of all Dharmaśāstras. In the case of *Rāmāyaṇa*, *Mahābhārata*, etc. which portions of it were later extrapolations are matters of much disagreement among the researchers. The other important question is about the time of origin of these literatures. The Vedas as we have already pointed out were Śrutis, i.e. revealed (truth) and in that sense originally the Vedas were not written or were

---

[16] The Purāṇas are originally recited by the *sūta*s (bards) before the kings narrating stories of their ancestors. It is a matter of debate as to whether Purāṇas are books or performances. For details on Purāṇas, vide Kane 1977.

not texts. When were the Vedas textualized, at what point of time had the Purāṇas originated – many such unresolvable questions have been sought to be resolved by the scholars by calculating inferentially probable or approximate times of origin. Any attempt to map out the range of Śāstra incorporating all its divisions and sub-divisions may be looked upon with suspicion by the sceptics. The taxonomy of Śāstra, a particular specified way of classification of Śāstra in the manner successfully attempted by science, is difficult to realize. A layout of Śāstra, however may be drawn along with its major branches and sub-branches after Pramath Nath Tarkabhusana,[17] as shown in the next page.

Thus, we find that the Vedas and Smṛtis or Dharmaśāstras are taken to be records of principles or truths given to us by highly gifted and elevated scholars known as *ṛṣi*s (seers). Both of these sources are often regarded as unquestionable or beyond faults. Those two sets together may be called scriptural authorities, i.e. works which state what is morally right or wrong, obligatory or forbidden, virtuous or vicious. These constitute according to Manu and many others sources of moral knowledge. In our account so far we have mainly tried to touch upon these sources of moral knowledge. The other source is the behaviour of moral exemplars or heroes. The assumption is that there are some individuals who are morally perfect or incorruptible and their behaviour can also function as certificates of morality. *Rāmāyaṇa* and *Mahābhārata* however, often presented various instances of lapses of so-called *mahājana*s (moral exemplars). The other organ for certifying the morality of an action is its satisfying or being approved by our moral sense or sensibility, or to be more accurate by our moral conscience. *Manu Saṁhitā* adds *ātmatuṣṭi* (satisfaction or conviction) of moral conscience as a mark for determining morality. But the question remains about the very sense of moral sense or moral conscience. Some scholars have tried to establish a link between the notion of *ātmatuṣṭi* and deliberation or reasoning.

---

[17] Tarkabhusana 1936: 216.

Śāstra

Four Vedas Four Upavedas Six Vedāṅgas Four Upāṅgas

1. Ṛg
2. Yajur
3. Sāma
4. Atharva

Ayurveda Dhanurveda Gandharvaveda Arthaśāstra

Cikitsā Kāmaśāstra Nīti Śilpa Āśava Sūpakāra Kalā ityādi asaṁkhya

Purāṇa
Mahāpurāṇa
Upapurāṇa

Nyāya
1. Gautamīya Darśana
2. Vaiśeṣika Darśana

Mīmāṁsā
1. Karma-Mīmāṁsā Darśana
2. Brahma-Mīmāṁsā Darśana

Dharmaśāstra

Mantra
1. Ṛg
2. Yajur
3. Sāma

Brāhmaṇa
1. Vidhi
2. Arthavāda
3. Anuvāda

Śikṣā
1. Sarvaveda Sādhāraṇa Yathā-Pāṇinīya
2. Pratiśākhā

Kalpa

Vyākaraṇa
1. Secular
2. Vedic

Nirukta
1. Nirukta
2. Nighaṇṭu

Chanda
1. Laukika
2. Vedic

Jyotiṣa
1. Saṁhitā
2. Jātaka
3. Praśna

Smṛti Mahābhārata Sāṁkhya Darśana Pāśupata Others

Śrautasūtra Gṛhyasūtra Dharmasūtra Rāmāyaṇa Pātāñjala Darśana Vaiṣṇava

While outlining sources of moral knowledge in the discourse of Dharma-Ethics, we are really moving round the corpus of knowledge formed centring the four Vedas, *R̥g*, *Yajur*, *Sāma* and *Atharva*; their four subsidiary or minor Vedas (Upavedas) dealing with the art of healing (Ayurveda), archery (Dhanurveda), music and aesthetics (Gandharvaveda) and Arthaśāstra; six branches of Vedas (Vedāṅgas) namely Śikṣā, Kalpa, Vyākaraṇa, Nirukta, Chanda and Jyotiṣa; and four minor sub-branches (*upāṅga*s) including Purāṇas, Dharmaśāstras, Nyāya and Mīmāṁsā. What is important to note that the whole corpus of these literatures is not providing materials only for Dharma-Ethics. In spite of there being different subjects of concern in these literatures, there are large materials also in some literatures relating to *dharma* and *adharma*. In course of our discussion we will get some idea about the specific sources out of this body of knowledge which is relevant for Dharma-Ethics. The rootedness of the Vaidika Dharma-Ethics, however, in the Vedas, is undeniable. The discussion of good or bad, virtue or vice, right or wrong whatever would be discussed in Dharma-Ethics must be rooted in the Vedas finally. The sources of moral right, good and virtue have to be traced back to the Vedas. But some questions arise as to if a certain thing is considered morally right or obligatory by some Veda or Vedas, then does it become morally right necessarily? Or, if something is accepted as good, right or virtuous does it mean that it has been accepted to be so because the Vedas say so-and-so? Under such situations what would be the relevance for Dharma-Ethics? Does not such authoritarian viewpoint reduce Dharma-Ethics to a dogma? These are indeed serious snags to our proper understanding of Dharma-Ethics. Philosophers do not close the door for further enquiry and analysis: it may be suggested, instead of accepting the first premise without deliberation, there is a scope for accepting the second premise and to look into its acceptability.

1. Something is accepted as good, right because the Vedas said so.

2. Something is said to be good or right by the Vedas, because that is the Truth.

Some Basic Metaphysical Presuppositions of Dharma-Ethics

In order to grasp what is Dharma-Ethics and what is its objective, we need to have some clear idea about its basic metaphysical presuppositions. In fact, it is hardly possible to have pristine pure Dharma-Ethics which is absolutely free from any sort of qualifications whether of Vedic-Upaniṣadic, Buddhist or Jaina and thus paving the way to focus exclusively upon the features of Dharma-Ethics. These are contents of Dharma-Ethics and devoid of these contents it becomes an empty idea. The Dharma-Ethics is the very inalienable core of Indian philosophy except the Cārvāka philosophy. Two primary requisites for any ethical discourse are its notion of a moral agent and its notion of action or to be more specific, free actions. The notion of agency and notion of autonomy of the agent in the performance of his actions are two pivotal concepts in any moral discourse and Dharma-Ethics is no exception to this demand.

One of the fundamental presuppositions of ethics is the belief in the freedom of will. The discovery of the principle of indeterminacy in the field of modern physics has given a unique twist to the age-old controversy over the freedom of the will. Science, which itself behaved to be the foe of any kind of indeterminism, has gone into the reverse and has acknowledged a certain kind of freedom even in the world of physical reality. This change of perspective in science has led to the reassessment of the question as to what it is to be free? The question is, whether a person's actions are free in the sense that they are not necessitated, determined and made certain, predictable by antecedent factors in the total situation. From the opposite side, it may also be asked are not human actions, like everything else in nature, under the reign of natural law, which rigidly determines whatever happens in the world, including human behaviour? Are we not all caught in the clutches of the law of cause and effect, so that every act of ours is caused by some preceding event or condition?

Two schools of psychology, particularly behaviourism and psycho-analysis, tend to teach that human activities are entirely determined by events taking place before hand in nature. The determinist argues that human acts like all other events in nature obey nature's laws. Seen from this deterministic perspective the idea of freedom seems to conflict with every scientific canon. The concept of freedom of will has been discussed at great length in different literatures on Western ethics. The freedom of will expresses through such actions where the choice or selection of the agent is involved in the performance or non-performance of the action. Thus broadly speaking voluntary acts, intentional acts come within the purview of such acts where the freedom of the agent has been admitted. These actions are definitely supposed to be different from other actions where the provision for freedom has been sealed. In Dharma-Ethics the problem of free will has never been so elaborately discussed. It is quite evident from the discussions of Indian philosophers on the nature of voluntary actions as distinguished from automatic or reflexive actions,[18] that they also recognized the importance of free will. One of the basic presuppositions of Dharma-Ethics is its commitment to the law of *karma*. The law of *karma* is a law pertaining to purposive or intentional action done with the intention to achieve some goal or end. It has an aim or objective which could be positive or negative. But when we come to Karmavāda, the question naturally arises as to whether the adherence to such a theory leaves room for freedom of will in Dharma-Ethics? Before addressing this question, some basic observations about the law of *karma* may be attempted. In the first place, the law of *karma* means that whatever action is done with desire (*sakāma-karma*) by an individual leaves behind it some sort of potency *karmāśaya*, *apūrva* or *adr̥ṣṭa* which has the power to lay down for him joy or sorrow in the present life or

[18] This has been discussed in detail in Chap. 5, "The Nature of Human Motivation and Agency".

future according as it is good or bad. The necessary corollary to it is the law of conservation which implies that there is no loss of the effect of work done, or *kṛtapraṇāśa* and that there is no happening of events to a person except as the result of his own work (*akṛtābhyāpagama*).

The *karma* doctrine holds not merely that the events of our life are determined by their antecedent causes, but also instills the spirit of the proverbial phrase, "As you sow, so you reap", thus creating the impression of getting justice through the rewards and punishment, in the form of joys and sorrow, that fall to our lot. This claim of the theory about what the doer deserves, or, is entitled to get back in the form of reward or punishment, which makes the law of *karma*, a moral law or a postulate of morality, and not merely the claim that good actions lead to happiness.[19] In Dharma-Ethics one important way of classifying actions is on their "effectuating potential, their effect-producing capacity, or consequential preparedness or readiness".[20] The actions that have been performed with the desire for some consequences are classified broadly into two categories according to their effect-producing "readiness" is as follows:

Actions Performed with Desire (*Sakāma-karma*)

↓

Prārabdha-karma (already effectuating actions) | *Anārabdha-karma* (not-yet-effectuating actions)

Prārabdha-karma ↓

Sañcita-karma (already-done-but-not-yet-effectuating actions) | *Sañcīyamāna-karma* (actions which-are-being-done)

The consequences of the *prārabdha-karma*s can in no way be avoided. The results of *sañcita-karma* may be avoided by attaining

[19] This aspect of Karmavāda has been very clearly elucidated by Rajendra Prasad in his *Karma, Causation and Retributive Morality* (1989).

[20] Prasad 2008b, *A Conceptual–Analytic Study of Classical Indian Philosophy of Morals*, p. 407.

right knowledge. Śaṅkarācārya has said that the attainment of highest knowledge, i.e. knowledge of the self when attained, the *sañcita-karma* and *sañcīyamāna-karma* lose the capacity to produce effects. In this regard the agreement of Rāmānuja with Śaṅkarācārya is evident from his remark, IV.i.15 of *Brahmasūtra* as follows:

> Only those previous deeds are destroyed, the effects of which have not yet begun to bear fruits.

The notion of *karma* was prevalent from the Vedic period, though from the very beginning was not present in its fully analysed explicit form as it is found in recent time. In the Vedic literatures prior to the Upaniṣads, in the Saṁhitās and Brāhmaṇas, the expression *karman* occurred meaning thereby "any religious act or rite" as sacrifice, oblation, etc. The other expression used simultaneously for *yajña-karma*s is *iṣṭapūrta*. The expression, *iṣṭa* means "what is sacrificed" and *pūrta* means "filled up". In the Vedic perspective, generally sacrificial performances are presumed to go up in the heaven and are stored up there in the heaven and are to be taken possession by the sacrificer on his arrival in heaven. Thus here what are stored are like transcendental treasure (*nidhi*) acquired by the performer of those rites.[21] Some authors[22] have emphasized that the origin of the notion of *karma* has taken place from the Vedic concept of *iṣṭapūrta*. However, there are some differences of opinion among the interpreters about the exact meaning of the expression *iṣṭapūrta*. According to Monier-Williams *iṣṭapūrta* means "filled up or stored up sacrificial rites" or "the merit of sacrificial rites stored up in heaven".[23] This sense of *iṣṭapūrta* is found in *Ṛgveda* and *Atharvaveda*. Thus interpreted, *iṣṭapūrta* is taken as a word, consisting of expresions *iṣṭa* and *apūrta*. But Śaṅkarācārya in his commentaries on Upaniṣads, *Chāndogya* V.10.5, *Kaṭha* 1.8, *Muṇḍaka* 1.2.10, and *Praśna* 1.9, and Sāyaṇācārya

---

21 In Chap. 2, an elaborate discussion will be made about *yajña* as representing all *karma*s.

22 Y. Krishnan 1997, *The Doctrine of Karma*, pp. 3-16.

23 *A Sanskrit-English Dictionary*, p. 169.

(fourteenth century CE) in his commentary on the Saṁhitās interpret the expression *iṣṭapūrta* as a compound expression consisting of terms *iṣṭa* and *purta; iṣṭa* is taken to mean Vedic sacrifices or *yajñas* (*vaidikahotrādikarman*), such as *śrauta karma, yāga, homa, dāna,* etc. and *pūrta* as works of public charity such as construction of pools or reservoirs of water, wells, tanks, temples, rest houses (*vāpi, kūpa, taḍāga, devāgāra, ārāma*). In this sense the expression *iṣṭapūrta* is a compound of expressions *iṣṭa* and *pūrta,* meaning thereby sacrifice and public works.[24] In whatever way the expression *iṣṭapūrta* is interpreted, it is implied that following three common features are ingrained in the very concept of *iṣṭapūrta*:

1. Religious rites or works (*karman*) whose performance has been enjoined.
2. Enjoyment of benefits of performance of *karman* in the highest heaven.
3. The transmigration of the soul of the individual.

These three features also describe the tenet of Karmavāda, which was explicitly later formulated. Even if the expression *iṣṭapūrta* is interpreted in the second sense, it does not go against the hypothesis that the germ of Karmavāda was inherent in the notion of *iṣṭapūrta*. This much is not difficult to establish that *iṣṭapūrta* stands for actions that are performed by individuals with certain end or purpose in view. It is needless to reiterate that the doctrine of *karma* is founded upon the notion of actions performed under some desire, *sakāma-karma*. The notion of *yajña* has acquired some specialized sense, but the interpretation of it as a substitute for the notion of *karma* will be discussed in the next chapter. In the Upaniṣads, the notion of *karma* assumes more markedly its ethical profile. The distinction between good (*śubha, sukṛta, puṇya*) and bad (*aśubha, duṣkṛta, pāpa*) was discussed in the Upaniṣads in terms of their generating good or bad consequences. We may allude to *Bṛhadāraṇyaka Upaniṣad*, which maintains: "By good deeds

---

24 Krishnan 1997, op. cit., pp. 3-5.

good consequences are produced and by bad deeds bad consequences are produced".[25] From the following excerpt from *Praśnopaniṣad* we come across its viewpoint maintaining:

> . . . *puṇyena puṇyaṁ lokaṁ nayati pāpena pāpam ubhābhyāmeva manuṣyalokam* ||[26]

According to the nature of deeds performed by individuals three *loka*s (worlds) are apportioned among them, thus

> . . . by virtue taken to the heaven of virtue, by sin to the hell of sin, and by mingled sin and righteousness back to the world of men restoreth.[27]

Quite similar ideas find expression through *Kaṭhopaniṣad* II.ii.7 saying:

> For some enter a womb to the embodying of the Spirit and others follow after the Immovable; according to their deeds is their goal and after the measure of their revealed knowledge.[28]

It has been observed that in the Upaniṣads the use of the expression *punarmṛtyu* (re-death) that occurred more frequently, though gradually, such usage of the expression was replaced by the expression *punarjanma* (rebirth).

The *karma* theory emphasizes only those effects which relate to the doer. Any action may produce several kinds of effects, some of which may relate to the doer, some to someone else, and some to none. But the *karma* theory leaves out of its concern any such effect that does not directly relate to the doer. Rajendra Prasad has very explicitly brought out that the law of *karma* presupposes

---

25 *Bṛhadāraṇyaka Upaniṣad*, 3.2.13: *puṇyo vai puṇyena karmaṇā bhavati pāpaḥ pāpeneti* |

26 *Praśnopaniṣad* III.7.

27 Aurobindo 2004b: 183.

28 Ibid.: 121

yonimanye prapadyante śarīratvāya dehinaḥ |
sthāṇumanye 'nusaṁyanti yathākarma yathāśrutam ||
— *Kaṭhopaniṣad* II.ii.7

a retributive theory of morality.[29] Generally, the word "retribution" is taken in the sense of punishment and just getting retribution does not ensure complete justice. The law of *karma* also is a theory that ensures that good actions are also rewarded. This aspect of Karmavāda is equally in need of emphasis for finally then only the saying that Truth triumphs (*satyam eva jayate*) makes any impact. The law of *karma*, no doubt, gives prominence to consequences, for according to it, whatever consequence or result one deserves, as reward or retribution for having done an action, good or bad, he gets it simply because he has done that action (which leads to that consequence or result). The law of *karma* has been advocated as a theory of just deserts in morality. No comparison can be drawn with the Western ethical theory of consequentialism or utilitarianism. There are some who consider law of *karma* as thwarting the possibility of Dharma-Ethics; their position may be summed up by the following propositions:

1. One of the presuppositions of morality is freedom of will.
2. Determinism and the freedom of will are antagonistic to one another.
3. Karmavāda involves determinism.

But this sort of easy logical conclusion does not apply to the law of *karma*. On the law of *karma* various discussions have been done and there are philosophers who do not admit the law of *karma* to be a just mechanical principle operating blindly. Some systems of Indian philosophy like the Nyāya-Vaiśeṣikas, for instance, believe that the law of *karma* is under the guidance and control of God, the Supreme Being who creates the world in accordance with the law. It is a law which is centred in God and is sustained by his infinite consciousness and will. The Vedas and Upaniṣads do not subscribe to a mechanistic view of nature. In some other systems, e.g. the Jaina, Bauddha, Sāṁkhya and Mīmāṁsā, the law of *karma* is autonomous and works independently of the will of God. These systems believe that the

[29] Rajendra Prasad, 1989, *Karma, Causation and Retributive Morality.*

origin and order of the world may be explained by the law of *karma* without the supposition of God. The philosophers have argued that the law of *karma* does not totally deny an individual freedom to choose his way of life and act accordingly.

In the fold of Dharma-Ethics, it would be pertinent to draw attention to the distinction that has been admitted between fate (*daiva*) and human effort (*puruṣakāra*). It is difficult to suggest any unanimity among all thinkers on this subject. Within the scope of Dharma-Ethics altogether three broad perspectives are identifiable regarding the importance attributed to *daiva* and human *puruṣakāra*. There are passages from *Mahābhārata* which suggest primacy of human effort over destiny (*daiva*). In *Mahābhārata* 13.6.22,[30] it has been said:

> *kr̥taḥ puruṣakārastu daivamevānuvartate* ।
> *na daivamakr̥te kiñcit kasyacid dātum arhati* ॥

Mahābhārata 13.6.23 goes to the extent of suggesting that in the absence of human effort *daiva* remains unstable: *katham karma vinā daivam sthasyate*. The dialogue between Rāma and Lakṣmaṇa in the Ayodhyākāṇḍa of *Rāmāyaṇa* is worthy of observation regarding the place of fate vis-à-vis *puruṣakāra*. In *Rāmāyaṇa* 2.22.15, while Rāma was consoling Kausalyā and Lakṣmaṇa, prior to his exile in the forest, on many occasions he referred to *daiva* to account for many events. Rāma tells Lakṣmaṇa:[31]

> *kr̥tānta eva saumitre draṣṭavyo matpravāsane* ।
> *rājyasya ca vitīrṇasya punareva nivartane* ॥[32]

Rāma further suggests all those rude words uttered by Kaikeyī to hinder coronation of Rāma and to send him to exile were done under the influence of *daiva*. Rāma says:[33]

---

30 "Human effort follows destiny (*daiva*), that is *daiva* is moulded by human effort. Without effort, *daiva* cannot give anything to anyone." – Krishnan 1997, op. cit., p. 104.

31 *Rāmāyaṇa*, Ayodhyākāṇḍa 22.15, ed. Dhyanesh Narayana Chakraborty, 241.

32 "O Saumitri! It is worth considering destiny as the cause behind my being ascended to the throne, being refused from it and sent into exile."

33 Ibid. 2.22.18.

so 'bhiṣekanivr̥ttyarthaiḥ pravāsārthaiśca durvacaiḥ |
ugrairvākyairahaṁ tasyā nānyaddaivāt samarthaye ||

Whatever strong and rude words uttered by her (Kaikeyī) for preventing my coronation and for sending me into exile cannot be explained without accepting fate to be the cause.

In the case of Rāma, in Ayodhyākāṇḍa particularly, he succumbs very much to the clutches of *daiva* and does not say anything favourably about the role of human effort or *puruṣakāra*. He goes on saying to Lakṣmaṇa thus:

O Saumitre! Who has the perseverance to fight with destiny?
Prior to the enjoyment of consequences of karma, *nothing can be seen of it.*
In the cases of joy or sorrow, fear or anger, gain or loss, origination or destruction,
Whatever strange and unthought of events happen, these are all due to fate.[34]

He concludes this by saying:

Dear Lakṣmaṇa, because of the obstacle to my kingship neither younger mother nor father is to be blamed. They have done all these under the influence of destiny. You know that the power of fate is boundless.[35]

On the other hand, Lakṣmaṇa does not approve Rāma's surrender to the force of destiny, rather he speaks very much in favour of human effort, i.e. *puruṣakāra*. Lakṣmaṇa says:

The person who is able to check the (power) of destiny by his

---

34 *Rāmāyaṇa* 2.22.21-22:

kaśca daivena saumitre yoddhumutsahate pumān |
yasya na grahaṇam kiñcit karmaṇo 'nyanna dr̥śyate ||
sukha-duḥkhe bhaya-krodhau lābhā-labhau bhavā-bhavau |
yasya kiñcittathābhūtaṁ nanu daivasya karma tat ||

35 Ibid. 2.22.30:

na lakṣmaṇāsmin mama rājyavighne mātā yavīyasyabhiśaṅkitavyā |
daivābhipannā na pitā kathañcitjānāsi daivaṁ hi tathā prabhāvam ||

effort, does not lose enthusiasm even if he is imperiled by fate.[36]

The science of health (Ayurveda) which is also considered as a supplement to the *Atharvaveda*, in spite of admitting the doctrine of *karma* also speaks about the cure of diseases, and that has given, according to some, rise to a paradox. The question has been raised as to if diseases and sufferings are due to *karma* performed by an individual, how can there be provisions for the remedy of these diseases and suffering by medicines? The resolution of similar paradoxes may be attempted by utilizing the important distinction adhered to in the domain of the Ayurveda and many other literatures between the concept of fate and human effort.[37] The fate (*daiva*) consists of previously done actions out of which some bear fruits in the present life of the agent. In other words, what is called *daiva* comes closer to the notion of *prārabdha karma*s (already-effectuating actions). Ayurveda also has no way of escape from accepting all sorts of diseases and sufferings thereof (*vyādhi* and *rogabhoga*) are due to actions done earlier. But they also talk of *puruṣakāra*. To quote from *Caraka Saṁhitā*:

daivam ātmakr̥tam vidyāt karma yatpūrvadaihikam |
smr̥taḥ puruṣakārastu kriyate yadihaparam ||

To put it in other words, *daiva*, according to this viewpoint stands for *karma*s which were performed by the previous bodily existents and *puruṣakāra* stands for *karma* performed in this life. Another *sūtra* from *Caraka Saṁhitā* may as well be quoted to bring out the distinction between the two concepts:

daivam purā yat kr̥tamucyate tattam pauruṣam yattvīha karma iṣṭam |
pravr̥ttiheturviṣamaḥ sa iṣṭo nivr̥ttiheturhi samaḥ sa eva ||[38]

---

[36] *Ramayaṇa* 2.23.17:

daivaṁ puruṣakāreṇa yaḥ samarthaḥ prabādhitum |
na daivena vipannārthaḥ puruṣaḥ so 'vasīdati ||

[37] Aditi Patra, 2009, "Ayurveda śāstre svīkr̥ta karmavāda o kichu samasyā", in *Dharmaniti O Sruti*, pp. 245-55.

[38] *Caraka Saṁhitā*, *sūtra* 44, Adhyāya 2, Śārīrasthāna.

All actions of previous lives are to be regarded as fate, and all actions of this life directed towards some end or avoiding some consequence are all to be included within the fold of human effort. Ayurveda gives due importance to both fate and human effort in the success of any action in producing the desired goal of the agent. But it is plausible that sometimes in some context in an agent's life fate becomes more powerful than human effort or vice versa. From all these discussions we can argue that Karmavāda leads to determinism is not a fully acceptable conclusion. However, this commitment to Karmavāda, which ensures that nobody can beat a hasty retreat from experiencing any consequences of any of his actions, is one of the theoretical assumptions of classical Dharma-Ethics. Hence Karmavāda has to be understood in its true perspective to avoid unwarranted interpretations of it. The law of *karma*, as it is clear from our discussion, does not deny man freedom to choose his way of life and act accordingly. If it is interpreted in the sense that the will of man and all his actions are determined, then it is likely to lead to a fatalistic interpretation of the law of *karma*. Further, the law of *karma* is applicable to an individual and not to a society.

However, in the present chapter, I do not want to enter into any further discussion about Karmavāda as a basic presupposition of Dharma-Ethics. But there are other important corollaries of Karmavāda upon which we need to focus. One such corollary is the hypothesis about rebirth. The doctrine of rebirth of soul after death into another body follows logically from the law of *karma*. If a man is destined to enjoy the results of his actions good or bad and if he does not experience them in his present life, he has to experience them in the next life. Krishnan comments:

> Retributive justice is dispensed through *punarjanma,* rebirth of the soul (*ātmā*) of the doer.[39]

We have already touched upon three sorts of *karma* such as *sañcita-karma, sañcīyamāna-karma* and *prārabdha-karma* and different ways

[39] Krishnan, 1997, op. cit., p. 3.

of recurrence of their fruits in the lives of individuals. Thus, from this viewpoint, the transmigration of soul into another body in accordance with the good and evil actions of the individual becomes a necessity. In this connection to substantiate rebirth, we may quote *mantras* from *Śvetāśvatara Upaniṣad:*[40]

> Equipped with qualities, a doer of works and creator of their consequences, he reaps the result of his actions; he is the ruler of the life and he moves in his journey according to his own acts; he has idea and ego and is to be known by the qualities of his intelligence and his quality of self. Smaller than the hundredth part of the tip of a hair, the soul of the living being is capable of infinity. Male is he not nor female nor neuter, but is joined to whatever body he takes as his own.[41]

The doctrine of rebirth constitutes an important feature of Sri Aurobindo's view of man and his theory of spiritual evolution. As he observes:[42]

> Rebirth is an indispensable machinery for the working out of a spiritual evolution: it is the only possible effective condition, the obvious dynamic process of such a manifestation in the material universe.

According to Sri Aurobindo, belief in rebirth "is an inevitable logical conclusion if there exists at the same time an evolutionary principle in the earth–nature and a reality of the individual soul born into evolutionary Nature".[43] It constitutes, says Sri Aurobindo, "the rational and philosophical foundation for a belief in rebirth". He observes:

> It is rebirth that gives to the birth of an incomplete being in a body its promise of completeness and its spiritual significance.[44]

---

40 V.7-10.

41 Sri Aurobindo, 2001, *The Life Divine*, p. 825.

42 Ibid., p. 773.

43 Ibid.

44 Ibid.

The other theoretical background for Dharma-Ethics is its belief in soul as an eternal entity which from one birth to another is connected with a body suitable to its merit or demerit. Therein lies the final presupposition behind all these claims as to the notion of moral agency in terms of eternal but embodied self. The unseen force of destiny or previously performed action has been accepted to effect the formation of the body.[45] The body is the result of persistence of the effect of the previous acts.[46] It has been clearly stated by Uddyotakara that the birth of a being is not a mere physiological process. Uddyotakara says:

> The *karma* of the parents who have to enjoy the experiences resulting from the birth of the child, as well as the *karma* of the person who has to undergo experiences, both of these conjointly bring about the birth of the body in the mother's womb.[47]

Radhakrishnan summarizes basics of birth–death cycle as follows:

> The concrete history of each soul embraces a number of lives.[48]

Long back the same theme recurred in the discussion of the Upaniṣads; according to the Upaniṣadic view, an individual is possessed of body–mind organism but is essentially *ātman* (self). *Kaṭhopaniṣad* 1.3.3 says:[49]

> Know the self as the lord of the chariot and the body as the chariot. Know the intellect as the charioteer and the mind as the reins.

Kaṭhopaniṣad also describes the Self (*ātman*) as residing in the city of eleven gates. The human body is compared to a city (*pura*). It is possessed of eleven gates. The seven gates are located in the upper portion of the body, they are the two eyes, two ears, two nostrils

---

45 *Nyāyabhāṣya* III.2.60-72.

46 Ibid. III.2.60: *pūrvakṛtaphalānubandhāt*.

47 *Nyāyavārtika* III.2.63.

48 S. Radhakrishnan, 1913, *Indian Philosophy*, vol. II, p. 150.

49 *ātmānāṁ rathinaṁ viddhi sarīraṁ rathameva tu* |
buddhiṁ tu sārathiṁ viddhi manaḥ pragrahameva ca ||

and one mouth. The three others are located in the lower portion of the body. They are the naval, anus and the generating organ. One gate is located at the top of the skull (*brahmarandhra*). This city (the human body) belongs to the Self who is unborn, unchanging and self-luminous.[50] All schools of Indian philosophy are not unanimous in detail about the nature of self, but they are unmistakably committed to the eternality of the self, of course excepting the Cārvākas. However, when we enter into more details, we will find that schools of Indian philosophy including both the orthodox and the heterodox philosophers, except the Cārvākas, admit the existence of eternal soul, distinct from the mind–body organism, though they may have some differences in details. All these presuppositions including belief in the law of *karma*, belief in rebirth and belief in eternal self, whatever be the manner of explaining selfhood, are behind the working of the Dharma-Ethics in general. This is the very distinguishing feature of Dharma-Ethics. Neither the Vaidika Ethics, nor the Buddhist ethics nor the Jaina ethics has legs to stand upon, if from those ethical discourses, presuppositions regarding Karmavāda, rebirth and conscious agency are segregated. The *āstika* philosophers agree in holding that when all the consequences of the past deeds are exhausted completely through experiences of births and deaths in the shape of pain or pleasure, no more new desert in the form of merit or demerit accrue to the individual, the individual gets freedom from the phases of *saṁsāra* and rebirth and is liberated (*mukta*).[51] There are different arguments also offered in favour of the thesis proclaiming eternality of self. However, for the present volume, I need not enter into all such discussions. This chapter concludes by quoting the *Gītā śloka*s II.20, 22-24,[52] wherein Kṛṣṇa tutors Arjuna reiterating the immortality of the self:

---

50 *Kaṭhopaniṣad* 2.2.1.

51 *Nyāyabhāṣya* iv.i.64.

52 S. Radhakrishnan, 2005, *The Bhagavadgita*, pp. 107-09:

"He is never born, nor does he die at any time, nor having (once) come to be will he again cease to be. He is unborn, eternal, permanent and primeval. He is not slain when the body is slain.

→

na jāyate mriyate vā kadācin nāyaṁ bhūtvā bhavitā vā na bhūyaḥ ।
ajo nityaḥ śāśvato 'yaṁ purāṇo na hanyate hanyamāne śarīre ॥20॥

vāsāṁsi jīrṇāni yathā vihāya navāni gr̥hṇāti naro 'parāṇi ।
tathā śarīrāṇi vihāya jīrṇāny-anyāni saṁyāti navāni dehī ॥ 22 ॥

nainaṁ chindanti śastrāṇi nainaṁ dahati pāvakaḥ ।
na cainam kledayanty āpo na śoṣayati mārutaḥ ॥ 23 ॥

acchedyo 'yam adāhyo 'yam akledyo 'śoṣya eva ca ।
nityaḥ sarvagataḥ sthāṇur acalo 'yaṁ sanātanaḥ ॥ 24 ॥

← Just as a person casts off worn-out garments and puts on others that are new, even so does the embodied soul cast off worn-out bodies and take on others that are new.

Weapons do not cleave this self, fire does not burn him; waters do not make him wet; nor does the wind make him dry.

He is uncleavable. He cannot be burnt. He can neither be wetted nor be dried. He is eternal, all-pervading, unchanging and immovable. He is the same for ever."

2

Basic Concepts of Dharma-Ethics and Their Interconnectedness

ONE of the preliminaries to the beginning of any study is to provide some explanation of the basic concepts to be embraced in that discourse. The study of Dharma-Ethics is no exception to that requirement and it needs an initial explanation of the basic concepts of the proposed discourse. *Dharma*, *ṛta* and *yajña*, these are the three concepts that have prepared markedly the ground for the Vaidika Dharma-Ethics. The expressions, *dharma*, *ṛta* and *yajña*, though not uncommon in popular usages, contain specialized senses in the context of the Vaidika Ethics. We must suggest what is to be meant by these basic terms to avoid much of the allegations regarding the complexities of these expressions. The first task here is to unravel the semantics of *dharma*, *ṛta* and *yajña* and second, to figure out interconnectedness of these concepts in the province of the Vaidika Dharma-Ethics. No doubt, what is meant by clarity of an expression and how to arrive at such clarity are issues bothering philosophers from time immemorial. To arrive at a compatible solution the clarity of an expression may be sought from the origin of the word, tracing its lexical or other sources, and its uses by reference to the contexts within the discourse.

The fact that the concept of *dharma* is ambiguous has already been pointed out. In fact, the attempt to disambiguate the notion of *dharma* is also not uncommon. Is it possible to conceive one core meaning among the many meanings of *dharma* as its primary meaning? Or are we to accept all these meanings to be on a par as its basic meanings? The enquiry into the meaning of *dharma* may be carried on a three-tier order beginning with the Vedic–Upaniṣadic concept of *dharma*, the Dharmaśāstra concept of *dharma* and the concept of *dharma* as interpreted by the philosophical schools, and finally showing whether these concepts of *dharma* are inclusive of one another or not. It should not be supposed that it would be possible always in a clear-cut way to demarcate even all the major senses of *dharma*. There is not much ground for over-ambitiously planning to arrange different senses of *dharma* in clear-cut compartments. Notwithstanding, the senses of the expression *dharma* overlap from one domain to another, a modest attempt is made to present broad taxonomical divisions of the usages of *dharma*.

Vedic and Upaniṣadic Concept of Dharma

If we trace back to *R̥gveda*, the expression *dharma* is found to occur. Derivatively speaking, the expression *dharma* is from the verbal root *dhr̥*, meaning thereby to hold back, to sustain, to maintain, etc. In *R̥gveda*, often *dharma* is explained as the sustainer of everything, i.e. *sarvasya dhārakam*. In *R̥gveda* also we find *dharma* signifies meritorious actions, thus rituals like Agnihotra are called *dharma*. *Yajña*, widely understood signifying the act of worship or offering especially with reference to sacrifices or oblation, is also of the nature of *dharma*. In *R̥gveda*, it has been stated (*R̥V* X.90.16) that as the first symbol of *dharma*, gods engaged themselves in the act of offering with scarifies (i.e. *yajña*). To quote the following *mantra*:

> *yajñena yajñamayajanta devāstāni dharmāṇi prathamānyāsan* |

In many instances of *R̥gveda*, the expressions *dharma, vrata, r̥ta* are synonyms. In *mantra*, it has been stated that wise Mitra and Varuṇa by *dharma* saved the Vrata from the trick (*māyā*) of the *asuras*; *r̥ta* or the truth prevails in the whole of the universe, *bhuvana maṇḍala*. The vastness of the expression is enormous. In some instances *dharma* is also understood as a sort of spiritual power or energy. A *mantra* of *Br̥hadāraṇyaka Upaniṣad* (I.5.23) states:[1]

---

[1] *yataścodeti sūryo 'stam yatra ca gaccati prāṇādvā eṣa udeti* |
prāṇo 'stemeti tam devaścakrire, dharmam sa evādya sa uśva iti ||

> *Dharma* is that *śakti* (energy/force) by which sun rises and sets in. The life comes forth and ceases by the influence of *dharma*. That force has been created as *dharma* by gods. (Whatever is) the *dharma* for the present is the *dharma* for the future.

Dharma has a spiritual (or *ādhyātmika*) sense, in the sense of being related to *Brahman* (Self) is evident from the *mantra* of Madhu-Brāhmaṇa section of *Bṛhadāraṇyaka Upaniṣad* (2.5.11) which emphasizes that everything in this world is mutually helpful (*madhu*) towards the sustenance of one another. In the same *mantra*, while mentioning sky, fire, water, as examples of *madhu* (nectar), the mention of righteousness (*dharma*) has also been made as one of the examples of *madhu* (honey), to convey the idea of interconnectedness, as all these emerge from the same cause, the *Brahman*.

> *ayaṁ dharmaḥ sarveṣāṁ bhūtānām madhvasya dharmasya, sarvāṇi bhūtāni madhu. . . .*

Through the creation myth of *Bṛhadāraṇyaka Upaniṣad*, the notion of *dharma* has been introduced. Here *dharma* has been accorded a spiritual and metaphysical status. In *Bṛhadāraṇyaka Upaniṣad* 1.4.14: *dharma* has been identified as a form of *Brahman*.[2] In order to control injustice and regulate the affairs of the world, the *Brahman* assumes a particular form, which is of *dharma*. In the beginning there was only *Brahman*, because it was single. It has been further stated: it "did not become fully developed" (*na vyabhavat*). Thus *dharma* is conceived as righteousness, justice or the regulating principle for ensuring equally to all living beings the best of life

---

2 "Yet he did not flourish. He specially projected that excellent form, *dharma* (righteousness). This righteousness is the controller of the kṣatriya. Therefore, there is nothing higher than that (*tasmāddharmāt param nāsti*). So even a weak man hopes to defeat a stronger person through righteousness, as one contending with the king. That righteousness is verily truth. Therefore, they say about a person speaking of truth, 'He speaks of righteousness' or about a person speaking of righteousness, 'He speaks of truth', for both these are but righteousness."

– Swami Ranganathananda (ed.), 2005, *The Message of the Bṛhadāraṇyaka Upaniṣad*, pp. 90-91

experience. *Brahman* did not display itself but he assumed that excellent form of *dharma*. The idea is that this universe consists of various centres of power. Kṣatriya is the representative of the state power, brāhmaṇa is the representative of the priest power, vaiśya is the representative of money power. *Dharma* is spoken of as the controller of *kṣatra* (*kṣatrasya kṣatram yat dharma*). After each creation, it has been repeatedly stated *'na vyabhavat'* (i.e. it still did not become fully developed). The final act of creation made *Brahman* fully to develop and reach its full potential, when it created *dharma*.

Dharma is accorded the highest power. Therefore there is nothing higher than *dharma*.

All other powers like that of brāhmaṇa or of vaiśya are controlled by the power of *dharma*. Thus the Upaniṣad says power which governs all other powers is called the *Brahman* and this power is the supreme power. Thus equating *dharma* and *Brahman* it has been stated in the Upaniṣad: *tasmāt dharmāt param na asti* (there is nothing superior to this power of *dharma*). In this manifested universe thus it is believed that *Brahman* manifests itself as *dharma* and governs human's day-to-day activities. *Dharma* has some characteristic features: *atho abalīyan baliyaṁsama āsaṁśate dharmeṇa*[3] (through *dharma* even a weak person hopes to defeat a strong person in an encounter). Thus *dharma* is admitted as the controller of all the powers in this world. Further the passage from *Bṛhadāraṇyaka Upaniṣad* says: *yaḥ vai saḥ dharmaḥ satyam vai tat* (*dharma* is the truth). Thus here *satya* and *dharma* are taken to be identical. *Dharma* is identified with truth; it has been stated that if one speaks the truth, it is said that one is speaking what is right or *dharma* (*tasmāt satyam vadantam āhu, dharmam vadati iti*). It has been said that *dharma* which is of the nature of truth is most excellent and *dharma* by nature beneficial. Because it has originated from *Brahman*, it is the strongest among all and controls everything.

---

[3] I.e. through the *dharma* even a weak person hopes to defeat a strong person in an encounter. – *Bṛhadāraṇyaka Upaniṣad* 1.4.14

In other Upaniṣads also we come across the notion of *dharma*. The most significant occurrence of the notion of *dharma* in *Chāndogya Upaniṣad* is in the famous section known as Dharmaskandhas (2.23.1):

trayo dharmaskandhā yajño 'dhyayanam dānaṁ iti prathamaḥ
tapa eva dvitīyaḥ brahmacārya ācāryakulavāsī tṛtīyaḥ

In *Chāndogya Upaniṣad* threefold divisions of *dharma*s are spoken of: of which the first one speaks of *yajña* (act of performing oblation), *adhyayana* (act of the Vedic recitation) and *dāna* (act of charity). The secondfold division of *dharma* incorporates *tapasyā* (act of austerity and penance). The third form deals with the act of maintaining celibacy and studying in the residence of the teacher. It has been stated that by performing these actions one is able to attain merit or even able to attain immortality. From this statement of *Chāndogya Upaniṣad* we find the performance of a particular type of action, no doubt contains implicit reference to the *āśrama-dharma* which produces virtue and enables human beings to share a better world is regarded as *dharma*. It is clear that in this passage *dharma* specifically refers to modes of religious life, probably to the life of a Brāhmanical householder, an ascetic and a Vedic student. Here for the first time in Vedic literature we have an unambiguous passage that uses *dharma* in a way very close to its usage in the later Dharmaśāstras.

In *Taittirīya Upaniṣad*, it has been specifically said *dharmam caro* (follow the path of *dharma*). In his parting words to the student (*TU* 1.11.1.) the teacher tells him: *satyam vado/dharmam caro* (speak the truth/practise *dharma*). This is the first time that the term *dharma* is used with *caro*, indicating here the use of the term in the classical sense of Dharmaśāstra in its association with *dharma*. In the *mantra*: *dharmānna pramāditavyam*, *dharma* word signifies *anuṣṭeya-viṣayatva*, i.e. the action that has to be performed, for the non-performance which incurs *pramāda* (negligence or mistake).

In this brief discussion, we find that *dharma* has been a significant expression in the context of the Vedas and Upaniṣads, and is loaded with different connotations. *Dharma* as the truth,

Brahman, the transcendental energy, the sustainer of everything and the prime source has been principally acclaimed. Thus understood, *dharma* as the truth is static, foundational and metaphysical. The other important sense of *dharma* as a cosmic power is also derived from the Vedas and Upaniṣads. *Dharma* in its ethical sense, *dharma* as duties to be performed by the human beings is also contained in the Vedic–Upaniṣadic texts. These three senses of *dharma* are, however, not to be treated as three disjointed senses, rather these three, understood in a holistic tie, explain the basics of the Vaidika Ethics.

In the context of Smr̥tiśāstra, all these Vedic–Upaniṣadic senses, except one in the sense of duties, obligatory actions, hardly find any mention. In the Smr̥tiśāstra, the pronounced notion of *dharma* became synonymous with works that are binding upon individuals both as an individual and also as a member of a society. Thus *dharma* came to be identified with duties, both relative duties (*varṇāśrama-dharma*), i.e. duties relative to one's *varṇa,* and stages of life and common duties (*sādhāraṇa-dharma*), i.e. duties irrespective of one's *varṇa* and stages of life. Manu clearly stated that Smr̥tiśāstra texts were written to control activities and duties of individuals of all *varṇa*s and *āśrama*s (stages of life) from birth to death. If we turn to the pages of any Smr̥tiśāstra text, their objective will become clear. *Yājñavalkya Saṁhitā* begins as follows:

> *yogeśvaram yājñavalkyam sampūjya munayo 'brūvān* ।
> *varṇāśrametaraṇām no bruhi dharmān aśeṣataḥ* ॥[4]

Vyāsa Saṁhitā begins by saying:

> The holy sages approached that repository of penitential sanctity, Veda Vyāsa, . . . and asked him questions regarding the duties of the members of different social orders.[5]

---

[4] *Yājñavalkya Saṁhitā*, in *The Dharamśāstra,* vol. I, p. 1.
"Having adored Yājñavalkya , the lord of the *yogin*s (ascetics), the *munis* (sages) said: Do thou describe unto us in full the religious rites of *varṇa*s (four castes), *āśrama*s (four orders), and (those of) other inferior castes."

[5] *The Dharamśāstra*, vol. III, p. 501.

Again in *Parāśara Saṁhitā,* we find Vyāsa is asking the respected Sage Parāśara to enlighten in respect of *dharma* (rules of duties) to be followed by the fourfold social order and acts of virtue to be performed in the Kali-yuga. Thus it is clear that *dharma* includes *varṇāśrama-dharma.* But in all these Smṛti literature prescriptions about general duties are also spoken of as *dharma.* Another important thing to note that in the Smṛti literatures the sense of *dharma* was also understood as related to the time period. It has been clearly stated in *Parāśara Saṁhitā,* that according to the contingency of the period (*yuga*), nature of different rules and codes of actions are to be interpreted. What has been recognized as *dharma* (rules of conduct) in the Satya-yuga may not be considered as *dharma* in the periods known as Tretā-, Dvāpara- and Kali-yugas. In *Parāśara Saṁhitā,* it has been stated:

> Practice of penitential austerities was the virtue in Satya-yuga, knowledge of Self in the Tretā; celebration of religious sacrifices in the Dvāpara-yuga and practise of charity in Kali-yuga.[6]

It has been appropriately pointed out that "the contexts of proper actions (*dharma*) are not unlimited."[7] The Dharmaśāstra tradition puts more importance to action and this feature of Dharmaśāstra led some interpreter of Dharmaśāstra to comment:

> More important in fact than the actor is the action. One's primary concern should be the propriety of the act.[8]

The sense of *dharma,* in terms of actions or duties, is not wholly unrelated to *dharma* as truth, goodness or merit. *Dharma* as action is mostly empirical, consisting of physical, mental and speech actions through which an individual makes contribution to the goodness or merit of the society.

When we enter into the discourse of professional philosophers, we find the ambiguity still persists about the meaning of *dharma.*

---

6 *Parāśara Saṁhitā,* in *The Dharamśāstra,* vol. III, p. 537.

7 D.R. Davis, 2010, *The Spirit of Hindu Law,* p. 66.

8 Ibid.

Different schools of philosophers offer notions of *dharma* from their respective metaphysical positions. The notion of *dharma* as righteousness as merit acquired from the right performance of duties (*karmas*) persists among philosophers. In other words, that the performance of *dharma* (duties/obligations) produces *dharma* (merit) was another corollary to this conception of *dharma*. Philosophers, however, are not unanimous about the nature of *dharma*. For some schools of philosophers *dharma* does not require a theistic agency for appropriation of results to actions. As Mīmāṁsakas show that action generates a new quality (*apūrva*) in the subject which leads to future consequences. Or as the Sāṁkhyas hold every action brings about changes in the three *guṇas* which give objective results at a later time. Thus *dharma* may as well be conceived as an autonomous order without any need for external interference. The idea of an autonomous and objective moral order which meaningfully explains human condition and destiny is the strongest foundation of Indian ethics.

Sāyaṇācārya also accepted the division of the Vedas into Karmakāṇḍa and Jñānakāṇḍa or Brahmakāṇḍa. Sāyaṇa points out that Karmakāṇḍa deals with *dharma* and Jñānakāṇḍa or Brahmakāṇḍa deals with *Brahman*. Karmakāṇḍa comes first, for without the purification of mind which is attained by the performance of *karma* as enjoined by the Vedas one is not entitled to attain knowledge of *Brahman*. Thus *dharma* in the sense of *karma* and *Brahman* constitutes the subject matter respectively of Karmakāṇḍa and Jñānakāṇḍa.

Jaimini defines *dharma* as that which is characterized by injunctions, technically called *codanā*. *Codanā* is that which enjoins action. The performance of sacrifices, rituals, rites, worship, etc. in accordance with the injunctions as enjoined by the Vedas is called *dharma*. Kaṇāda defines *dharma* as that by which *abhyudaya* and *niḥśreyas* are attained. The word *abhyudaya* here means heaven (*svarga*). It also means happiness and prosperity of the individual and society. Śaṅkara Miśra in his *Vaiśeṣika Sūtropaskāra* has interpreted *abhyudaya* as meaning knowledge of the Real, *tattva jñāna*. It is this knowledge which enables one to attain *niḥśreyas* (liberation). This meaning of the word *abhyudaya* applies to that aspect of *dharma* which is called *nivṛtti-lakṣaṇa-dharma*.

The Vedas according to Śaṅkarācārya reveal two kinds of *dharma* – *pravṛtti-lakṣaṇa* and *nivṛtti-lakṣaṇa*. Jaimini defines *dharma* in the sense of *pravṛtti-lakṣaṇa*. It is *dharma* which expresses itself through actions as enjoined by the *vidhi*s, injunctions of the Vedas. *Nivṛtti-lakṣaṇa-dharma* is characterized by freedom from or withdrawal from action. Kaṇāda's definition covers both the aspects of *dharma*, *pravṛtti-lakṣaṇa* and *nivṛtti-lakṣaṇa*. According to the Vedānta, *pravṛtti-lakṣaṇa-dharma* paves the way for *nivṛtti-lakṣaṇa-dharma*, if the former is practised without any desire or attachment for its fruits. In this way it brings about the purification of mind which is necessary for the attainment of knowledge of the real, freedom from suffering and liberation. But it is the cultivation and practice of *nivṛtti-lakṣaṇa-dharma* which can enable one to attain this supreme goal. Thus *dharma* as laid down in the Veda, including the Upaniṣads, is all-inclusive. Kaṇāda's definition of *dharma* is also all-inclusive. Jaiminī's definition of *dharma* is essentially one-sided as he identifies it with *kriyā* (action) only. It can hardly be denied the importance of the notion of *dharma* in Dharma-Ethics and a close study of the notion of *dharma* has the potential of revealing interesting and unknown contours of ancient Indian culture, history and philosophy.

Ṛta*:* The Cosmic Order

The expressions *satya* (truth) and *ṛta*, i.e. the universal moral order of goodness and justice, are often tied together and presented as two fundamental ideas of Indian culture. In *Muṇḍaka Upaniṣad*, it has been maintained that the truth triumphs (*satyam eva jayate*) and what is not *ṛta* does not triumph. The literal meaning of the word *ṛta* signifies the course of things or natural ways of the world. The regular movements of sun, moon and stars, the alternatives of day and night and the regular successions of seasons, these are all signified by *ṛta*. *Ṛta* is the unalterable universal law behind the running of the universe. The dawn (*uṣā*) follows the path of *ṛta*, and appears always after nocturnal darkness. The lovely dawn (*uṣā*), "true to eternal order", is sublime by law (*R̥V* V.80.1). The sun follows the path of *r̥ta*, the moon follows the path of *r̥ta*. There are Vedic hymns praising sun, moon, etc., for following the path of order. *Anr̥ta* is the violation of the cosmic order. Varuṇa is the god who maintains the cosmic order or *r̥ta* (*r̥tasya gopta*). The Vedic prayers are often addressed to gods for the maintenance of *r̥ta*. But it is mostly taken to signify cosmic order governing the universe. The gods are described as *r̥tavān* (possessor of *r̥ta*). The gods are there in order to carry out the purposes of *r̥ta*. As the gods do, so should the humans follow the law of *r̥ta*. The preservation of *r̥ta* depends on the proper relation between the earth and the heaven.

The semantics of *r̥ta* does not remain confined to one meaning. *R̥ta* is also used in the moral level. *R̥ta* at this level is understood as opposed to evil (*adharma*). The demon Vr̥tra whom Indra destroys is the power of evil, who obstructs the working of *r̥ta*. *Dāsa*s and *dasyu*s are followers of evil laws. Gods are identified with *r̥ta*. Br̥haspati, who rides the awe-inspiring car of *r̥ta*, destroys evil. Indra identifies himself with *r̥ta* and says to his worshippers that eternal law of *r̥ta* has made him mighty. *R̥ta* has two sorts of applications, one at the cosmic level where *it* signifies victory of light over darkness and in the moral level *r̥ta* signifies victory of good over evil. A willing acceptance of *r̥ta*, the cosmic moral order, brings joy to the follower of *r̥ta*. *R̥gveda* I.90.6-8 sings:

> *madhu vātā r̥tāyate madhu kṣaranti sindhavaḥ* ।
>
> . . .
>
> *madhumānno vanaspatiḥ* . . . ।
>
> To the man who lives by law (*r̥ta*), the earth is sweet, the rivers shed sweetness, the trees and forests become nests of sweetness.

On the basis of this idea of *r̥ta*, *R̥gveda* anticipated the law of *karma*. *R̥ta* became identified with irrevocable law of *karma*. With the growing of ritualistic rites and sacrifices the semantics of *r̥ta* changed to *yajña*. But in the Upaniṣads, *r̥ta* was connected with truth. The *r̥ta* has been also identified with *dharma*. In later Sanskrit literatures, *ṛta* has been described as the child of *dharma*, probably in the sense of truth. Sri Aurobindo in his *The Secret of the Vedas*, interprets *ṛta* as the principle of the *bṛhat* (vast) and is truth of things and it leads upwards to *māyas* (bliss). In another passage he has rendered the translation of *satyam*, *ṛtam* and *bṛhat* as the truth, the right and the vast. He further elaborates that it is *satyam*, the truth of being, it is in action *ṛtam*, the right – the truth of divine being regulating right activity both of mind and body; it is *bṛhat* – the universal truth proceeding direct and without being deformed out of the Infinite. Thus according to Sri Aurobindo, *ṛta* transforms the truth of being into a divine truth and in turn is transformed into a universal truth. *Ṛta*, is an endless journey from truth to truth. There are differences of opinion among different interpreters regarding the semantics of *ṛta*. Kane in his *History of Dharmaśāstra* (vol. IV), maintained that the primary meaning of *ṛta* is cosmic movement. The secondary meaning is a regulated cosmic order, tertiary meaning is laying out of sacred rites and finally it comes to have a general meaning of moral conduct. Both *ṛta* and *satya* are one reality, *ṛta* is the flow of time and *satya* is the expanse of space. Both are mutually dependent.

The Concept of Dharma in Jainism and Buddhism

In the history of Jaina philosophy, the concept of *dharma* has been the subject of extensive elaboration and taken on a plurality of meanings. In the late canonical period (CE 200–300) in the Jaina ontology, category of *dharma* as motion with its opposite *adharma* signifying "rest" are found. There are also other uses of the notion of *dharma* in the Jaina philosophy. In one of the senses of *dharma*, it is taken to mean something related to ethics, religions and social behaviour of the lay person on the one hand and the mendicant on the other. In the third sense *dharma* is linked with the conception of the eternal self (*jīva*) thus locating *dharma* in the transcendental sphere. Over the course of the medieval period (400–1200), these two denotations were synthesized to form a definition of correct conduct or behaviour in keeping with one's intrinsic nature or essential self (*svabhāva*). On the basis of this definition, *dharma* has twofold significance including both the behaviour that accords with moral rules and virtues (*pravṛtti-dharma*) and the behaviour that accords with one's intrinsic nature (*nivṛtti-dharma*). Towards the end of this period *dharma* obtained yet an additional meaning: that of a universal order governing all activity in the cosmos. From the early canonical period, as evidenced in the Jaina texts like *Ācārāṅgasūtra* and *Sūtrakṛtāṅgasūtra*, the term *dharma* has been employed as a designation for the Jaina teaching as a whole. In *Tattvārthasūtra*, the first Jaina text penned in Sanskrit and the earliest systematization of the canonical teachings, *dharma* was defined as the "highest forbearance, modesty, uprightness, purity, truthfulness, restraint, austerity, renunciation, non-attachment and continence". The word *dharma* was thus employed to designate ten constituents of righteous character which closely paralleled the five vows (*mahāvrata*) that have formed the basis of Jaina ethics since early canonical times: non-violence (*ahiṁsā*), truthfulness (*satya*), honesty (*asteya*), continence (*brahmacarya*) and propertylessness (*aparigraha*). Both *Tattvārthasūtra* and *Pravacana Tattvārthasūtra* emphasize the necessity of adopting a particular state of mind as a basis for moral conduct. The meditation on Jaina doctrine (*dharma-dhyāna*),[9] often considered as an item of austere practice (*tapas*), was regarded instrumental in the cultivation of virtuous behaviour (*samyak-caritra*), one of the paths to liberation.

In *Śāstravārtāsamuccaya*, Haribhadra describes *dharma* in two ways:

1. *dharma* as behaviour characterized by activity (*pravṛtti*) resulting in merit (*puṇya*) and enjoyment (*bhoga*), and
2. *dharma* as cosmic order.

At the close of the medieval period, Jainism came to embrace the notion of *dharma* as a universal order. It was supposed to consist of uncreated, eternal, impersonal laws that constituted the intrinsic nature of each that determined the activity of all that

---

[9] *Tattvārthasūtra* 9.37-38.

existed. The Jaina cosmic order rested upon an ontological plurality (*dravyas*). The Jaina cosmos is comprised of (eternal self) *jīva, dharma, adharma, pudgala, ākāśa* (space) and *kāla* (time), with each substance having its own distinct *svabhāva* and its own specific governing rules. In *Pravacanasāra, dravya* is defined as:

> That which, whilst it does not forsake its innate nature, is connected with creation, maintenance and destruction and which possesses qualities and modifications, is called a substance.[10]

To trace the trajectory of the concept of *dharma* in Buddhism is none the less a tough attempt. The concept of *dharma* in Buddhism has undergone profound changes in meaning. *Dharma* is interpreted as doctrine, the law of a specific teacher and his school, that is, as the world order that has been recognized and proclaimed by the great teacher. *Dharma* means principally the doctrine of the Buddha. The expression, "wheel of the law" is noteworthy, the *dhamma-cakka-pavattana-sutta* (i.e. *dharma* is taken to set in motion the wheel of the law). This expression emphasizes the dynamic character of *dhamma*. Concept of natural law on the one hand and concept of moral law on the other hand flow together completely into one concept; this sort of striving to cancel the dichotomy between the natural and the moral may appear alien to the Western thought. Corresponding to the existential world-view, the Buddha's *dhamma* principally refers to actions of people, especially to the law of actions (*kamma*), which with inescapable necessity determine the future form of life in the wheel of existence (*saṁsāra*).

The Buddha acknowledges no god as the creator and guide of the world, nor any metaphysical source in the sense of *ātman* or *Brahman* of the Upaniṣadas, and no existence of absolute being as the supreme truth, but according to him only *dharma*, the abstract world-law, has determined the course of all phenomena since beginningless time. Whoever has understood profoundly in its

---

10 *Pravacanasāra* II.3, cited in "Dharma in Jainism".

essence the universal conditionality of all events, is released, so that the Buddha's *dharma* is simultaneously a law of liberation.

The Concept of Yajña

In this section an attempt will be made to explain another important concept of the Vaidika Dharma-Ethics, which is of *yajña*. The close association with *yajña* has been both a matter of praise and condemnation for Hindu ethics. *Yajña* is another elusive expression about which it is not uncommon to find a man in the street claims authority whereas a specialist may shy away from making any outspoken comment about the true nature of *yajña*. This is another intricate concept and is not easy to explain. Here, an attempt will be made to bring out the most relevant facet of *yajña* that would apprise us about the true spirit of Dharma-Ethics. My analysis of the notion would concentrate on the *Gītā* text. It is needless to add that there are at least nine classical interpretations of *Gītā* apart from its myriad interpretations by contemporary thinkers like Bankim Chandra, Bal Gangadhar Tilak, Sri Aurobindo, Gandhiji and others. In this section the analysis of the concept of *yajña* has been done after Sri Aurobindo's interpretation of *Gītā*, which is one of the most appropriate account suitable to the spirit of Vaidika Dharma-Ethics.

Before entering into straightforward analysis of the notion of *yajña*, we need to deal with the concept of action (*karma*) and specifically the concept of *karma-yoga*. *Gītā* has emphasized on *karma-yoga*, which implies action done with self-control. The sense of action done as *yoga*, has been variously described as performance of action with non-attachment, as performance of actions without any mental attachment to the objects of sense and fruit of the actions. In the Western ethical theories there are paradigms of consequentialist theories or deontological theories to provide guidance for judging which sort of human actions are good or bad. The hedonist would urge that the action promoting the pleasure of the agent is the right action, morally justified action. The other consequentialist would introduce utility or the greatest good of the greatest number as the criterion for determining moral worth of an act. Deontologists deviate from these consequentialist approaches to morality and promulgate that duty for duty's sake is the standard for the evaluation of the moral worth of an action. In Dharma-Ethics no such clear-cut moral standards for right and wrong about an action have been provided. But it would not be correct to say that in Dharma-Ethics no such guidance is available. The *Gītā* text has provided ample scope for such discussion, though such terminologies or similar such terminologies for expressions such as consequentialism or deontology are not in use. Questions have been raised as to whether this *karma-yoga* suggests some kind of inaction? In *Gītā,* the teacher Kṛṣṇa has made a clear-cut distinction between the idea of inaction and the idea of action done as a *yoga*. The idea of inaction, in one of the common-sense interpretations of the expression "inaction", i.e. *akarma,* is inconsequential from the perspective of *Gītā,* for it is supposed to be an error, a confusion, a self-delusion. When it has been advised by Kṛṣṇa to perform action, according to the interpreters of *Gītā,* it has been a self-controlled action: *niyatam kuru karma tvam*. But he has also emphasized as suggested by the interpretors, the importance of knowledge and intelligence.

To grasp the proper implication of the lesson of *karma-yoga* preached by *Gītā,* we need to focus on the background of *Gītā*. The distinction between two expressions the Sāṁkhya and Yoga recurred in *Gītā*. The expressions Sāṁkhya and Yoga have some special connotations in *Gītā*. There are differences of opinion among the interpreters of *Gītā*. Śaṅkarācārya in his commentary has emphasized that the path *jñāna* of *jñāna-yoga* has been recommended in *Gītā* for the recluse (*saṁnyāsīs*). According to Śaṅkarācārya there is no provision for considering knowledge and action simultaneously (*jñānakarma-samuccaya*) to be effective in the context of *Gītā*. The teaching of *Gītā* as has been interpreted by Śaṅkarācārya is that *jñāna* and *karma* are recommended for individuals with different capabilities. There are strong critics to the position of Śaṅkarācārya in this regard. The explanation of the notion of Sāṁkhya as given by Śaṅkarācārya is not acceptable to Sri Aurobindo. Neither the expression Sāṁkhya does stand for the Sāṁkhya school of philosophy that has been elaborated by the author of *Sāṁkhyakārikāra,* Īśvara Kr̥ṣṇa. Again in the case of *Gītā,* we also come across the notion of Yoga, but it has already been pointed out that this *yoga* does not signify the Yoga system of Patañjali. Sri Aurobindo has explained clearly the difference between the Yoga of Patañjali and the Yoga of *Gītā*. The Yoga of Patañjali is based on the subjective method of *rāja-yoga*: this practice of *rāja-yoga* involves an internal discipline by which the mind is gradually quietened so that it can gain *samādhi. Samādhi* enables mind to attain both temporal results and eternal results: the temporal results consist in soul's great expansion in knowledge and powers. But this result is temporal. It can also attain result which is eternal when there is divine union of the soul.

Sri Aurobindo makes a contrast between the Yoga of Patañjali and the Yoga of *Gītā* on the ground that the method of Yoga of Patañjali is "limited, rigidly cut out, severely and scientifically graded"[11] but referring to the Yoga of *Gītā,* he thinks that "This *yoga* does not adopt any strict and scientific gradation but it is a process of natural soul-development".[12] No doubt, to say that the method of *yoga* is a process of natural soul-development gives rise to many questions as to its real implications. Sri Aurobindo perceives *yoga* as a method of renovation of the soul which is brought about by the "subjective poise and action".[13] The notion of *samādhi* that is delivered by *Gītā* is also different from that of the Patañjali Yoga. The Yoga of Patañjali and the Yoga of *Gītā* are in disagreement with one another on the issue regarding the significance to be accredited to action. In the Yoga of Patañjali the importance of action has been highlighted for moral purification. Hence it would not be inaccurate to say that in the system of the Patañjali action has been considered as only "preliminary" towards fulfilling some other goal. In *Gītā,* the role of action is not

---

11 *Essays on the Gita*, p. 63.

12 Ibid.

13 Ibid.

preliminary, but "it is a permanent foundation". *Rāja-yoga* does not require to be continued when its result keeps in view which action has been performed. Sri Aurobindo quite categorically maintains that for *Gītā, karma-yoga* "is a means of the highest ascent and continues even after the complete liberation of the soul".[14]

Sri Aurobindo writes:

> In the *Gītā* the Sāṁkhya and the Yoga are evidently only two convergent parts of the same Vedāntic truth or rather two concurrent ways of approaching its realization, the one philosophical, intellectual, analytic, the other intuitional, devotional, practical, ethical, synthetic, reaching knowledge through experience.[15]

The notion of Sāṁkhya and Yoga of *Gītā* acquires a more positive interpretation that views the two – Sāṁkhya and Yoga – in a non-hostile relatedness. Sri Aurobindo relentlessly emphasized that

> Sāṁkhya and Yoga are not two different, incompatible and discordant systems, but one in their principle and aim; they differ only in their method and starting point.[16]

Sri Aurobindo continues:

> This *Gītā* provides by bringing into its Vedāntic Sāṁkhya the ideas and principles of Vedāntic Yoga.[17]

It was commonly believed as we have already discussed that Sāṁkhya and Yoga are two diverse and opposite methods, of which Sāṁkhya proceeds by knowledge while Yoga proceeds by actions. This sort of viewpoint has also given rise to the belief that Sāṁkhya leads to entire passivity and the renunciation of works, *saṁnyāsa*, while Yoga is required for inner renunciation of desires through action towards God. Arjuna, positioned at the battlefield, was perplexed as to which path, whether of Sāṁkhya

---

14 Sri Aurobindo, 1970, *Essays on the Gita*, p. 62.

15 Ibid.: 64

16 Ibid.

17 Ibid.: 70.

(knowledge) or of *yoga* (action), he was to follow because hard line was drawn during that time between these two paths. The perplexed Arjuna asks Kṛṣṇa:

> If thou holdest the intelligence to be greater than works, why then dost thou appoint me to a terrible work?[18]

According to Kṛṣṇa,

> Renunciation and Yoga of works both bring about the soul's salvation, but of the two the Yoga of works is distinguished above the renunciation of works.[19]

Thus from the point of view of *Gītā*, we find that notion of *saṁnyāsa* is a different notion from what is commonly understood by it. Some thought that to get liberation one will have to renounce family life, all works. But that is not the proper sense of renunciation. Just by giving up external works no proper renunciation can be attained. So long an individual is embodied, the works of *prakṛti* will go on. The embodied souls live through their doing of works. In this connection we may refer to *Īśopaniṣad* 2 where it has been said:

> *kurvanneveha karmāṇi jijīviṣet śatam samāḥ* ।
>
> In this empirical world you should will to live for hundred years by doing works.

Apart from the distinction between the Sāṁkhya way of knowledge and the Yoga way of works, another quite similar sort of opposition between Jñānakāṇḍa and Karmakāṇda prevailed within Vedānta itself. It is evident that two sorts of interpretations of the Vedas focusing on Jñānakāṇḍa and Karmakāṇḍa were current since the period of the Smṛtiśāstra. The belief that Karmakāṇḍa and Jñānakāṇḍa were meant for different types of people with different capacities and qualifications (*adhikārī-bheda*) had gained considerable ground. It was thought by some that a person, who took the path of action (*karma*), could not be

---

[18] Aurobindo, 1970, op. cit., p. 76.

[19] Ibid.: 76-77.

considered suitable for taking the path of renunciation (*saṁnyāsa*). The philosophers who overemphasized the action-centredness (Karmakāṇḍa) of the Vedas are known as the Pūrva-Mīmāṁsakas who finally arrived at Vedavāda (so-called Vedism). On the other hand, philosophers who emphasized the knowledge aspect (Jñānakāṇḍa) of the Vedas are known as the Uttara-Mīmāṁsakas and their viewpoint is known as Brahmavāda. This sort of interpretation when carried to the extreme gave rise to a sharp dichotomy between Vedism and Vedāntism. It has often led to extreme viewpoints in either direction. It has been thought that action is very much antagonistic to knowledge; the intelligent people who concentrate upon *Brahman* supposedly required forsaking desire and action, for action is born out of desire and the result of action leads to bondage. Situated at this juncture of conflicting paradigms, perplexed Arjuna asked Kṛṣṇa as to why does he call upon him to participate in a dreadful action, like battle.[20] To remove Arjuna's doubt and misgivings Kṛṣṇa presented his positive thesis about *karma*. The actionless state of soul (*naiṣkarmya*) is a different state, and this is not to be confused with refraining from works.

> Not by abstention from works does a man enjoy actionless, nor by mere renunciation (of works) does he attain to his perfection.[21]

This brings in the important distinction that has been highlighted in *Gītā* between the theory of action (*karma*) and the theory of inaction (*akarma*). In the discourse of Dharma-Ethics it is an important discussion for two reasons: in the first place, the question may be raised as to whether *akarma* is possible at all? Second, the other related question is as to why inaction was supposed to be needed? As regards the first question *Gītā* answer is quite straightforward. The embodied individuals as empirical beings cannot desist from performing actions, for the very being of embodied beings are always in action. It is impossible to allocate

---

20 *tat kiṁ karmāṇi ghore māṁ niyojayasi keśava* | – *Gītā* III.1

21 Aurobindo, 1970, op. cit., pp. 98-99.

a moment or a second when these embodied individuals could have suspended acting in one way or other. The physical empirical existences of embodied beings are always involved in actions.

> Our physical life, its maintenance, its continuance is a journey, a pilgrimage of the body *śarīrayātrā*, and that cannot be effected without action.[22]

Under no circumstances an embodied individual can be said to be existing without performing any action. Commonly, if anything is supposed to be devoid of action, it is wrongly understood in terms of immobility. A person even if he sits idle or motionless like a stone, or even in a comatose state, the person is not without actions. Physical activities, mental activities all account for action of embodied existents. The action has never been taken to be identical with only physical actions, the concept of action is inclusive of mental actions, speech actions over and above physical actions. A person may control his senses from being stimulated by external stimulus, and thus may prevent himself from indulging in any sorts of objects of desire. But his mind may continue harping on those objects of desire and objects of senses through thinking and remembering. That person's physical withdrawal from the appeasement of senses, however, does not establish him as self-disciplined. Understood, at this point, the very notion of *akarmakṛt*, (one who does not work), turns out to be an absurd idea.

Gītā has taken into account the role of mind in truly accomplishing the required self-discipline. It enjoins control of action at the physical level and at the mental level. The mind must bring the senses under its control and organs of actions must be rightly used for action, but for action as *yoga*. Thus comes in the notion of action done as *yoga* or *karma-yoga* which, of course, requires to be further elaborated. But why according to some inaction was also suggested to be indispensable? The primary reason is the fear of rebirth and recycles through the processes of

---

22 Aurobindo, 1970, op. cit., p. 100:
na hi kaścit kṣaṇamapi jātu tiṣṭatyakarma-kṛt । —III.5

birth and death. The logic that worked was a very simple logic: do not act, then you will not acquire fruits of actions; then you will not be reborn. But that has been shown to be a faulty logic from the perspective of *Gītā*.

From the standpoint of *Gītā* it has been categorically rejected that the notion of inaction is superior to action. On the contrary, it has been asserted by *Gītā* that *karma jyāyo hyakarmaṇaḥ* (action is better than inaction). The notion of desireless action (*niṣkāma-karma*) is the most fascinating and complex teaching of *Gītā*. The performance of desireless action characterizes the *karma-yoga* of *Gītā*. *Buddhi-yoga* (*yoga* of self-liberating intelligent) presupposes *karma-yoga*, the necessity of desireless actions. Thus we may remember once again the advice of Kṛṣṇa to Arjuna, *niyatam kuru karma tvam*. The expression *niyatam* is a significant expression, however loosely speaking, *niyatam* may be taken to imply insistence on regular performance of work.

But here an important question arises, how can there be action in the absence of desire? We will discuss elaborately the role of desire in motivating an individual to action in Chapter 5. Ordinarily, it is well-accepted that desire is the motive of all actions, and if that be the accepted position, then in the state of desireless existence of an individual without any desire or devoid of desire, how would his motivation for action is to be accounted for? If desire is accepted as the conditioning factor for motivation, then in the absence of desire, i.e. the conditioning factor, there should not have been any motivational action. To answer this question, it may be supposed that in the event of desireless actions, no subjective element can be held accountable as the motivational force of all human actions. In that case, some may propose that instead of locating the motivational force in human subjectivity, it may be located in *nitya-karma* (Vedic duties) like ceremonial duties and social duties. Thus the advice, *niyatam kuru karma tvam,* may be taken to suggest *nitya-karma kuru tvam. Nitya-karma* stands for sacrificial actions, ceremonial rites and duties pertaining to stages of life and *varṇa*, i.e. *varṇāśrama-dharma*. No doubt, it is also one of the interpretations suggested to account for human action as desireless actions. Sri Aurobindo, however, expresses his unwillingness to accept *niyata-karma* as *nitya-karma* enjoined by the Vedas. Sri Aurobindo avoids interpreting *niyata-karma* of *Gītā* as *nitya-karma*, i.e. duties or *kartavya karmas* pertaining to the rules of society. From Sri Aurobindo's point of view, *Gītā* does not provide room for any external interference in its account for moral actions. If *Gītā* were thus fettered by Aryan norms of ceremonials and social duties, then Sri Aurobindo would say the universal vision of *Gītā* would be jeopardized. *Gītā* would then be restrained by narrow outlook and dogmatism.

The doubt still persists as how to truly explain the possibility of desireless action. Sri Aurobindo also explains that generally what are called by many as desireless actions or disinterested actions are really instances of such actions where petty self-centred desires are replaced by other larger desires, which are supposed to be impersonal, as related to mankind, country, etc. Sri Aurobindo does not support any reading of *Gītā* as promoting utilitarian values. In the *Gītā*, however, it has been maintained quite convincingly that action has to be performed in a desireless state. How that desireless action is to be brought about is a different question. The answer to this question brings in the other most important concept of Dharma-Ethics, i.e. *yajña* (sacrifice). This also prepares the ground for answering the question as to why *yajña* has been considered to be of great import in the context of the Vaidika Ethics. We shall find that the notion of sacrifice in *Gītā* and its different interpretations are all very suggestive in our exploration of the true spirit of Dharma-Ethics. Kṛṣṇa tells Arjuna:

> *yajñārthāt karmaṇo 'nyatra loko 'yaṁ karma-bandhanaḥ* ।
> *tadarthaṁ karma kaunteya muktasaṅgaḥ samācara* ॥[23]

> By doing works otherwise than for sacrifice, this world of men is in bondage to works; for sacrifice practice works, O son of Kuntī, becoming free from all attachment.

[23] *Gītā*, III.9.

The notion of *yajña* in *Gītā* in the above-mentioned *śloka* stands for *karma* that does not cause any bondage. Here we need to find out what sort of connection is there between the notion of *yajña* and *karma* that does not lead to bondage. In the Smr̥ti literature it has been stated, *karmaṇā badhyate jantuḥ* (by works all men are in bondage). To a person who is desirous of obtaining liberation (*mumukṣu*) and is guided by the belief that performance of actions is the cause of bondage, the performance of actions may turn out to be a discouraging factor. The desire to abandon all actions as being not worthy of performance may seem acceptable to such a *mumukṣu* person. But we have already discussed that Kr̥ṣṇa does not encourage *akarma,* i.e. refraining from works as remedy for keeping oneself free from bondage. This *akarma* theory fails to provide any solution to the problem of bondage. The other suggested alternative capable of eliminating the fetters of *karma* is by considering action as *yajña*. Actions that lead to bondage are such which are performed by agents as qualified by a sort of *kartr̥tva-abhimāna* which is supposed to be an erroneous conception regarding self as the doer of all actions. The expression *yajña* signifies Viṣṇu, i.e. the Supreme God (*maheśvara*), which is also corroborated by the statement of Śruti: *yajña vai viṣṇuḥ* (*yajña* is Viṣṇu). So long individuals are dominated by ego-sense (*kartr̥tvābhimāna*), individuals act for the satisfaction of their ego. All actions performed from the ego sense, whether narrow or enlarged, are not regarded as equivalent with acting for the Divine. Thus the teaching of *Gītā* is that "egoism is the knot of the bondage"[24] and "by acting godwards without any thought of ego, we loosen this knot and finally arrive at freedom".[25] This also makes it clear that actions done godwards are actions that are performed for the sake of sacrifice (*yajñārtha-karma*). This also explains Kr̥ṣṇa's advice to Arjuna, ". . . for sacrifice practice works". When actions are done out of self-interest whether in a narrow sense of the self or the enlarged sense of self, that leads to

[24] Aurobindo, 1970, op. cit., p. 104.

[25] Ibid.

consequences whether pleasurable or painful. The cases of actions guided by the ego-sense presuppose distinction among the subject (*kartā*), object (*karma*) and *karaṇa* (instrument) of actions. "Works done godwards" is interpreted as works done for the sake of duty.

Sri Aurobindo has maintained that when actions are thus done for the sake of delight of God or the absolute, the consequences of actions whether pleasurable or painful does not touch the individual agent concerned. Whenever any action is done, since action is an event, there is no point in saying that action does not produce any consequence. The insight of *Gītā* is to establish that as consequences all these are not of the same level in the context of morality. If anybody seeks to judge the consequences just by their physical appearances the subtle but impressive differences among the consequences would be overlooked. Much emphasis has been laid on the psychology of the agent; the psychology of the agent would be so moulded that it would cause enormous difference to the consequence, so that such a consequence, even though similar in physical appearance with the another consequence, would not bind the individual. Thus Kr̥ṣṇa's advice to Arjuna to fight for the sake of fight expects that sort of psychological turn in the internal mental state of Arjuna, so that in spite of his participation in the war and resulting consequences consisting of innumerable cases of death, destructions there from he would not bear any fruits of action. This is also important to notice that in the case of Dharma-Ethics, sometimes it may seem that the boundary of ethics and psychology coalesce. This close connection between Dharma-Ethics and psychology is both its merit and, according to some, its demerit.

Gītā gives to the notion of *yajña* wider significance, implying by *yajña* all sorts of works, *sarvakarmāṇi*. Thus by extending the range of *yajña* as equivalent with all actions, *Gītā* perspective stands out to be unlike the perspective of the Buddhist, in this context particularly, for *Gītā* instead of rejecting the concept of sacrifice, provides a deeper significance to it. In the *Gītā* view, the sacrifice is the very condition of life.

The notion *yajña* has been taken in the sense of desireless action. The main teaching of *Gītā* is that all works have to be done in the sense of *karma-yoga* meaning thereby without any desire. Thus *Gītā*'s explanation of the necessity for desireless actions, *niṣkāma-karma*, depends on the belief that the life of man is not for his personal enjoyment and for the fulfilment of his desires and hope. The example of *yajña* is very illuminating here in giving a more concrete shape to some extent to the notion of *niṣkāma-karma* or *karma-yoga*. We may analyse different senses of *yajña* to arrive at a right notion of *yajña* suitable to the spirit of *Gītā* and Vaidika Ethics as well. The three broad-ranging ways of analysing the very notion of *yajña* is undoubtedly important. The popular notion of *yajña* in the sense of ritualistic action, the sense in which it was championed by the proponents of *karmakāṇḍa* has been described by *Gītā* as the peculiar amalgamation of diverse actions (*kriyāviśeṣabahulam*). The Vedas as a whole, reveal the mystery of *karma* or *dharma* and *Brahman*. According to the Vedic tradition the major portions of the Vedas, Saṁhitās and Brāhmaṇas deal with *karma*. The sacrificial rite strictly viewed from the ritualistic point of view, is not a simple work; but it is a complex activity of various ancillary acts like building altar for the rite, setting up three to five fires, pouring of offerings into fire such as butter (ghee), food grains and other substances, chanting *mantra*s simultaneously – by the Hotās reciting invocations from *Ṛgveda*, by the Udgātā chanting hymns from *Sāmaveda*, measuring the ground by the Adhvaryu and building altar after *Yajurveda* and over all supervising and co-ordinating by the Brahmā, associated with *Atharvaveda*. The performance of these sacrifices is meant to fulfil different desires and needs of man. But each of the part-action (*aṅga-karma*) of the complete sacrifice requires to be performed rightly to get the desired result. The right performance of sacrifices enables men to get sons, crops, cattle, wealth both material and spiritual. The performance of sacrifice also frees man from evils and sins. The supreme goal of the sacrifice, according to Brāhmaṇas is the attainment of *svarga*. This may be called a ceremonial interpretation of *yajña*. Thus understood *yajña* is a *sakāma-karma*, i.e.

karma that is performed with some desire mainly for the benefit of self and sometimes may be for the benefit of the greater self. This interpretation of *yajña* has not been accepted when *yajña* has been identified with actions which are desireless, i.e. *niṣkāma-karma*. Thus in *Gītā* we find a deeper reflection on the nature of *yajña*. Even those who offer a richer significance to their interpretations of the notion of *yajña* are divided into two groups: some interpret in terms of cause–effect relation on the basis of reciprocal altruistic symbiosis and some other provide spiritual interpretation of the notion of *yajña* in terms of deeper psychological allusion.

Yajña has been in the sense of reciprocal symbiosis viewed as a universal creative activity. The cosmos, including the living beings, is brought into existence by *yajña*. In this vein in *Gītā* a story of creation by Prajāpati has been stated. At the beginning of creation, Prajāpati created human beings by sacrifice (*yajña*) and asked human beings to achieve their vigour and prosperity through the performance of *yajña*. The sacrifice would contribute towards the prosperity and fulfilment of all desires of human beings.[26] According to some interpretation of the concept of *yajña*, it has been maintained that here by *yajña* is signified the traditional scheme of *varṇāśrama-dharma*, i.e. duties that have been prescribed for individuals to perform according to their inherent capabilities (*varṇa*) and their stage of life (*āśrama*). Thus, according to this reading, individuals are advised to perform their *varṇāśrama-dharma* and thus to attain their growth and prosperity. According to some by *yajña* is meant rituals, as stated in the Smṛtiśāstras: *pañcasūnā kṛtam pāpam pañcayajñairvyāpohati*, i.e. five sorts of *pāpa* (demerits/guilts) may be done away with the performance of five types of sacrifices (*pañcayajña*). Here reference is to five types of places or utensils where animals are liable to be killed accidentally. In course of working with five articles of household uses such as fireplace (*culli*), slab for grinding condiments (*peśanī*), broom (*mārjanī*), pestle and mortar (*kaṇḍanī*) and water pot (*udkumbha*) these may

---

[26] *saha-yajñāḥ prajāḥ sṛṣṭvā purovāca prajāpatiḥ* |
anena prasaviṣyadhvam eṣa vo 'stv iṣṭa-kāmadhuk || – III.10

become instrumental for the killing of animal life and thus users of those articles may be subjected to incurring demerits (*pāpa*). For that reason five types of sacrifices (*yajña*s) such as sacrifice towards gods (*devayajña*), towards ancestors (*pitṛyajña*), towards human beings (*nṛyajña*), towards other animals and birds (*bhūtayajña*) and towards Brahmā (*brahmayajña*) are directed, this is known as *vaiśvadeva-yajña*, religious ceremony which ought to be performed especially before midday meal by offering small portions of cooked food to all the gods and especially to the god of fire who cooks the food and bears the offering to the heaven.[27] This interpretation of *yajña* puts more emphasis upon external performance of action, thus may come closer to Vedism. But there are other interpreters who offer different interpretations of *karma* and *akarma*, ignorance is equated with *karma* and knowledge is equated with *akarma*. Thus it has been stated that when one has placed himself at the level of knowledge then from that situation of *jñānabhūmi* whatever *karma*s are performed are to be reckoned as *akarma*. This, however, is not the *Gītā* view.

One of the most significant features of Vedic ritual (*yajña*) is reciprocal exchange. Thus interpreted *Gītā* notion of sacrifice comes closer to the idea of symbiotic relation that is beneficial to all the participants. The term symbiosis is one of the expressions popular in the domain of biology which covers ways in which organisms relate and live together to some advantage of each other. The concept of *yajña* has been described in terms of cause–effect relation in which participants depend upon each other and thus benefit. By performing sacrifice, men strengthen the gods and they in turn give prosperity to men by causing rains, etc. at the right time.[28] The sacrifices bring into being an amiable relation between gods and men and facilitate men to enter into a harmonizing relationship with the gods. It also provides a link between men, gods and the Supreme Being Īśvara. The sacrifice is based on the universal law of causation, and operation of cause and effect is

[27] Monier-Williams, 1986, *A Sanskrit-English Dictionary*, p. 1027.

[28] *Gītā* III.11.

admitted in the phenomenon of sacrifice. This is the universal law of *ṛta*. The ritual procedure thus represents an eternal cycle which functions within the bounds of *ṛta*. Reciprocity is not confined to sentient beings only but also found in the phenomenal world as a system of constant recycling: phenomena originating in heaven such as sun come to earth and nourish and are even transformed into other entities such as plants and other living beings, semen, milk that ultimately make their way to heaven again (as offering). In this cycle nothing is wasted or lost. In *Gītā*, the causal picture of sacrifice and rainfall cycle has been poetically projected. The living beings would not survive without food and *Gītā* mentions: "From food all living beings are born (*annād bhavanti bhūtāni*)". But foods are themselves effect of something else. *Gītā* says: from the rainfall foods are produced (*parjanyād anna sambhavaḥ*). Without rainfall grains, vegetables and other crops would not grow, then there would be no food. But rainfalls themselves are caused phenomena. To produce rainfalls clouds are required. From the smoke rising from the sacrificial fire clouds are formed and these clouds cause rainfall; rainfalls facilitate the production of foods and living beings are sustained by food. These living beings again enter into the cycle of cause–effect relation. The ritual of oblations and the hymns of praise are just *one* act in an endless cycles of exchanges of *anna* (food) between the humans and the gods.

Throughout the world a stupendous *yajña* is going on. Whatever results we get, whatever enjoyment we receive, it seems this to be the adequate description of *yajña* in the sense of Śrauta ritual. Expressed in a religious tone, the fire is posited as the carrier of the offerings to the gods. Fire also transmutes the offerings, not only by changing these offerings from one condition or state of substance into another, i.e. from a raw uncooked state into a cooked palatable one, but also by changing these from one sort or nature of substance into another sort, i.e. from a mundane substance into one with divine characteristics. Foods are supposed to reach gods in the form of smoke and essence of oblations and are also acknowledged by gods. The remains here on earth, which are glorified as marks of graciousness of god, are return gifts from the gods who tasted the food while being seated at the sacred fire through invocation and spitted out of their mouth remnants of food (*ucchiṣṭa*) making these consumable by human beings. The gods also give other return gifts to men, e.g. rain, sons, food, long life – the standard wishes of a Vedic person. Apart from the gods, the ancestors and the ancient sages and poets, *ṛṣis*, are part of the system of exchange as well. Offering to all of them is regarded as delivering oneself from the innate *ṛṇa* (debt, obligation)[29] that is inherent to all men. The ritual procedure thus represents an eternal cycle which functions within the bounds of *ṛta*. This brings forth a picture of correlation between spheres of humans, society gods and universe through *yajña*. Thus ritual is based on the strictly logical application of the rule of cause and effect.[30]

Sri Aurobindo interprets the passages explained above as the symbolic use of the words and the psychological character of the sacrifice. Sri Aurobindo commented that there are always in the Vedic system a double sense physical and psychological, outward and symbolic, and psychological and the inner meaning as well. The whole anecdote of sacrifice as stated earlier assumes a whole new meaning when interpreted after Sri Aurobindo. In the episode of sacrifice, fire is important, but according to Sri Aurobindo behind the outward symbol of fire:

> The fire of sacrifice, *agni* is no material flame, but *brahmāgni*, the fire of the *Brahman* or it is the *Brahman*-ward energy, inner Agni, priest of the sacrifice, into which the offering is poured; the fire is self-control or it is a purified sense-action or it is the vital energy in that discipline of the control of the vital being through the control of the breath which is common to *rāja-yoga* and *haṭha-yoga*, or it is the fire of self-knowledge, the flame of the supreme sacrifice.[31]

29 Malamoud, 1989, *Cuire le monde: Rite et pensée dans I'inde ancienne*, cited in Michael Witzel (2003).

30 Michael Witzel, 2003, "Vedas and Upanisādas", in *The Blackwell Companion to Hinduism*.

31 Aurobindo, 1970, op. cit., p. 112.

Thus, the account of Sri Aurobindo differs from the prevalent traditional interpretation of the Vedas. He does not like to fall prey to Vedism and Vedāntism and he thinks actually that was not the spirit of *Gītā* also. The interpretation of *Gītā* very much depends on the sense given to expressions *yajña*, *karma* and Brahmā (*Brahman*). Sri Aurobindo does not subscribe to the ritualistic interpretation of *yajña*. He writes:

> If the sacrifice is simply the Vedic sacrifice, if the work from which it is born is the Vedic rule of works and if the *Brahman* from which the work itself is born is the *Śabda-Brahman* in the sense only the later of the Veda, then all the positions of the Vedist dogma are conceded and there is nothing more.[32]

Sri Aurobindo strongly rejects the ceremonial interpretation of *yajña*.

> Obviously, this cannot be the meaning of the *Gītā*, for it would be in contradiction with the rest of the book.[33]

Sri Aurobindo does not contradict the notion of *yajña* as a vindication of a greater mutual tie of cause–effect relation among all spheres of the universe and their residents. But his psychological interpretation of *yajña* has something more worthwhile to contribute towards our comprehension of Vaidika Ethics. Thus, through all these ways of characterizing fire, as (1) inner Agni or *Brahman*-ward energy, (2) as self-control, and (3) as self-knowledge, Sri Aurobindo shows the importance of the symbolic expression, "fire". In *Gītā* we find discussions about sacrifice both in the third chapter and fourth chapter. The metaphysical presupposition is that all-pervading *Brahman* (*sarvagatam Brahman*) is established in sacrifice. Sri Aurobindo as a Vedāntin admits absolute *Brahman* and he speaks in the terminology of *Brahman*. He says in the fourth chapter the wider sense of sacrifice has been indicated, where it is said that sacrifice is born from work, work from *Brahman* and *Brahman* from *akṣara*, and therefore the all-

---

32 Aurobindo, 1970, op. cit., pp. 108-09.

33 Ibid.: 109.

pervading *Brahman* is established in sacrifice. The sense of sacrifice, signifies losing our lower individual personality in the impersonal, and arriving finally at union with that supreme personality which is not separate and individual, yet assumes all individualities. Transcending the lower nature of the three *guṇa*s, we can ascend finally into the higher nature of the infinite godhead which is not bound by the three *guṇa*s even when it acts through Nature. Reaching the inner actionless state of the silent *puruṣa, naiṣkarmya,* and leaving *prakṛti* to do her works, we can attain supremely beyond to the status of the divine Mastery which is able to do all works and yet be bound by none. Sri Aurobindo finds in *Gītā* an attempt to maintain two things simultaneously, one is silent *Brahman*, actionless *naiṣkarmya,* and on the other hand, world with all its activities.[34] "The works of sacrifice are indicated as a means of liberation and absolute spiritual perfection, *saṁsiddhi.*"[35] In the light of Sri Aurobindo's interpretation the notion of *yajña* upheld in *Gītā* is not in the light of "the modern pragmatic tendency". Sri Aurobindo seeks to provide justification from the spiritual angle.

Dharma, Ṛta and Yajña

In course of the above discussion, one thing has been quite clear that these expressions, viz. *dharma*, *ṛta* and *yajña* are loaded with various meanings and interpretations. We may sum up the similarities, dissimilarities and interconnectedness of these three terms in the Dharma-Ethics discourse.

Dharma in its transcendental sense is the Truth, the ultimate. *Dharma* is also the order of not only cosmic reality but also of social and ethical realities. Theories of *karma* and transmigration constitute the ethical nucleus of *Dharma*. *Dharma* at the level of embodied individuals is not only action that is obligatory or to be accomplished, but also *dharma* is righteousness or merit resulting from the performance of the duty. *Dharma* at the cosmic level is

---

34 This is in line with Integral Advaita Vedānta of Sri Aurobindo. Vide Sanyal 2015.

35 Aurobindo, 1970, op. cit., pp. 126-27.

indicative of meteorological, astronomical regularity and periodicity of all natural phenomena, like the flow of rivers or the perpetual return of the reasons, and the alteration of day and night. *Dharma* is more comprehensive than *ṛta* in its appeal and covers all the spheres – social, religious, cosmic and spiritual – of human life. What is common to both *ṛta* and *Dharma* is their autonomy. In the case of *ṛta*, it is not guided by gods, rather it guides them. *Ṛta* is not born of gods, but gods are born of *ṛta*s. The gods are only guardians or functionaries of *ṛta* which is an eternal autonomous order. If we substitute gods with natural phenomena (gods are only defied natural phenomena), or if we strip the natural phenomena of deification we have a quite naturalistic autonomous order. *Ṛta* as a cosmic and moral order expresses itself through the workings of natural phenomena and the conduct of men. The parallelism between *dharma* and *ṛta* is remarkable. *Ṛta* has been derived from the cosmic sphere: *ṛta* meaning thereby "course" is produced from (to go). In this respect the lexicography of *ṛta* is different from that of *dharma*. *Dharma*, the older form in *Ṛgveda* is *dharman*, derived from the verbal root *dhṛ*, meaning thereby "to hold", "to maintain", "to preserve", derivatively meaning that which is established or firm. Thus, it is quite logical to surmise that the static aspect of reality is signified by *dharma* and the dynamic aspect of reality is signified by *ṛta*. The derivation of *yajña* is from the verbal root, *yuj* meaning of which is "to join" and also "to offer". In the context of Dharma-Ethics the significance of *yajña* lies in its interpretation as action (*karma*), *karma-yoga*, *niṣkāma-karma* (desireless action) which finally enables to reach the truth, the absolute. In the whole scheme of Dharma-Ethics, a man's quest for the morality is part and parcel of his embodied existence. The quest for morality gets satisfaction through the performance of actions that are volitional with desire for some goal or disinterested actions. The concept of *yajña* explains all these actions. But these are all inter-connected. What is really noteworthy here is that there is no dichotomy between "fact" and "value" or "is" and '"ought". There is only one order which sustains "is" and promulgates "ought".

3

Dharma as Universal and Specific Duties

In the Dharma-Ethics, whether Vaidika or non-Vaidika, one of the very common uses of the expression *dharma* is duties or obligatory actions. It is interesting to note that the Vaidika Dharma-Ethics as represented through diverse literatures is unanimous in accepting broadly two classes of duties known as *sādhāraṇa-dharma* (common duties) and *varṇāśrama-dharma* (specific duties relating to one's *varṇa* and *āśrama*). Praśastapāda also classifies duties in the similar manner like that of Manu into *sāmānya-dharma*s and *viśeṣa-dharma*s. The duties which are recognized as standard duties (*sādhāraṇa-dharma / sāmānya-dharma*) are obligatory for all men. The so-called *varṇāśrama-dharma* are also called relative duties; S.K. Maitra writes:

> The duties of *varṇa* and *āśrama* together constitute code of relative duties, the duties of station in life, the duties obligatory on the individual in consequence of social status, temperament, specific powers and capacities.[1]

The very ideas of *varṇāśrama-dharma* and specially *varṇa-dharma* are the specialities of the Vaidika Dharma-Ethics. The very naming of some duties as specific or relative duties brings out their difference from other duties which are held to be universal duties. In the scheme of Dharma-Ethics acceptance of some duties as universal has the implication of reckoning some duties to be obligatory on all individuals irrespective of their age, capacity or work. The expression *sāmānya-dharma* is quite self-explanatory, as its domain of application covers the full domain of human obligation whatsoever. The universal duties are binding upon

1 Sushil Kumar Maitra, 1963, *The Ethics of the Hindus*, p. 1.

individuals unconditionally, irrespective of their social class and status. These duties – *sādhāraṇa-dharma* and *varṇāśrama-dharma* – together constitute the foundation of Hindu morality. It is to be noted that the notion of *dharma* in the sense of duties is very much action-oriented. Here prescriptions and prohibitions centre round actions which are obligatory for the agent to perform as a moral agent, some unconditionally and some conditionally. The obligations are about the performance of some actions or avoidance of some actions. Apparently, the Dharma-Ethics may seem to deal with external actions. But that is not the right perception about Dharma-Ethics. This aspect of Dharma-Ethics has been carefully explained by Maitra, who calls this objective aspect of Hindu morality. This objective code of duties is necessary for preparing the individual for higher stages of morality and inner purification. Within the domain of Hindu morality no sharp demarcation is maintained between action and conduct or character. In the Western moral tradition the distinction between conduct or character and action has been sharply maintained giving rise to two different ethical traditions, that of character-oriented virtue ethics and action or duty-oriented duty ethics. No such nomenclatures of splitting or partitioning are found in the Dharma-Ethics discourse because of their acceptance of the notion of *dharma* both externally as objective codes and also resulting appropriation or internalization of these into conduct or character trait of the agent. The performance of *dharma*, i.e. prescribed actions produces good result, i.e. righteousness (*dharma*) and performance of prohibited actions, results in evil consequences, known as unrighteousness (*adharma*). These two aspects of *dharma* are condensed into one expression *dharma* in Dharma-Ethics: one of its aspects signifies duties (*dharma*) or obligatory actions as distinguished from prohibitory actions; the other aspect signifies *dharma* or virtue as distinguished from vice or *adharma* that resulted from objectively taking over injunctions or prohibitions in the semblance of subjective, internal character-traits of the performing agents. These actions are not wholly external for the performance of these actions also transforms the doer of such actions to beings of the same character-type or kind. Interestingly, the view expressing a close relationship between conduct and action is embedded in classical Upaniṣadic texts like *Bṛhadāraṇyaka Upaniṣad* and others. To quote from *Bṛhadāraṇyaka Upaṇisad* IV.4.5, where the Sage Yājñavalkya observes:

> *. . . yathākārī yathācārī tathā bhavati*
> *sādhukārī sādhurbhavati pāpakārī pāpo bhavati . . .*
>
> As a man acts, as he behaves, so he becomes;
> One who does good, becomes good, one who commits sin becomes evil.[2]

In the Vaidika Dharma-Ethics equal emphasis has been placed upon duties which individuals qua individuals are required to perform for the growth and development of one's own self; but also upon duties which individuals are required to perform as members of societies or communities, according to the age of the individual concerned and his capacity to perform certain action. In determining the obligations and duties of an individual to the society, the age of the individual and his capability to perform an action were also given due importance. The Vaidika Dharma-Ethics has no difference from other Dharma-Ethics such as Buddhist Dharma-Ethics or Jaina Dharma-Ethics in respect of individual's universal duties as such. But the Buddhist ethics and Jaina ethics upheld their strong reservations against accepting the so-called specific duties, especially *varṇa-dharma*. In discussing about *sādhāraṇa-dharma* and *viśeṣa-dharma*, in this chapter, main focus will be on Dharmaśāstra literatures. Among the authors of Dharmaśāstra, Manu's name occurs first for attempting to classify duties (*dharma*) into two broad categories: universal duties and specific duties.

Dharma as universal duties (*sāmānya-dharma*) has also been classified into different types. Manu has enumerated following *dharmas*: Patience (*dhṛti*), forgiveness (*kṣamā*), restraint (*dama*), non-

---

[2] Swami Ranganathananda (ed.), 2005, *The Message of the Bṛhadāraṇyaka Upaniṣad*, p. 658.

stealing (*cauryabhāva*), purity (*śauca*), repression of sense-organs (*indriya-nigraha*), wisdom (*dhī*), scholarship (*vidyā*), truthfulness (*satya*), absence of anger (*akrodha*).

In *Atri Saṁhitā*,[3] another Dharmaśāstra literature, the expressions *yama* and *niyama* are found as suggesting codes of actions which are obligatory for individuals. According to *Atri Saṁhitā*, absence of cruelty (*anṛśaṁsya*), forgiveness (*kṣamā*), veracity (*satya*), non-violence (*ahiṁsā*), charity (*dāna*), simplicity (*ārjava*), love (*prīti*), cheerfulness (*pramāda*), sweetness of temper (*mādhurya*) and mildness (*mārdava*) and the *yamas*. *Atri Saṁhitā* mentions the following *niyamas*: purity (*śauca*), sacrifice (*ijyā*), austerity (*tapa*), making gift (*dāna*), Vedic study (*svādhyāya*), restraint over sexual relations (*upastha-nigraha*), observance of vow (*vrata*), abstention from speech (*mauna*), fasting (*upavāsa*) and bathing (*snāna*). In *Atri Saṁhitā*, *yamas* are directives for daily practices but *niyamas* are not meant for daily practices.

Similarly in the classification of duties that has been provided by Praśastapāda, among the category of *sāmānya-dharmas* are included moral earnestness (*dharme śraddhā*), non-violence (*ahiṁsā*), welfare of creatures (*bhūtahita*), speaking the truth (*satya vacana*), non-stealing (*asteya*), sexual continence (*brahmacarya*), purity of motive (*anupadhā*), giving up of anger (*krodhavarjana*), cleanliness (*abhiṣecana*), devotion to the deities (*viśiṣṭa-devatā bhakti*), eating of purified food (*śucidravya-sevana*), observation of fast (*upavāsa*) and moral alertness (*apramāda*). These are some of the literary evidences suggesting codes of practices for individuals in general. The list of universal duties provided by Praśastapāda on many instances includes or overlaps duties enumerated by Manu: Or, the list of duties prescribed by Atri overlaps with that of Manu or Praśastapāda: thus, speaking the truth (*satya vacana*) and truth (*satya*), non-stealing (*asteya* and *cauryabhāva*), control over sense-organs and motor organs (*brahmacarya* and *indriya-nigraha, upastha-nigraha*), giving up of anger (*krodhavarjana* and *akrodha*), purity

[3] Manmath Nath Dutt, 1979b, *Atri Saṁhitā in the Dharamśastrā* (Hindu Religious Codes), vol. II.

(*abhiṣecana* and *śauca*) are such examples. Neither Manu nor Praśastapāda nor Atri has provided any clear-cut principle for enumerating the duties that they have actually enumerated. Whether all these duties are to be regarded as positive duties or negative duties, or both, have not been discussed anywhere. Among the duties mentioned, it is also difficult to accept all these duties as moral duties; to accept all these duties as falling under moral duties needs to be supplemented by adequate explanation. In the Buddhist ethics elaborate discussions are found about *śīla*s (good conduct) enumerated to be five (*pañcaśīla*) or sometimes ten (*daśaśīla*). In the Jaina ethics also the discussion about good conduct occupies an important place for according to Umāsvāti, *samyag-darśana-jñāna-caritrāṇi mokṣamārgaḥ*[4] (right awareness, right knowledge and right conduct) lead to liberation. In the Jaina tradition it is the individual's vow to abstain from violence, falsehood, stealing, carnality and possessiveness makes the mark. Broadly speaking both the Buddhists and Jainas belong to the śramaṇa tradition and in their model of conduct and actions recommended for such ideals always maintain a distinction between duties of a monk (*śramaṇa*) and a laity (*gṛhastha*). In the present volume, I avoid discussing about the Jaina Dharma-Ethics and the Buddhist Dharma-Ethics.

Coming to the discussion of specific duties, the Vaidika Dharma-Ethics presents before us two broad scheme of duties, in the first place, related to the different social classes (*varṇa*), known as *varṇa-dharma* and second, the duties related to the different stages of life (*āśrama*), known as *āśrama-dharma*. The concepts of *varṇa* and *āśrama* are two pivotal concepts of Hindu morality and over which lots of discussions and debates have taken place. The Vedic Dharma-Ethics views an embodied individual also in his social setting, as a member of a society or a community. Two factors, viz. *varṇa* and *āśrama*, both the concepts to be explained shortly, of an individual have been considered as the deciding factors about his situation in a social

---

4 Umāsvāti, 1994, *Tattvārthasūtra* 1.1, tr. Nathmal Tantia, p. 5.

setting. It is expected of each individual to accomplish his obligation to the society through proper performance of his duties. Here lies the significant distinction between the universal duties (*sāmānya-dharma*) and the specific duties (*viśeṣa-dharma*); *varṇa-dharma* and *āśrama-dharma* are specific duties required to take into cognizance the social class (*varṇa*) of the individual member of the society and also his stage of life (*āśrama*). Praśastapāda mentions that specific (*viśeṣa*) duties are relative to the social position of the individual founded upon the particular *varṇa* to which the individual belongs and his *āśrama*.

Varṇa-dharma

The most debatable portion of the Vaidika Dharma-Ethics is its notion of *varṇa-dharma*.[5] For the ideology of *varṇa-dharma*, as it has already been pointed out, is one of the differentiating features of the Vaidika Dharma-Ethics that makes its difference from the Buddhist Dharma-Ethics and the Jaina Dharma-Ethics most conspicuous. The ideology of *varṇa-dharma* from both the perspectives – either from its accreditation or from its repudiation – it tends to fracture the discourse of Vaidika Dharma-Ethics. No doubt the ideology of the institution of *varṇa* order and the subsequent extensive practice of caste system in India have given rise to varied speculations. The perennial problems of caste that afflict Indian society are considered to be essentially Hindu phenomena that had its origin in the ancient ideology of *varṇa-vyavasthā* (institution of class order). The notion of caste, its origin and structure are none the less complex and defy any sort of short-cut characterization. One of the identifying features of the caste model is to uphold hereditary specialization in pursuing a profession. The underlying demand is that the son can only continue the profession of his father and son cannot choose any other occupation than that of his father. The fall out of such practice is being witnessed by India for centuries in the form of economic

---

[5] See Indrani Sanyal, 2010, "Varna and Jati", in *Ethics and Culture: Some Indian Reflections*.

inequality and social deprivation. In the present section, however, discussions relating to the empirical, social and economic repercussions of casteism are not incorporated. The grave repercussions of caste system necessitate a re-look into the ideology of *varṇa-dharma*. The Vedic tradition especially is held responsible for caste and all the issues relating to caste that we experience in the present India. Puruṣasūkta,[6] one of the hymns of *Ṛgveda*, has been specifically cited by many interpreters as responsible for sowing the seeds of thoroughly obnoxious caste system in India. Some writers have gone to the extent of nicknaming Puruṣasūkta as the "ideology of class exploitation".[7]

The full text of Puruṣasūkta (*ṚV* X.90) is without doubt intended to establish the divine origin of the four-tiered class structure of the prevailing Vedic society, to legitimize and sanctify it in the eyes of the people and thus create a pseudo-religious disguise for the oppression and exploitation of the masses by the ruling class.[8] The caste system that developed in India no doubt was extremely exploitative, oppressive and ruthless. Ambedkar making a close study of the institution of caste ascribed most of the evils of Hinduism to this institution of caste and called for its annihilation. Ambedkar speaks about the complexity of caste, mysteries of caste and calls it a "hoary" institution.[9] But Ambedkar has also admitted:

> The principle underlying caste is fundamentally different from the principle underlying *varṇa*. Not only are they fundamentally different but they are also fundamentally opposed.[10]

The deliberation on the characteristics of *varṇa-dharma* leaves no choice but to proceed with extreme caution. First, we may

---

6 *brāhmaṇosya mukhamāsīt | vāhu rājanyaḥ kṛtaḥ |*
uru tadasya yad vaiśyaḥ | padābhyām śūdro 'jāyata ||

7 Jayanatanuja Bandyopadhyaya, 2007, *Class and Religion in Ancient India*, p. 20.

8 Ibid.

9 Valerian Rodrigues (ed.), 2007, *The Essential Writings of B.R. Ambedkar*, p. 242.

10 Ibid.: 279.

summarize basics about the nature of *varṇa,* types of *varṇa* and types of duties ascribed to each of the *varṇa*s. Second, we need to see what actually was there in that famous Puruṣasūkta also which has often been cited as the source of all evils. The actual socio-empirical conditions establish that caste model thrives upon the matter of heredity and birth as the determiner of profession and thereby of socio-economic existence of the successors. The main task in this section is also to find out whether the ideology of *varṇa* is intrinsically bonded with the principle of *varṇa* division based on heredity and birth or some other principle. To be very sincere, it has to be acknowledged, if *varṇa-dharma* is elaborated as one of the pillars of Vaidika Dharma-Ethics then ideology of *varṇa* and practice of caste system should not go hand in hand.

In the Smṛti literatures including *Manusmṛti,*[11] frequently elaborated reference to all these *varṇa*s are available. In the writings of Manu we find lots of praises are bestowed on the brāhmaṇas. It is stated in 1.96:

> Among the created beings, living beings are superior, among the living beings rational beings are superior and among the rational beings, brāhmaṇas are superior.[12]

It is found in *Manusmṛti* further:

> Brāhmaṇa is the lord of all created beings,[13] brāhmaṇa, who is conversant in the Vedas, is the ruler of the world (*īśa sarvasya jagato brāhmaṇa vedapāragaḥ* – 9.245).

In *śloka* 10.3 Manu says clearly that among all *varṇa*s, brāhmaṇas are superior to all others for their nature, for upholding laws and for performing some specific sacraments (*saṁskāra*s).[14] Thus we

---

[11] It is maintained that the current *Manu Saṁhitā* is based on the ancient *Mānava Dharmaśāstra* with the later additions and alterations.

[12] *bhūtānām prāṇinaḥ śreṣṭhāḥ prāṇinām buddhijīvinoḥ* |
buddhimatsu narāḥ śreṣṭhāḥ nareṣu brāhmaṇāh smṛtāḥ ||

[13] *sarvasyaivāsya sargasya dharmato brāhmaṇaḥ prabhuḥ* | – 1.93

[14] *vaiśesyāt prakṛtiśraiṣṭhyāt niyamasya ca dhāraṇāt* |
saṁskārasya viśeṣācca varṇānām brāhmaṇaḥ prabhuḥ || – 10.3

find that in the writings of Manu clearly brāhmaṇas are granted superior status. It has been stated that it is the duty of the king to look after the well-being of brāhmaṇas. No true brāhmaṇa ought to suffer from hunger.[15] It is the duty of a king to make provision for the maintenance of the dependents of brāhmaṇas. If the king does not take cognizance of brāhmaṇa's hunger, then that would torment the kingdom. However, the brāhmaṇa also needs to be a true brāhmaṇa. If the brāhmaṇa deviates from his duty, then he is considered to be a *brāhmaṇabruva* (one who is called brāhmaṇa but is not a true brāhmaṇa). *Atri Saṁhitā* mentions certain characteristics which are specifically of a brāhmaṇa.[16] These are purity (*śauca*), doing good to others (*maṅgalam*), absence of exertion (*anāyāsa*), absence of jealousy (*anasūya*), absence of acquisitiveness (*aspṛhā*), self-restraint (*dama*), charity (*dāna*) and mercy (*dayā*). In the text some explanation is also provided about these features. First, an account is provided about what is meant by *anasūya.* A person who does not try to belittle another person's achievement, rather speaks highly about that person's achievement or does not joke with anybody's defects is considered to be one devoid of jealousy. In the Indian *dharma* tradition especially in accounting for *varṇa* we will frequently come across the notion of *śauca. Atri Saṁhitā* says:

> *Abhakṣyaparihāraśca,* i.e. rejecting those food which are not to be eaten, avoiding interaction with those who are criticized, and *ācāreṣuvyavasthānam,* i.e. committed to the established rule of conduct are the determiners of *śauca.*[17]

The expression *ācāra* may mean conduct, behaviour as well as established rule of conduct. In my rendering of *ācāra,* my preference is for "established rule of conduct". While explaining the concept of *maṅgala,* it has been maintained that *maṅgala* is synonymous with *praśasta ācaraṇa. Praśasta* literally means what is recommended

---

[15] *yasya rājñastu viṣaye śrotriyaḥ sīdati kṣudhā* |
tasyāpi tatkṣudhā rāṣṭramacirenaiva sīdati || 7.134

[16] *Atri Saṁhitā, śloka* 35.

[17] Ibid. 1.35-39.

or considered to be fit or good. Hence this explanation of *maṅgala* in terms of *praśasta,* i.e. good behaviour or activities, does not add anything more to our intuitive understanding of *maṅgala.* A brāhmaṇa should not torment his body with over exertion whether good or bad, for a brāhmaṇa *anāyāsa* is a distinctive mark. A Brāhmaṇa must be satisfied with whatever he has. He should never covet for another person's wife and this sort of lewd mentality is called *spṛhā. Dama* is a quality which marks a brāhmaṇa for even if anybody either externally or spiritually brings harm upon him, he does not take any revenge for that for he is a self-restrained personality. Charity (*dāna*) that has been spoken of here refers to an altruistic trait of a brāhmaṇa and in order to be benevolent one need not give huge amount of wealth. What has been stated in *Atri Saṁhitā* that the brāhmaṇa should donate (even) from a limited income regularly infused with zeal and internal feeling. A brāhmaṇa is supposed to be compassionate (*dayā*), he is supposed to look upon his friend or foe as his own self (*ātmavat-vartitavyam*). A brāhmaṇa is required to perform certain actions which are called *iṣṭa.* Maintenance of sacred fires or adoration of Vaiśvadeva is such a work. The excavations of tanks, wells and other watery expanses, the construction of temples, the distribution of food, laying out of pleasure gardens are called *pūrta* (acts of pious liberality). A brāhmaṇa should do both the *iṣṭa* and *pūrta karma*s that are prescribed for his performance. A śūdra must perform *pūrta karma*s but śūdra has not been allowed to perform Vedic rites.

In *Mahābhārata* it has been stated that a kṣatriya is one who protects from being afflicted with wounds, in other words, kṣatriya is the redresser of wrongs (*saḥ eva kṣatriya proktaḥ kṣatrāt trāṇamkarati yaḥ*). It has been further stated that it is the duty of a kṣatriya not merely to be ready for the defence of the country but to actively seek the evil out and crush it. It is the duty of a kṣatriya to engage himself in just violence. If an enemy attacks, he should be killed. It is honourable for a kṣatriya to die in a battlefield. It has been very specifically mentioned that *svadharma* (duty of a kṣatriya) is not to run away from the battlefield. According to *Hārīta Saṁhitā,* a kṣatriya is required to be proficient in laws relating to the administration of a polity (*nītiśāstrārtha kuśala*) and to be knowledgeable about the means to be adopted for making peace and dissention if, and when, required by the context (*sandhivigrahaḥ tattvavid*).[18] Apart from that a kṣatriya is also expected to be righteous in his dealings with his subjects.

Vaiśyas were allocated a separate class of duties. Agriculture, rearing of cattle, looking after business – these were considered to be the duties of a vaiśya. It is stated in *Manusmṛti* that it is the duty of vaiśyas to make the provision for food for every living creature. *Hārīta Saṁhitā* also echoes more or less the same functions as the activities of the vaiśyas. It has been said quite categorically that the vaiśyas should feed *brahmāṇḍa* with their wealth and priests at the time of sacrifice. But a vaiśya should not be proud of his wealth (*dambha-moha-vinirmukta*) and because he would be feeding *brahmāṇḍa* with his wealth, he should never try to exercise control over religious matters (*aprabhūtvaṁ ca vartet dharmeṣu dehapatanāt*). Vaiśyas and kṣatriyas are required to be religious and to participate in sacrifices in their own ways.

The work of śūdras is to serve all communities. According to *Atri Saṁhitā*, like all other Smṛti Saṁhitās, śūdras are required to serve all other communities (*varṇatrayasya suśrusaṁkuryāt śūdraḥ prayatnataḥ*). A śūdra should earn his livelihood with hardship and zealously worship the deity according to the rules of *pāka-yajña*, (a simple domestic sacrifice). A śūdra should adore śūdras who followed righteous and just ways. Śūdras are required to adjust with all sorts of hardship and deprivations. He should put on a tattered cloth, eat the remnant of brāhmaṇa's food, find pleasure only in own wife, and avoid another person's wife.[19] All these oppressive codes and rules of conduct are found in the Dharmaśāstra literatures and *Manusmṛti* is the foremost in this matter. But it has been argued by the scholars that it is wrong to thing that Manu is the originator of caste and in this regard the remark of Ambedkar is worthy of note:

---

[18] *Atri Saṁhitā* 2.4.

[19] *Hārīta Saṁhitā* 2.13.

> One thing I want to impress upon you is that Manu did not *give the law* of caste and that he could not do so. Caste existed long before Manu. . . . His work ended with the codification of existing caste rules and the preaching of caste *dharma*.[20]

To decipher the link between Purusaṣūkta and caste ideology we need to concentrate upon the mentioned *sūkta* and its implications. Puruṣasūkta presents a story of creation referring to the Supreme Being *Puruṣa*, who is self-conscious being and the ultimate cause of all creations. The present hymn conceives the act of creation as representing the self-sacrifice of *Puruṣa*. The first born *Puruṣa* undergoes sacrifice in order to create the world or cosmos. From the oblation smoke first *R̥k–Yajur–Sāma* appeared. From the body of *Puruṣa*, horse, cattle, goat, sheep, etc. were born. In the same *sūkta* it was stated that from the mouth of *Puruṣa* brāhmaṇa was born, from two arms of *Puruṣa* kṣatriya was born, from his two thighs vaiśya was born and from his two feet śūdra was born. The story of creation does not end here. Among the older texts, mention must be made of *Br̥hadāraṇyaka Upaniṣad* (1.4.11-15), wherein we come across a story of creation of brāhmaṇa gods, kṣatriya gods, vaiśya gods and śūdra gods. Puruṣasūkta, however, to many, turned out to be quite acceptable as proponent of class division on the basis of birth. Without raising any question about the real motive of Puruṣasūkta, or proposing any liberal non-rigid interpretation of that *sūkta*, many people straightforwardly considered Puruṣasūkta as the proponent of the theory of *jāti* on the basis of birth. Sāyaṇācārya has interpreted the meaning of the *mantra* as follows:

> From the mouth of the *Virāt Puruṣa* brāhmaṇas were born, from the limbs the kṣatriyas were born, from two thighs vaiśyas were born and from his feet the śūdras were born.

Again there is another *śruti-vākya* as the following which supports the determination of *jāti* on the basis of birth:

---

[20] Rodrigues, 2007, op. cit., p. 254.

prajāpati akāmayeta prajāyeya, sa mukhataḥ . . . nirmimita . . .
brāhmaṇo manuṣyāṇām ।
uraso bāhubhyām . . . nirmimita rājanyo manuṣyāṇām ।
madhyataḥ . . . nirmimita . . . vaiśyo manuṣyāṇām ।
paṭṭaḥ . . . nirmimita śūdro manuṣyāṇām ।[21]

The following statement from *Mahābhārata*[22] also speaks in the same vein:

brāhmaṇo mukhataḥ sṛṣṭo brāhmaṇo rājasattām ।
bāhubhyām kṣatriyaḥ sṛṣṭaḥ urubhyam vaiśyo eva ca ॥

varṇānām paricaryārtham trayānām bharatarṣabha ।
varṇaścaturthaḥ sambhūtaḥ padbhyām śūdro vinirmitaḥ ॥

In the later Smṛti literatures,[23] in *Mahābhārata* and also in *Gītā* we find reference to *varṇa*. Again there are many statements speaking in favour of classification of *varṇa*, which later came to be known as *jāti*, on the basis of *guṇa* (potentiality) and *karma* (action). In *Bṛhadāraṇyaka Upaniṣad*, the creation process has been stated as follows:[24]

brahma vai idamagra āsīt ekam eva, sanna vyabhavat
tacchreyarūpam asṛjata kṣatram
saḥ naiva vyabhavat saḥ viṣam asṛjata
saḥ naiva vyabhavat sah śaudram varṇam asṛjata.

These *mantras* narrate that *brāhmaṇa* was alone and could not flourish, so He created kṣatriya. He could not flourish, so He created vaiśya. (Still) He could not flourish, so He created śūdra *varṇa*. According to some interpreters of these *mantras*, brāhmaṇa was alone existing as the brāhmaṇa, prior to the origination of kṣatriya, vaiśya and śūdra. But as a brāhmaṇa, brāhmaṇa was not able to perform the work of a kṣatriya, so he created the kṣatriya. The brāhmaṇa himself was not able to perform the work

---

21 *Taittirīya Saṁhitā* 7.1.1.4-6.

22 *Mahābhārata*, Śāntiparva, 72.4-5.

23 *Manusmṛti* 12.26: *sattvam jñānam tamohjñānam rāgadveṣau rajaḥ smṛtam* ।
etad vyāptimadeteṣām sarvabhūtaśritam vapuḥ ॥

24 *Bṛhadāraṇyaka Upaniṣad* 1.4.11-13.

of a vaiśya. The brāhmaṇa himself was a brāhmaṇa, and created kṣatriyas and vaiśyas, but still found some essential works were left unaccomplished. Hence He created śūdra to perform the service-work. From this creation story presumably we get to know about the importance of four major types of work. In Śāntiparva of *Mahābhārata* it has been maintained that whole world is brāhmaṇa and there was nothing special about the *varṇas*. Beings which were earlier created by the *Brahman* acquired different colourization (*varṇatā*) because of their actions.[25]

In *Taittirīya Brāhmaṇa*, a *mantra* states:

> *Brahman* created gods, *Brahman* created this world. From *Brahman*, the kṣatras are created, *Brahman* created brāhmaṇa out of itself.[26]

In *Aitareya Upaniṣad* in a straightway the theory of creation has been described as follows:

> *He brought unto them Man . . .*
> *It was this bound that He cleft, it was by this door that He entered in.*[27]

These three quoted statements from *Bṛhadāraṇyaka Upaniṣad*, *Mahābhārata* and *Aitareya Upaniṣad* are narrating the kernel of creation in unanimous way as follows: At first men were created, the creator himself entered into the body of men, these men were known as brāhmaṇa, because Brahmā himself assumed the form of the brāhmaṇa. In course of time Brahmā as brāhmaṇa *jāti* through

---

25 *Mahābhārata*, Śāntiparva, 188.10-14:

na viśeṣo 'sti varṇānām sarvam brahmamidam jagat |
brāhmaṇa pūrvasṛṣṭam hi karmabhir varṇatām gatam ||

26 *brahma devanajānayat brahma viśvamidam jagat* |
brahmanaḥ kṣatram nirmitam brahma brāhmaṇamatmāna ||
– *Taittirīya Brāhmaṇa* 2.8.8.9

This reference is derived from Viśvarūpānanda 1988, vol. 1: 767.

27 Sri Aurobindo 2004b: 198, 201.

tābhyoḥ puruṣamānayat |
. . . *sa etameva simānaṁ vidāryetayā dvārā prāpadyata* |
– *Aitareya Upaniṣad*, 1.2.3, 1.3.12

the successive births of children and grandchildren, after the *Bṛhadāraṇyaka* described way, for easily doing different types of work, got himself divided into four different *varṇa*s (classes) according to the ways people preoccupied themselves in carrying on each of these works. In *Mahābhārata* also it has been mentioned that the core of four *varṇa*s is four types of *karma*s.[28] In *Mahābhārata* there are passages that suggest absence of any difference among individuals on the ground of *varṇa*. No doubt there is some metaphysical twist to this belief, to which we have just referred, which suggests that this world is born of *Brahman*, so initially there was only one *varṇa*, that is brāhmaṇa. The passage from *Mahābhārata* also supports the view that gradually the criterion for deciding who is brāhmaṇa, or kṣatriya or vaiśya or śūdra depended on the type of *karma* performed by an individual.[29] In *Gītā* Kṛṣṇa said:[30] *brahmakarma svabhāvajam*. It has also been said by Kṛṣṇa, *kṣatram karma svabhāvajam*. Thus, here *guṇa* or natural potency (*svabhāva*), not birth, has been mentioned as a determining factor of *varṇa*. The *śruti-vākya*s unambiguously mentioning *karma* and *guṇa* (quality) as marks of *varṇa*-determination are not easy to find out, but statements from Smṛti literatures abound mentioning *guṇa-karma* as the basis of *varṇa*-determination. There are statements from *Manusmṛti* saying that one has acquired the quality of being śūdra, for his forsaking the study of the Vedas.[31] Again in *Mahābhārata*, it has been said:[32]

> One who has given up practices prescribed by the Vedas is remembered as a śūdra.[33]

---

28 *cāturvarṇasya karmāṇi cāturvarṇyaṁ ca kevalam* |
asṛjata sa hi yajñārthe pūrvameva prajāpatiḥ || – Anuśāsanaparva 48.3

29 *nahi viśeṣo 'asti varṇānām sarvam brahmamidam jagat* |
brāhmaṇam pūrvasṛṣṭam hi karmabhirvarṇatām gatām || – Śāntiparva 188.10

30 XVIII.42-43.

31 *yo 'nadhītya dvijo vedamanyatra kurute śramaṁ* |
sa jīvanneva śūdratvamāśu gacchati sānvayaḥ || – *Manu Saṁhitā* 2.168

32 *Mahābhārata*, Śantiparva 189.7.

33 Ibid.

In *Bhagavadgītā* we find a metaphysical speculation and a normative exposition about *varṇa*. *Gītā* tells about three *guṇa*s, viz. *sattva, rajas* and *tamas* as qualities of *Prakṛti*; these three *guṇa*s, according to the Sāṁkhya philosophers, represent latent potentialities of which *sattva* is the principle of assimilation, harmony and equilibrium, *rajas* is the principle of creative endeavour, motion and impulsion, and *tamas* is the principle of inertia, passivity and is responsible for creating disharmony and thwarting dynamicity. *Gītā* maintains further that these three qualities of nature are evidently present and active in all existences including human beings and none can be said to be devoid of any one *guṇa*s or free from any one of three *guṇa*s; none is cast in the mould of one *guṇa* to the exclusion of the other. These three *guṇa*s are juxtaposed or combined in a very complex manner in all existents in all aspects of their existence – physical, mental and moral. These three *guṇa*s are present in all existents including human beings but the order is not the same wherever one *guṇa* predominates and the other *guṇa*s play subservient role to it. There is a general rule of mind and action for all men, but each individual acts not only according to the common laws, but according to his own nature constituted by the inherent potentiality, tendency or whatever bestowed upon him by the order of the constituting *guṇa*s; each man fulfils different functions or follows a different bent according to the rule of his own circumstances, capacities, character, power. What place is to be assigned to this variation, this individual rule of nature in the moral discipline? It lays it down that one's own nature, rule, function should be observed and followed – even if it is defective, it is better than the well-performed rule of another's nature.

> To follow the law of another's nature is dangerous to the soul, contradictory as we may say, to the natural way of his evolution, a thing mechanically imposed and therefore imported, artificial, and sterilizing to one's growth towards the true stature of the spirit.[34]

[34] *Gītā* XVIII.47: *śreyān svadharmo viguṇaḥ paradharmāt svanuṣṭhitāt* |
svabhāva-niyataṁ karma kurvannāpnoti kilbiṣam ||

This *svadharma* is of four general kinds formulated outwardly in the action of four orders of the old Indian social culture, *cāturvarṇya*. In other words, there are four distinct orders of the active nature or four fundamental types of the soul in nature *(svabhāva)*, and the work and proper function of each human being correspond to his type of nature. The actions of brāhmaṇas, kṣatriyas, vaiśyas and śūdras are divided according to the qualities (*guṇa*s) born of their own inner nature, spiritual temperament, essential character (*svabhāva*). Moral actions performed under the predominance of *sattva guṇa* are called *sāttvika-karma*s; similarly we see there are provisions for *rājasika-karma* and *tāmasika-karma*. Thus if we look into the *Gītā* text, we do not find any reference to birth or hereditary feature in accounting for *varṇa*. In *Mahābhārata* also we find that it has been asserted that *varṇa* is not hereditary. It has been said that *varṇa* depends solely on natural temperament or inborn vocational aptitude. It has been very clearly said that neither birth, nor *saṁskāra*, nor *vidyā* nor family is the cause of being a brāhmaṇa, but only profession. In Vanaparva of *Mahābhārata* it has been further stated that a śūdra, if he has acquired good character traits may be treated as a brāhmaṇa and a brāhmaṇa by his defiling attitude may be turned into a śūdra.

In *Bṛhadāraṇyaka Upaniṣad*, as already mentioned, the story of creation begins with the creation of four types of gods belonging to brāhmaṇa *varṇa*, kṣatriya *varṇa*, vaiśya *varṇa* and śūdra *varṇa*. One interesting thing has been said about the śūdra *varṇa* god who is Pūṣā, i.e. Pṛthivī and whose task is Pūṣaṇam.[35] The Sanskrit word *pūṣaṇam* is derived from the root *puṣ*, which means to cause to prosper, thrive, nourish, fulfil, etc. Hence there is enough scope for interpreting the work of śūdras in a nobler way. There is also an encouraging line about śūdras in *Hārīta Saṁhitā*. In the same Saṁhitā it has been said that a śūdra should work always with his mind, words and deeds. It has been further said that having performed religious deeds and having his sins dissipated

[35] *sa naiva vyabhavat sa śaudram varṇamasṛjat pūṣaṇamiyam vai puṣeyam hidam sarvam puṣyati yadidam kiṁ ca* | – *Bṛhadāraṇyaka Upaniṣad* 1.4.13

(thereby), he attains the dignity of Indra.[36]

Now, we come to the most difficult part of the enquiry regarding the principle that works behind the division into different *varṇa*s. There are many literary evidences to suggest that division of different *varṇa*s are not rigidly determined by birth. In the Vanaparva of *Mahābhārata*, we also find illuminating statements relevant for this context, wherein a *ṛṣi* had made the following statement:

> A brāhmaṇa, who indulges in vicious acts and is very haughty, in spite of his intelligence, is to be considered as a śūdra; and a śūdra who is always truthful and dutiful and has self-restraint to be considered as a brāhmaṇa.

In Ajagarādhyāya of Vanaparva, Rājarṣi Nahuṣa is found to remark that if truth, charity, forgivefulness, mercifulness, which are said to be qualities of a brāhmaṇa, are discovered in a śūdra, then that śūdra should be regarded as a brāhmaṇa. In reply to this remark of Nahuṣa, Yudhiṣṭhira admitted that in many instances qualities of a brāhmaṇa are discoverable in a śūdra and qualities of a śūdra are discoverable in a brāhmaṇa. Hence it may be contented that just by birth one is not brāhmaṇa or śūdra, rather it is by his *vyavahāra* (mode of action) one person may acquire the qualities of a brāhmaṇa or that of a śūdra. In *Mahābhārata* there are instructive suggestions at places in favour of accepting a non-rigid stand regarding classification of *varṇa*. Passages have been cited from *Mahābhārata* specifically suggesting that a person born of śūdra parents if pursues good practices is not to be regarded as śūdra.[37] Thus, it is quite arguable that in one of the senses *varṇa* signifies character or inner trait of an individual.

---

[36] This may be interpreted as a hint towards *guṇakarmagatajātivāda*. This will be discussed subsequently.

ittham kuryāt sadā śūdra manovākyakarmabhi |
sthānamendramavāpnoti naṣṭapāpa supuṇyakṛt || – *Hārīta Saṁhitā* 2.14

[37] *śūdra caitadbhavellakṣam dvije cecca na vidyate* |
na vai śūdra bhavecchudra brāhmaṇo brāhmaṇo na ca || – Vanaparva 151.25

However, the question remains how do we then justify *varṇa-bheda* (difference among *varṇa*s), which is also an accepted matter? In this regard we also have some suggestive hints from the epics and other Dharma literatures. It has been stated that among the original brāhmaṇas some were regarded as kṣatriya for they became interested towards material property, and were rough by nature, more prone to anger and were adventure-loving and gave up their own *dharma* and the colour of their body was red.[38] Among the brāhmaṇas some earned their livelihood by animal husbandry, agriculture and were yellow in colour were called vaiśyas.[39] Lastly, those brāhmaṇas who were fond of violence and falsehood, used to perform those work in order to assist other people, were devoid of tidiness and were black in complexion were śūdras.[40] True brāhmaṇas were sincere to Vedic rites and rituals and they observed the Vedic tradition and kept themselves busy in penance (*tapasyā*).[41] Thus, from the above consideration, it would not be too rash to conclude that birth was not the only deciding factor in case of determining difference between one *varṇa* and another. The intellectual capacity of a person, his temperament, his ethical nature, his spiritual stature all are important factors in determining *varṇa-bheda*.

The interesting point to note that within the tradition itself the justification for maintaining difference among various *varṇa*s was questioned. In Mokṣaparva of *Mahābhārata*, in the section entitled "Bhṛgubharadvājasaṁvāda" we find Bharadvāja questioning the legitimacy of *varṇa-bheda*. His argument is as follows: since each of us has desire, anger, fear, greed, sorrow,

---

[38] *kāmabhogapriyāstīkṣṇāḥ krodhanāḥ priyasahasāḥ* |
tyaktasvadharmā raktāṅgaste dvijāḥ kṣatratām gatāḥ ||
– *Mahābhārata*, Śāntiparva 181.11

[39] *gobhyo vṛttim samāsthāya pitāḥ kṛṣyupajivināḥ* |
svadharmānnānutiṣṭhanti te dvijā vaiśyatām gatāḥ || – Ibid. 181.12

[40] *hīṁsānṛtapriyālubdhāḥ sarvakarmopajīvinaḥ* |
kṛṣṇāḥ śaucaparibhraṣṭānte dvijāḥ śūdratām gatāḥ || – Ibid. 181.13

[41] *brāhmaṇā brahmatantrastāḥstāpasteṣām na naśyati* |
brahmadhārayatām nityam vratāni niyamāṁstathā || – Ibid. 181.16

thought, hunger and labour, how can we be diffcrent from one another?[42] Further it is argued, since equally all of us have experience of excreting perspiration, urine, stool, cough, bile and blood from our body, how should we be different from one another?[43]

One concept that frequently occurs in connection with castes and sub-castes is *varṇasaṁkara* (admixture of *varṇa*), which may remind one of the criteria of purity and pollution as admitted by sociologists as criteria for maintaining difference among the castes. In *Manusmr̥ti* X.12 and 24 the word *varṇasaṁkara* is used in the sense of mixed castes, mixture or intermingling of *varṇas*. On account of the great emphasis laid on the prevention of *varṇasaṁkara*, the Smr̥tis ordain that it is one of the principal duties of the king to punish people if they transgress the rules prescribed for *varṇa*s and to punish men and women if guilty of *varṇasaṁkara*. *Bhagavadgītā*, the normative text par excellence of the Hindus, outlines collapse of the social and moral order when there are leakages in the closed structure of marriages. Ideally both parents must be of the same caste. Most polluting are those castes which are the products of reprehensible unions between women of a higher caste and men of a lower caste. In fact, in later Dharmaśāstras concern about purity of *varṇa* became very important.

No doubt there are mixed responses about the status of śūdra in the context of Dharma-Ethics. In the context of classical Vedānta philosophy the question, "Does the śūdra have the right to *brahma-vidyā*?" (*śūdrodhikriyate vedavidyām athavā na hi*?) became one of the most debatable issues. From these sorts of controversies the basic question that again and again comes to the surface regarding the real foundation of the *varṇa* theory in the Dharma-Ethics. What is the real foundation of *jāti* division that is playing havoc in India for centuries? The Dharma-Ethics deserves to be retained or

---

42 *kāmaḥkrodhobhayamlobhaḥ śokościntākṣudhāśramaḥ* ।
sarveṣām naḥ prabhavati kasmādvarṇa vibhajyate ।। – Śāntiparva 181.7

43 *svedamutrapurīṣāni śleṣmāpittam saśonitam* ।
tanuḥ kṣarati sarveṣām kasmādvarṇa vibhajyate ।। – Ibid. 181.8

abandoned on its competence to handle this bizarre notion of *varṇa/jāti* debate.

In course of the present discussions we have already found two distinct sorts of spirit are prevailing regarding the notion of *jāti* in the huge body of literatures that goes by the name of Dharma-Ethics literature. According to one theory, *jāti* is determined on the basis of *guṇa* (constitutive element) and *karma* (action), which may be called *guṇakarmagatajātivāda*. The other opposite theory which supports the division of *jāti* on the basis of birth (*janma*), may be called *janmagatajātivāda*. It has been already clarified from our discussion that the proponents of theory of *jāti* based on birth or, in other words, *janmagatajātivādin*s admit that from the different body parts of the creator individuals belonging to four different *jāti*s, such as brāhmaṇa, kṣatriya, vaiśya and śūdra have originated. As believers in law of *karma*, these theoreticians, of course, would admit that the past deeds of those individuals were responsible for their present birth. But they do not admit possession of any quality or performance of any action in their present life, have effect upon the class (*jāti*) of his present life. The supporters of the theory of *jāti* on the basis of *guṇa* and *karma* would argue that in the beginning everybody was brāhmaṇa but because of performance of different types of *karma* and because of different *guṇa*s working as motivating factors to different types of actions, brāhmaṇas were according to the convention of the period, got themselves classified into four *varṇa*s or *jāti*s. Both of these theories attempt to explain the phenomenon of *jāti*, that is the basis of class division and also later caste division. The problem of caste is no doubt one of the most baffling problems of Indian society. It is also not easy to establish simply any one of the theories as supported by the Vedic tradition. The problem has been aggravated by the fact that there are Vedic statements and statements of Smṛti supporting both the alternatives. The conflicting statements are all Vedic statements or statements from Smṛti which also owe their roots to the Vedas. Among these conflicting statements – all statements cannot be regarded to be the same in their truth-value nor are they the same in being means to valid knowledge. It has to be admitted that among these statements some are true others are false; or some are *pramāṇa* and others are *apramāṇa*. Otherwise the Veda itself as a body of conflicting statements would be deprived of its validity (*prāmāṇya*). For these statements as *śruti-vākyas*, in spite of contradictions among themselves, require to be of the same strength (*samabala*).

The speculation that during one *kalpa*[44] of creation, Brahmā created the brāhmaṇas, kṣatriyas, vaiśyas and śūdras from the different parts of his body and in another *kalpa* of creation he created brāhmaṇas, kṣatriyas, vaiśyas and śūdras on the basis of their quality and *karma*, may not be credible. If one subscribes to this hypothesis, then it has to be admitted that the nature of creation varies from one *kalpa* to another, then it would amount to admitting that there is no determining principle behind creation. This would further lead to the admission that in each creation, a thing that did not exist before, *apūrva* is created. Then that would lead to the collapse of nature and essence of objects. The words (*śabda*) that were in the previous *kalpa* would not be able to reveal objects in the later *kalpa* in the absence of objects. From the point of view of those who believe in eternality of words (*śabda-nityatvavāda*) this would amount to giving up the hypothesis about the eternal relation between the words and objects. Finally, this would lead to accepting that the Vedas are not eternal. The authority of the Vedas under such circumstances gets jeopardized. This cannot be a favourable position for an *āstika* thinker. However, from the perspective of other schools, some other ways of arguing may be forwarded, which are not included in the present discussion.

To arrive at a decisive conclusion either in favour of the theory supporting division of *jāti* on the basis of quality and *karma*

---

[44] "A fabulous period of time (a day of Brahmā, or one thousand *yugas*, a period of four thousand, three hundred, and twenty millions of years of mortals, measuring the duration of the world)." – Monier-Williams 1986, p. 262

(*guṇakarmagatajātivāda*) or in favour of the theory supporting division of *jāti* on the basis of heredity and birth (*janmagatajātivāda*) is indeed a difficult task for there are many supporting or opposing Vedic and Smṛti statements corroborating both the viewpoints; we need to ponder basically over the possible ways of resolutions of conflicts, if possible, keeping within the framework of the Vedic tradition. To abandon a theory or to reject a theory by taking the perspective of an external critique would in no way be beneficial in the context of Dharma-Ethics. To a large number of interpreters *varṇa* and caste are just two sides of the same coin. But persons like Ambedkar spoke in opposite direction by admitting that *varṇa* and caste are not the same: according to Ambedkar the underlying principle of *varṇa* is worth.

In the domain of Vaidika Dharma-Ethics, the Vedic statements are authoritative and are regarded as source of knowledge. If all Vedic statements were unanimous in speaking either in favour of the hypothesis that the division of *jāti* is done on the basis of difference in birth or on the basis of quality and action, then which thesis is to be accepted would have been settled amicably. With reference to *varṇa*, there are many Vedic statements, but are not unanimously speaking in favour of either one of the positions.[45]

---

45 Broadly speaking, depending on the division of the Vedas into Brāhmaṇa and *mantra*, *śrutivākya*s can as well be a *brāhmaṇavākya* or a *mantravākya*. When two *śrutivākya*s are in conflict with one another, that conflict situation can be of at least three sorts: (a) a *brāhmaṇavākya* is at variance with another *brāhmaṇavākya*, (b) a *mantravākya* is at variance with another *mantravākya*, (c) a *brāhmaṇavākya* is at variance with another *mantravākya*. Again this does not cover all the instances of conflicting Vedic statements for there may be opposition between a *śrutivākya* and a *smṛtivākya* and how that opposition is to be overridden, according to the instructions of the Śāstra, needs to be discussed. These are no doubt significant discussions about the procedure for finding out which of the statements is to be finally acceptable as the stronger. By taking into consideration all these technicalities for deciding which of the statements is stronger Viśvarūpānanda has categorically established that the theory suggesting *varṇa* or *jāti* is determined by quality and action is more cogent and acceptable. For these discussions in detail, one may refer to Vedāntadarśana, vol. I, with Swami Viśvarūpānanda's *Bhāvadīpikā*.

It has been objected that if the *guṇakarmagatajātibheda*-alternative is accepted then this will lead to the contradiction with the viewpoint of Kumārila Bhaṭṭa. In Tantravārttika of the *Mīmāṁsasūtra* 1.2.2 it has been stated that there is no epistemological justification in favour of the claim that according to *karma, varṇa*s are determined: i.e. *varṇa*s are *ācāranimitta*. The acceptance of this viewpoint that classification of *varṇa* or *jāti* depends upon the quality and action of individuals, as argued by the critics, entails the following: If the *jāti* of brāhmaṇas is settled, then on the basis of that admission the requisite duties or actions of brāhmaṇas are prescribed; on the other hand from the observation of actions which are worthy of being brāhmaṇas, *jāti* of brāhmaṇa is settled. The critics, however, bring the charge of arguing in a circle or *itaretarāśrayadoṣa* against this explanation. The same explanation would be applicable with regard to other *varṇa*s such as kṣatriya, vaiśya and śūdra and their respective manner of actions established as rules of conduct or good behaviour. Hence in all such instances no valid epistemological justification can be adduced in favour of the theory that proposes *varṇa* or *jāti* to be accomplished on the basis of *guṇa* and *karma* of the individuals.

It has further been objected that if one and the same person performs actions befitting prescribed rules of conduct of one *varṇa* or *jāti* on one occasion and on another occasion performs actions befitting the rules of conduct prescribed for another *varṇa* or *jāti*, then the same person has to be treated as belonging to different *varṇa*s or *jāti*s in his same lifespan. Bhaṭṭapāda is of the opinion that if a person does good action then he has to be regarded as a brāhmaṇa and if he does bad action then he has to be regarded as a śūdra. Thus simultaneously the same person has to be treated as a brāhmaṇa and a śūdra in the same life. In reply to this objection it may be pointed out that it is not possible for any individual to strictly follow all the rules of good conduct and all the norms of good behaviour. Often at times lapses are quite usual and conceivable. Just by depending upon instances of temporal behaviour, if Śruti proceeds to determine who belongs to which *varṇa*, it will also become difficult to ascertain which person is capable (*adhikārī*) for which work. In that case in the absence of any fit person or *adhikārī* for any work, the injunctions of Śruti would turn out to be useless (*vyartha*). Viśvarūpānanda does not concede to these objections as necessarily following from the adherence to the theory of *guṇakarmagatajātivāda.*

From the point of view of Kumārila Bhaṭṭa who is the supporter of *varṇa* determination on the basis of birth (*janmagatajātivāda pakṣa*), it seemed that the acceptance of the other alternative would lead to endorse the postulate that the performance of *karma* (religious rites) like penance (*tapasyā*) and impressions (*saṁskāra*) born out of such penances have no role in determining the characteristic of being a brāhmaṇa (*brāhmaṇya*) and are not effective in manifesting or expressing the *varṇa/jāti* of the individual. By raising similar such objections Bhaṭṭapāda seemed to have expressed his reservation against accepting *guṇakarmagatajātivāda* as a viable alternative. Viśvarūpānanda, however, tries to account for Bhaṭṭapāda's antagonism towards the *guṇakarmagatajātivāda*. It has been suggested that Kumārila Bhaṭṭa made a sort of bold and pompous assertion, *prauḍhivāda*, guided by the urge for checking any sort of opposition that would have been labelled against the Brāhmanical tradition due to the resurgence of Buddhism – a historical contingency of the period.

How far the objection of arguing in a circle is convincing against the proponents of *guṇakarmagatajātivāda* requires to be explored. It has been explained that the sort of fallacy known as *anyonyāśraya* occurs when in providing an explanation, the term used for explanation and the term to be explained – these two entities are reciprocally dependent. An example may be given to explain the context where the charge of *anyonyāśraya* would be feasible. In *Mahābhārata*[46] it has been said:

satyam dānam adroha anr̥saṁśyam trapā ghr̥ṇā |
tapaśca dr̥śyate yatra sa brāhmaṇa iti smr̥tāḥ ||

---

[46] Śāntiparva, 182.4.

The suggested yardstick for recognizing a brāhmaṇa is truthfulness, charity, non-malevolence, mercy, pity and modesty. Wherever austere endeavour is observed in a person, say in respect of truthfulness in speech, charity, non-malevolence, etc. he is recognized to be a brāhmaṇa. For example, let us suppose that the prescribed rule of action for a brāhmaṇa is to speak the truth, to be charitable, to be non-malevolent, etc. Thus, it may be presumed a sort of arguing in a circle is taking place here, for from the observation of certain traits or actions, such as speaking of truth, performing charitable act, being non-malevolent in action a person is recognized to be a brāhmaṇa; and for a brāhmaṇa the prescribed rules of action suggestively are speaking the truth, performance of charitable actions, performance of non-malevolent action, etc. On the belief that a reciprocal dependence is there between being a brāhmaṇa and speaking the truth and the speaking the truth and being a brāhmaṇa, the charge of *anyonyāśraya doṣa* has been brought in.

Viśvarūpānanda however, does not concede to this objection. Viśvarūpānanda pointed out that, if it were found that both the instances of speaking the truth are of the same order, then in that context this sort of objection about *anyonyāśraya doṣa* would have been valid. "Speaking the truth" (*satyakathanaṁ*) may be used as a mark of a character trait (*jātijñāpaka*) of a brāhmaṇa or may be used as a rule of direction or prescription for action (*vihitācāra*) for a brāhmaṇa; and these two uses of the same expression are not the same. When it has been observed in a person the trait of speaking the truth is present, "the speaking the truth" may be predicated of that person. Thus considered, in this case, "the speaking the truth" is a predicable. It has been shown that to be a prescription and to be a predicable are not the same or to be in the same level. What has been prescribed, has not yet been realized, but it is to be realized (*sādhya*). On the other hand, the predicate signifies something that has been realized (*siddha*). The important distinction between the notion of being *vidhyāka* (directing or prescribing) and *vidheya* (a predicate or predicable) may throw some light on the distinction between two sorts of uses of the expression "speaking the truth" (*satya kathana*).

How far Bhaṭṭapāda was a whole-hearted supporter of *janmagatajātivāda* may be questioned. Viśvarūpānanda thinks that it cannot be said that Bhaṭṭapāda was an outright supporter of the view that *varṇa* or *jāti* is determined by birth. In some instances remarks of Bhaṭṭapāda seemingly divert from the staunch *janmagatajātivādī* alternative. This has reference to *Ślokavārttika*, 5th *sūtra*, *vanavāda*, 29, which runs as follows:

> In some cases from the actions of subjects who are rightly protected by kings the quality of being a brāhmaṇa is ascertained.[47]

The story of Satyakāma Jābāla goes very much against the stance of *janmagatajātivāda*; Satyakāma Jābāla, as we learnt from *Chāndogya Upaniṣad*, was one of the great teachers of the time prior to the composition of *Chāndogya Upaniṣad*. When Satyakāma decided to lead the life of a *brahmacārin*, he asked his mother what was his *gotra*. His mother had no glorious story to share about the birth of her son; rather she conceded her inability to tell his *gotra*. The mother of Satyakāma was a serving girl, serving for hire at various houses, and was unable to name her son's father. When Satyakāma came to Haridrumatā the Gautama and expressed his desire to be his student, he was asked to tell his *gotra*, and he straightforwardly narrated all that he had learnt from his mother about his lineage and introduced himself as Satyakāma Jābāla. But in the case of Satyakāma Jābāla, who had the "meanest possible birth", to whom who was his father not known, was recognized by his teacher to be a brāhmaṇa, i.e. his *brāhmaṇatva* was determined by his virtue of speaking the truth. His teacher accepted him as a *brahmacārin* impressed by his truthfulness, and remarked, "None but a brāhmaṇa would have a moral strength to make such an avowal". In *Chāndogya Upaniṣad* it is stated: *naitad abrāhmaṇo vivaktum arhati* (4.4.5). To be more

---

[47] *kvacidācārataścāpi samagrājānupālitāt* |

explicit, from this remark of *guru*, it does not follow that *guru* had found that Satyakāma's father was a brāhmaṇa. He accepted Satyakāma because he had a brāhmaṇa quality. Thus from this story we find that Satyakāma's physical birth was of no importance but his quality of truthfulness that mattered most in determining whether he was a brāhmaṇa or not. The supporters of *janmagatajātivāda* in that case may be accused of going against the Śruti. Viśvarūpānanda proposes a liberal reading of the position of Bhaṭṭapāda; Bhaṭṭapāda's inclination towards *janmagatajātivāda* may be interpreted as a descriptive record of the then timely practice of an ancient society.

Some have argued that if *varṇa* is supposed to be determined by *guṇa* and *karma*, some problems would arise regarding the performance of ritual practices related to the birth-ceremony (*jātakarma saṁskāra*): When a child is born or when it is in its tender age, the capabilities or potencies of a child for any action are not discernible. Therefore, it has to be admitted that the *varṇa/jāti* of a newborn child has to be kept on hold till it attains sufficient maturity for the attribution of a *varṇa/jāti* worthy of him. A child's existence has to be presumed to be in a state of no-*varṇa* or no-*jāti*-state. Hence in those cases the performance of rituals relating to birth-ceremony cannot be performed for such performances are conditioned by the specific rules of conduct prescribed for different *varṇa/jāti*s. But this objection has not daunted the supporters of *guṇakarmagatajātivāda* for they have shown with supportive citations from the Śāstra that *jāteṣṭi karma* (rituals relating to after birth of a child) are enjoined by the Śruti on the parents. The father and the mother of the newborn child are enjoined to perform such sacrificial rites.[48] When a child is born, to celebrate its birth-ceremony, rituals are to be performed by the parents according to the *varṇa* of parents. In this regard there are various discussions in the Śāstra. Broadly speaking, the Śāstra is well-equipped to account for these types of cases: (1) when parents are of the same *varṇa*, (2) when parents are of different

[48] *Pūrvamīmāṁsā* 6.1.4. Cited in Swami Viśvarūpānanda, 1988, *Vedāntadarśanam*, vol. 1, p. 774.

varṇa,[49] and (3) when parents are unknown. There are also passages in the Smṛti literatures favouring the ascription of the *varṇa* of the parents as the *varṇa* of a foster child.[50] It is clear that for the performance of rituals at the time of birth, there is no necessity for the *karma* and action of the newborn. If *jāti* is determined only by birth and the principle of *janmagatajāti* was upheld, then all those discussions contained in the Śāstra turn out to be ineffective. Thus from all these considerations, Viśvarūpānanda comes to the conclusion that even if a child is baptized by rituals at the time of birth by the *guṇa*s of his parents, he may later on attaining maturity may acquire *varṇa* according to his *guṇa-karma*. This argument proposed in favour of *guṇakarmagatajāti* may be supposed to go rather against the position. Because, it may be argued that by all those statements relating to rituals after birth, there is no consideration about the *guṇa-karma* of the newborn. In all these cases more stress seems to be on the birth. But the proponents of *guṇakarmagatajātivāda* do not concede to this objection. They would go on arguing that with the maturity of the children, the character traits and potentiality that are in children become determining factors of their *varṇa*. But the question may be raised as to whether it amounts to admitting that the boy who has been assigned the *varṇa* of being a brāhmaṇa at birth may turn out to be a kṣatriya on account of his later *karma* and action. But *jāti* such as *brāhmaṇatva* or *kṣatriyatva* are *nitya* (eternal), how can there be change in *jāti*? One answer may be that here the expression *nitya jāti* is not to be taken as synonymous with the idea of *jāti* as *nitya* as has been propounded in the Nyāya-Vaiśeṣika metaphysics. If *jāti* is accepted as *nitya* there can be no question of creating that *jāti*. But it has been pointed out that there are also various statements which go in favour of substantiating the claim that *jāti* is the product of

---

49 *vipravadviprabinnāsu kṣatrabinnāsu vipravat* |
jātakarmāṇi kurvīta tataḥ śūdrāsu śūdravat |
vaiśyāsu viprakṣatrābhyām tataḥ śūdrāsu śūdravat | – *Vyāsa Saṁhitā*, 1.7-8

50 *mātāpitṛbhyām yastyaktaḥ pathi yastam prakalpayet* | *yo varṇa poṣayet tam ca tadvarṇaḥ tasya jāyate* | *tāvapi svāviva sutau saṁskāryāviti niścayaḥ* |
– *Mahābhārata*, Anuśāsanaparva 49.20-26

creation. The classic statement in *Gītā*, where Śrī Kṛṣṇa is announcing: *cāturvarṇyaṁ mayā sṛṣṭam guṇa-karma-vibhāgaśaḥ* (IV.13), i.e. "four *varṇa*s are created by me according to the difference in *guṇa* and *karma*" is worth recapitulating here. In *Mahābhārata* it has been said: *cāturvarṇyam bhagavatā pūrvam sṛṣṭam svayambhuvā* (Anuśāsana 143.2). Another similar statement from the Smṛti literature is as follows: *cāturvarṇyasya karmāṇi cāturvarṇyam ca kevalam asṛjat* (Anuśāsana 48.3). Thus on the basis of the quoted passages, there are enough corroboration of the stand that *varṇa* has been created by God; the supposition that *varṇa*s are determined according to the difference in quality and *karma* may imply the possibility of there being more than one *jāti* at different times in an individual.

In one sense of the term *varṇa*, it has been defined as *varṇyate iti varṇa* (what is being described is *varṇa*). This may be accepted as the minimum but the core of the concept of *varṇa*. Thus the four *varṇa*s are described as follows: *brahma-vedaḥ, tadadhīte iti brāhmaṇaḥ* (*Śabdakalpadruma*). The meaning of Brahma is Veda, those who study Vedas are described as brāhmaṇa. In this way brāhmaṇas are described, brāhmaṇa is one of the *varṇa*s. Similarly, in the *Śabdakalpadruma* a kṣatriya is described as follows: *kṣadati-rakṣati-janān iti kṣatraḥ* or *kṣatāt trāyate iti kṣatraḥ*. Thus kṣatriya is described as one who protects from injury, and so kṣatriya is a *varṇa*. Similarly, vaiśya is described as *paśūnvāṇijyadyupayoginaḥ labdhvā viśati pratiṣṭhām labhate, iti vaiśyaḥ* (*Mahābhārata*, Śāntiparva 189.7, Nīlakaṇṭha). Similarly, śūdra is described as *parasevādina śucaṁ śokoṁ abhidudrāva prāptavān iti śūdraḥ* (*Nyāyanirṇaya* 1.3.34). Because a śūdra is thus defined, śūdra is a *varṇa*. The literal meaning of *jāti* is birth: *satimūle tadvipāko jātyāyurbhogaḥ* (*Yogasūtra* 2.13). In later period due to *varṇa* being determined by birth, two expressions *jāti* and *varṇa* became equivalent.

Again, if somebody wants to retain the notion of *jāti* in the sense of the Nyāya-Vaiśeṣika as one, eternal and inherent in many, then also there will be no difficulty in accounting for changes in *jāti*s of individuals. Thus *guṇa*s and *karma*s are not the producer or destroyer of *jāti*s. These *guṇa*s and *karma*s are the determiners of the relation between an individual and an eternal *jāti*. The eternal *brāhmaṇatva jāti*, existed in the past, exist in the present and will also exist in future. Similarly *śūdratva jāti* is eternal and it had existence in the past, exists at present and will exist in future. Since *guṇa* and *karma* are the determiners of the relation between the eternal *jāti* and the individual, the latter acquires the requisite *jāti* according to the possession of his *guṇas–karma*s. Thus in the same individual with change in time, there can be different *varṇa*s. In that case *jāti* that is inherent in an individual may also get changed. But that does not imply the destruction of *jāti*.

It may however be asked, if *brāhmaṇatva* or *kṣatriyatva jāti* in spite of being eternal are admitted to have changes, then why are we not granting changes to *jāti*s such as *paśutva* and *manuṣyatva*? In answer to this question, attention has been drawn to the distinction between these two sorts of *jāti*s. In one case *jāti* of individuals are expressed (*abhivyañjaka*) by their *avayavasaṁsthāna* (arrangement of the parts of their body); and in the case of *varṇa*, *jāti*s are expressed by *guṇa* and *karma*. Thus the author draws a distinction between being implied by quality and action, in other words, *guṇakarma-vyaṅga* and being implied by arrangement of bodily parts, in other words, *avayava-saṁsthāna-vyaṅga*. When there is change in the *abhivyañjaka guṇa* and *karmas* there is change in the *jāti*. Why does *jāti* which is eternal requires *guṇa*s and *karma*s, as its *abhivyañjaka*? Thus it may be said by the objector that *jāti*s do not require *guṇa*s-*karma*s as their determiners. But Viśvarūpānanda asks if *jāti* as eternal does not require any determiner to determine the relation between the individual and the eternal *jāti*, then why should the proponents of division of *jāti* on the basis of birth, (*janmagatajātivādī*) require birth (*janma*) to determine *jāti*?

Hence he retains his position by saying that even if *jāti* is eternal, it may have changes in its locus. There are lots of passages in different Śāstras that admit the possibility of the changes of *varṇa* in the same individual in different times. The following statements support the claim regarding the possibility of change of *jāti* of an individual:[51]

ebhistu karmabhirdevi śubhairacaritaistathā ।
śūdra brāhmaṇatāmyāti vaiśya kṣatriyatām vrajet ॥

sarvo 'yam brāhmaṇo loke vṛtten tuvidhīyate ।
vṛtte sthitastu śūdro 'pi brāhmaṇatvamniyacchati ॥

The above-quoted passage is very clearly indicating *jātiparivṛtti*; literally speaking *parivṛtti* indicates moving to and fro of *jāti* or substitution of one *jāti* by another (without destroying the locus). Performance of good deeds by an agent substitutes the quality of being śūdra by the quality of being brāhmaṇa, or substitutes the quality of being vaiśya by the quality of being kṣatriya.

We may also quote the following statement maintaining that quality or potency and action determine *jāti*:

ekavarṇamidam pūrvam viśvamāsīt yudhiṣṭhira ।
guṇakriyāviśeṣeṇa cāturvarṇyam pratiṣṭhitam ॥

This passage also speaks in favour of *jātiparivṛtti* or exchanges of *jāti* for one another. Though initially there was one *varṇa* in the universe, four *varṇa*s are established on the basis of peculiarity of quality and action.

Āpastamba Dharmasūtra 2.5.11.10-11 says:

dharmacaryāya jaghanyaḥ varṇaḥ pūrvam pūrvam varṇamāpadyate jātiparivṛttau । *adharmacaryayā pūrvo varṇaḥ jaghanyam jaghanyam varṇamāpadyate jātiparivṛttau* ।

This passage also corroborates changes in *jāti* from a worse state to a better one or from a better state to a worse one according to the nature of quality acquired or action performed by the agent.

Viśvarūpānanda has cited enough evidence of instances of changes in *varṇa*. Gārgya, who was the founder of Gārgya *gotra*, Mudgal, who was the founder of the Maudgalya *gotra* and many others who were kṣatriya but later on changed to brāhmaṇa. He cites *Śrīmadbhāgavata* 9.19-21 and 9.30. Again from *Vāyu Purāṇa*

---

[51] *Mahābhārata*, Anuśāsana, 143.26.51, etc.

(92.4-5) and *Viṣṇu Purāṇa* (4.8.1), he alludes to a kṣatriya known as Śuṇaka in whose family brāhmaṇa, kṣatriya, vaiśya and śūdra – all were born. He alludes to *Śrīmadbhāgavata* (5.4.11) to cite the case of kṣatriya Ṛṣabhadeva, who had eighty-one brāhmaṇa sons.

Again there are instances where out of rage of brāhmaṇa or for their unwillingness to educate themselves many kṣatriyas were turned into śūdras (*Mahābhārata* 33.21-22). Again another kṣatriya called Vītahavya was turned into *brahmarṣi* by the favour of another sage, Bhṛgu (*Mahābhārata,* Anuśāsana 30.57). Again Viśvarūpānanda cites from *Rāmāyaṇa* of Vālmīki where in the womb of Manu, who is daughter of Prajāpati Dakṣa and wife of Kaśyapa, brāhmaṇa, kṣatriya, vaiśya and śūdra – these four types of men were born. This makes it clear that according to the principle of *guṇakarma* to the same couple children belonging to different *varṇa*s were born.

In *Mahābhārata* we know that Droṇācārya, Kṛpācārya are also such instances (*Mahābhārata,* Śāntiparva 296.13-14). The famous Veda Vyāsa and Maharṣi Viśvāmitra are all good examples good for substantiating that birth was not the determiner of *varṇa* but their quality and work. In *Vālmīki Rāmāyaṇa* elaborate descriptions are provided to show how strenuously kṣatriya Viśvāmitra endeavoured to control his sense-organs and acquire qualities requisite for being a brāhmaṇa (*Vālmīki Rāmāyaṇa* 1.57-65).

We need not, however, continue this endless debate. What I have tried to establish is that a broad-based and balanced account of *varṇa* and *varṇa-dharma* is rooted in the Vedic literatures but has not been properly explored or utilized. Sri Aurobindo counselled:

> The ancient *cāturvarṇya* must not be judged by its later disintegrated degeneration and gross meaningless parody, the caste system.[52]

No sane Hindu has anything to dissent from Ambedkar's scathing comment: "It (caste) has completely disorganized and demoralized

---

52 Sri Aurobindo, 1998, *The Foundations of Indian Culture*, p. 118.

the Hindus".[53] If *varṇa-dharma* is to be accepted as one of the pillars of Dharma-Ethics, the interpretation and the elucidation of *varṇa* after *Bhāvadīpikā,* or Sri Aurobindo[54] or Ambedkar[55] need not be overlooked as possible interpretations.

Āsrama-dharma

Maitra has made an important comment about *āśrama-dharma.* He writes:

> Through the education of the *āśrama* duties the individual becomes a useful member of his society or community and as there is a progressive unfolding of the power of the individual, the code of self-education also varies in the different stages.[56]

In Indian ethics we find that equal emphasis has been laid upon duties which individuals as qua individuals need to perform for the growth and development of one's own self; but also individuals are viewed as members of a society or a community taking into cognizance that an individual's relation to the society or community varies according to the age of the individual concerned. This also shows their awareness about the relation between the age of an individual and his capability to perform an action. The duties of *āśrama* (different stages of life) constitute the other class of these specific duties. There are four major *āśrama-dharma*s admitted in the Vaidika Dharma-Ethical system. These are duties relating to stages of life (*āśrama*) known as *brahmacarya, gārhasthya, vānaprastha* and *saṁnyāsa.*

The duties of a *brahmacārī* who practises sexual abstinence is to serve his preceptor (*guru-suśruṣā*), to collect fuel (*īndhana ahāraṇa*), to offer incense to the sacrificial fire (*agnau homaḥ*), to collect alms (*bhaikṣya*). Further it has been categorically stated in *Hārīta Saṁhitā*

53 Rodrigues, 2007, op. cit., p. 267.

54 Sanyal, 2010, op. cit.

55 In a seminar to Commemorate Centenary of the Publication of *Annihilation of Caste* at Jadavpur University, a lecture was delivered entitled, "Ambedkar on Varṇa and Jāti".

56 Maitra, 1963, op. cit., p. 24.

that "a *brahmacārī* should study [the Vedas] properly"[57] for without which he does not attain the fruit of Vedic studies. The person who performs righteous deeds disregarding the proper rules is called *durātmā* (wicked souls) for he fails to attain the fruits of the Vedic studies. In the Indian model study is not barren theoretical study for much emphasis has been placed both on the theoretical and practical applications of the Vedic studies. This is evident from *Hārīta Saṁhitā* 3.5:

> Therefore for attaining success in his Vedic study, he should perform rites laid down in the Vedas. He should learn from his preceptor, the many and varied rules for attaining purification.

A *brahmacārī* is always required to attain purity. Initially it may seem that importance has been given always upon physical or outer purification. There are *śloka*s where it has been told that *brahmacārī* should cleanse his teeth, rinse his mouth carefully everyday. Students during this stage of *brahmacarya* or practise of sexual abstinence are also required to maintain inner purity or *śauca*. In *Śaṅkha Saṁhitā* a student (*brahmacārī*) has been advised to be humble in spirit and devoid of arrogance. He should acquire all sorts of good habits like that of getting up early in the morning before his preceptor rises and must go to bed after his preceptor sleeps. The *brahmacārī* has been told to avoid use of honey, meat-diet, he should avoid all music, dancing and avoid all female company. He should observe continence and have self-control. Those who are wise should follow these rules while studying the Vedas.

The *brahmacarya āśrama* may be viewed as a period of learning restraint (*saṁyama*) and receiving education. Whenever in the context of Hindu culture the discussion about the pertaining of knowledge occurs, it must not be guessed that knowledge is always theoretical and about training in religion. Apart from logic, phonology, mathematics, trigonometry, etc. were also subjects with which disciples had to be acquainted. The Hindus in their

---

57 *kuryādadhyayanām brahmacāri yathāvidhi* – 3.3

search for the trans-life, they do not ignore the reality of the life. In *Hārīta Saṁhitā* the description of a *brahmacārī* is as follows:

> A *brahmacārī* who being self-controlled and devoted to the service of his preceptor, moves about on this earth, acquires an auspicious learning, so difficult of attainment, and comes by its fruit (i.e. virtue, worldly-profit, desire and emancipation) so easily attainable (by such a person).[58]

There are two sorts of *brahmacārīs*, one is an ordinary *brahmacārī* and the other is a *naiṣṭhika brahmacārī*. A *naiṣṭhika brahmacārī* does not enter into *gr̥hastha* life, he lead a celebate life and vows lifelong abstinence and stays with his spiritual preceptor. In the Smr̥tiśāstras there are various other directions for conducting a *brahamcārī*'s life. All these details are not important for our purpose.

When a student leaves his *brahmacaryāśrama*, his preceptor gives him advices to carry on his later life in the path of *dharma*, he also advises his student to keep his family lineage intact. In *Taittirīya Upaniṣad*, the teacher is instructing his pupil to lead family life in a proper way. This advice is quite remarkable: *prajā ca svādhyāya-pravacane ca* | *prajanaḥ ca svādhyāya pravacane ca* | *prajātiḥ ca svādhyāya pravacane ca* |[59] Previously during the student's stay at *ācāryāśrama* leading the life of austere practices and physical hardship he has also learnt to prepare himself for the life of enjoyment.

The stage of family life (*gārhasthya āśrama*), in a sense, is regarded as the most important among the four *āśramas*, because it gives a unity to the social frameworks and keeps them together. Other orders of existence depend upon this *gārhasthya āśrama* for their sustenance. In this *āśrama*, more stress is upon the ideals of

---

58 *yo brahmacārī vidhinā samāhitaścaret pr̥thivyām gurusevane rataḥ* |
samprāpya vidyāmatidurlabhām śivām phalam ca tasyāḥ sulabhantu bindati ||
– 3.16

59 *Taittirīya Upaniṣad* 1.9.

"Progeny with the study and teaching of Veda. Act of procreation with the study and teaching of Veda. Children of thy children with the study and teaching of Veda – *these duties*." – Sri Aurobindo, *The Upaniṣads* II, p. 212.

living a social life. It has been further stated in chap. 3.69 of *Manusmṛti* that with effort the *gṛhasthāśrama* has to be retained. One can enjoy unlimited pleasure in this worldly life because of *gṛhasthāśrama* and also can enjoy imperishable heavenly bliss in other world. In *Vyāsa Saṁhitā* we find enormous praise for the *gārhasthyāśrama* and Vyāsa is commenting that household is the best hermitage in the world; in the *Vyāsa Saṁhitā* much importance has been attached to the proper discharge of duties as a householder. *Vasiṣṭha Saṁhitā* pays compliments to the *gārhasthyāśrama*, as the most distinguished among the four *āśrama*s. The reason for praising the *gārhasthyāśrama* is that a householder alone celebrates life, and performs sacrifices and austerities. *Vasiṣṭha Saṁhitā* states: as all rivers and rivulets go to the ocean to be integrated, so (the spirit of) all orders are amalgamated within the life-stage of the householder.[60]

In the *gṛhasthāśrama*, the necessity for adopting one profession or another has been elaborately discussed in *Manu Saṁhitā*. Without entering into the details about the types of professions to be pursued, the general spirit of *Manu Saṁhitā* may be stated: everybody should perform actions that are according to his capacity and *adhikāra* diligently. It is also the duty of a married man to beget children by cohabitation with his wife, but it should be in proper season. The *gārhasthyāśrama* may be viewed as the period of activity and raising family.

In *Hārīta Saṁhitā* much emphasis has been laid on *atithi-sevā* by a householder.

> Thereafter he should offer *bali* (offerings of food) to the Viśvadevas according to the rite thereof: A householder should wait for a guest till the hour of milking the cow.[61]

---

60 *Vasiṣṭha Saṁhitā*, chap. 8.
yathā nadīnadaḥ sarve samudre yānti saṁsthitiṁ |
evamāśraminaḥ sarve gṛhasthe yānti saṁsthitiṁ ||

61 *viśvadevam tato kuryādvali karma vidhānataḥ* |
godohamātramakaṁkedatithiṁ prati vai gṛhi || – *Hārīta Saṁhitā* 4.55

Again it has been said, "... the guests should be daily worshipped by a householder with respect and according to his might."[62] It has been said that a householder should be such that he reveres his elders and preceptors, supports his servants, is kind, non-envious, truthful and self-controlled, daily performs his *homa* and *japa* (divine contemplation and mental recitation of *mantra*), is faithful to his own wife without coveting that of another; the householder by his activities should not bring any *dishonour* to his family. The right performance of his family duties brings to him the merit of a pilgrimage without travelling out of his own house.

Among other duties of a householder are not to steal, not to covet other men's wives and riches. The householder acquires merit by being hospitable to the brāhmaṇas and alms to the poor and offerings to the Viśvadevas. In *Vyāsa Saṁhitā* other duties of a householder have been elaborately stated. A householder has to pay off his different debts to different people. Debt to gods such as Indra or Prajāpati are paid off by offering food. It has been said in the same Saṁhitā that a householder who has subdued all his senses, his house becomes as holy as Kurukṣetra, Naimiṣa, Puṣkara, Gaṅgādvāra and Kedāra. The wealth is not only for his consumption. The emphasis has been put on the act of giving, i.e. charity. The wealth spent in the act of charity towards the good brāhmaṇas is only true wealth. Thus, encourages giving in charity.

A *brahmacārī* after finishing the studies of the Vedas should marry a girl not of the same *pravara* (spiritual clanship) or *gotra* (family) and not in any way related to him. The eight forms of marriage recognized by the Dharmaśāstras are: (i) Brāhma, (ii) Daiva, (iii) Ārṣa, (iv) Prājāpatya, (v) Āsura, (vi) Gāndharva, (vii) Rākṣasa, and (viii) Paiśāca. All these eight forms of marriage are discussed in detail in different Smṛti literatures. The first four forms of marriages are generally recommendable in respect of the brāhmaṇas and the Gāndharva and Rākṣasa forms are commendable in respect of kṣatriyas. The form of marriage in

---

[62] *tasmādatithaye kāryam pūjanam gṛhamedhina* |
bhaktyā ca śaktito nityam viṣṇorarccanādanantaram || – Ibid. 4.59

which the bride is ceremoniously given away to the bridegroom, without any solicitation on his part is called Brāhma. In *Gautama Saṁhitā*, it has been stated further that a form of marriage in which a girl, bedecked with ornaments, is given away in a marriage to an erudite man of good conduct and respectable connections is called Brāhma. The marriage in which a daughter is given to a priest officiating at a religious sacrifice in the form of honorarium is called Daiva; Ārṣa, a form of marriage derived from the sages (*ṛṣi*s): it is a form of marriage in which the father of the bride receives one or two pairs of *kine* from the bridegroom.[63] The form of marriage in which the bride is given to one who solicits her hands is called the *prājāpatya-vivāha*; the Prājāpatya is the common form of Hindu marriage that is still in practice. The form of marriage in which the bride is purchased or given away for money is called Āsura. In the Gāndharva form of marriage the bride and the bridegroom unite out of love. The Rākṣasa is a system of marriage in which the bridegroom kidnaps the bride or marries her by force. The most heinous form of marriage is the one which happens through the adoption of monstrous means or artful tricks is called Paiśāca. *Gautama Saṁhitā* states, in a Paiśāca marriage the bride is abducted even during her sleep. There are lots of prohibitions and restrictions regarding marriages with other *varṇa*s.

In the Smṛtiśāstra, in *Manusmṛti* and many other literatures also we find that a householder is instructed to perform five *mahāyajña*s. It has been said that a householder should everyday perform those five *yajña*s, though no specific time has been allotted for such performance. Hence these *yajña*s are to be performed so long a person lives. Hence these *yajña*s are regarded as *nitya-karma* for the householder. In *Śaṅkha Saṁhitā* it has been mentioned that in a household, a householder daily destroys animal lives in the oven, by the broomstick, by the grinding stone, in the pestle and mortar, and in the water pitcher. To expiate the sin of destruction of lives, a householder should daily celebrate the five

63 M. Monier-Williams, 1986, *A English-Sanskrit Dictionary*, p. 152.

domestic sacrifices known as *pañca-yajña*, whereby all his sins would be extinguished. These five *yajña*s are *brahmayajña*, *pitr̥yajña*, *daivayajña*, *bhūtayajña* and *nr̥yajña*. These are stated in *Manusmr̥ti* in detail. These five sacrificial ceremonies (*yajña*s) (*bhūta–manuṣya-deva–pitr̥–brahma-yajña*) are required to be performed by a householder every morning and evening by means of one's own earnings. These *pañca-yajña*s are for a married person and their observance is binding on him only if he has necessary strength or capacity (*śakti*) to undergo the hardship involved:

1. *Bhūtayajña* consists in offering of oblations to the *bhūta*s (elements).
2. *Nr̥yajña* consists in serving and entertaining guests. A person who has been invited cannot be regarded as an *atithi*.
3. *Devayajña* is offering of sacrifice to gods of the sacred fire (*homaḥ devayajñaḥ*).
4. *Pitr̥yajña* is paying respect to the dead by observing the funeral rites and other allied ceremonies (*śrāddham pitr̥yajñaḥ*).
5. *Brahmayajña* consists in the recital of sacred texts, i.e. the Vedas (*vedapāṭhas brahmayajñaḥ*).

The duties of a *brahmacārī-gr̥hastha* – who after having completed the duties of his married life is living a life of conjugal abstinence or celibacy at home – are as follows: wearing the bark of trees (*valkalādi-dhāraṇa*), betting the hair grow (*keśādi-dhāraṇa*), living on the roots and fruits of the jungle (*vanasya phalamūlasya bhojanam*) and dining on the surplus of the meal after entertainment of all the guest (*atithiśeṣa-bhojanam*). In a *Śaṅkha Saṁhitā* it has been said that a householder when he finds that his hairs have turned grey and the skin on his body has become loose and wrinkled, and that a son has been born unto his own son, should move to forest. By the practice of penance (*tapas*), he should cause his body to be emaciated. The *brahmacārī-gr̥hastha* is required to perform five types of penances (*pañca-tapas*) with great hardship sitting amidst fires on four sides with the summer sun burning over the head. During the rainy season, he should live in the open without any shelter or shade under the vast expanse of heaven, and take his meals at night, or at the fourth or the sixth part of the day. A self-controlled *brahmacārī*, he should live a life of penance and privation in the forest, whereby a twice-born one should become a member of the *brahmāśrama.*

In *Vasiṣṭha Saṁhitā*, a *vānaprastha* has been told not to enter a village. He shall not tread a ploughed land. He shall gather wild growing roots and fruits, i.e. he should live on raw fruits and roots (*akr̥tam mūlaphalam*). He is advised not to show his muscular strength, rather to be forgiving to everybody. He shall honour guest coming to his hermitage with alms of roots and fruits. He shall only give but never receive. He shall be free from attachment to any house. He should live under a tree. He who thus gives his due to the deities, departed ancestors and men, shall attend to the endless celestial region.[64]

Of the fourfold order of life we have already covered discussions about threefold orders of life as admitted in the Dharma-Ethics tradition. Is it necessary that one will have to strictly follow these four orders of life? A reply to this question may be provided from *Viṣṇu Saṁhitā*: it has been stated that one who has felt an aversion to the pleasures of the orders of life, may do *prājāpatyam* sacrifices and donate all his possessions and take recourse to the fourth order of ascetism (*pravrajyam*).

A *brahmacārī-gr̥hastha* or *vānaprastha* becomes *yati* (mendicant-seer on the attainment of *śraddhā* or *cittaprasāda* (mental serenity and equanimity). This is the stage of life when a man bears gentle and harmless attitude to all sentient creatures for at this stage he has accomplished destruction of all *karma* potencies of his works (*karmas*), and has performed with care without any lapse the acts of self-discipline as laid down in the *yamas* and *niyamas*.[65] The *yamas* are thus the duties of self-restraint, in this sense veracity

---

64 *dadyāddevapitr̥ manuṣyebhayoḥ* ।
sa gaccet svargamanantyam ॥ – *Vasiṣṭha Saṁhitā*, p. 775

65 *Yamas* and *niyamas* are very important notions and would be discussed elaborately in a later chapter.

(*satya*) implies restraint in this sense, i.e. restraint of the self's tendency to exaggeration and misrepresentation in the interest of momentary self-advantage. The *niyamas* on the contrary are rules of self-realization, i.e. the realization of the self's true essence as spirit. Thus while the *yamas* are negative and restrictive, the *niyamas* are positive and objective rules of self-expansion and development. The ideal of *saṁnyāsa* as preached by Indian thinker has often been misunderstood. It has been said that *saṁnyāsī* is regarded as the most respectable person by all, but it has been alleged that this ideal of *saṁnyāsī* has no connection with philanthropy or good of others. This ideal is very much self-created, and since it is duty of everyone to look into one's own goodness, so this sort of ideal does not tarnish anybody's character.

We see that the Hindu view of life emphasizes the claims of the present living state in the scheme of ethics. But they never consider that sort of human existence to be the final. The underlying presupposition is that man essentially transcends these limitations of space, time and circumstances. The institution of *saṁnyāsa* is the expression of this transcendental view of life. There are great debates among interpreters as to the exact notion of *saṁnyāsa* which is the pivotal concept in *saṁnyāsa aśrama*. In this regard we may concentrate upon the Upaniṣads to clarify the exact implication of *saṁnyāsa*. In this connection we need to understand the important distinction between *indriya-nigraha* and *indriya-niyantraṇa*. It is to be observed that the Upaniṣads in general harp upon *indriya-niyantraṇa*. *Niyantraṇa* (control) is a different idea from that of *nigraha* (prevention). According to the Indian conception a man's body and mind need to be controlled in order to lead a successful life. The Upaniṣads never encouraged one to avoid or flee away from family responsibility. The *saṁnyāsavāda*, rigidly interpreted, advises one to prevent his body and mind from being drawn towards external objects of delight. But the Upaniṣadic view is not the expression this sort of rigidity. It cannot be denied that a man has a natural attraction towards objects of enjoyment, his sense-organs, his mind draws him towards such objects. Now those who are protagonists of rigid *saṁnyāsavāda* have found that if this is allowed to happen this leads to distraction of mind (*cittavikṣepa*) and hinders concentration (*ekāgratā*). Hence *saṁnyāsavāda* to achieve concentration of mind generally recommends the path of (*kṛcchrasādhana*). Hence they attempt to dissociate sense-organs always from the objects of enjoyment, so that mentality for avoiding objects of sense-organs grows. They speak that there is no peace in the enjoyment of senses, no gratification, and the worldly life is temporary and non-substantial. They try to convince that objects of sense which attract us are ugly and unworthy. Thus they advise always to avoid women (*kāminī*) and gold (*kañcana*). Thus to these thinkers, who propound *saṁnyāsavāda, kṛcchrasādhana* (undergoing hardship) and *indriya-nigraha* (suppression of sense-organs) are the main objectives.

But in the Upaniṣads we find a remarkable difference from this sort of attitude towards sense-organs and their enjoyment. The other group does not deny the importance of seizure of sense-organs from objects. But that is not the proper end. The *saṁyama* of *indriya* is not the primary goal. If a person, proficient in bodily development, may enhance the development of his body; but if he forgets to utilize the body in the performance of actions is ridiculous. Thus same may happen with a *saṁnyāsī*, understood in a rigid sense, who trains his *indriya* to withdraw from objects. If such a person forgets about the secondary nature of this task, it would be nonetheless ridiculous.

Rabindranath Tagore very nicely describes the worthiness of *brahmacarya*. The observance of *brahmacarya* is not a mere practice for withdrawing senses from objects. Rabindranath says, that type of *brahmacarya* is only a sort of self-deception, because it does not make any use of the *vṛtti*s of human beings. He does not deny some positive role in the context of educating, for through the practice of undergoing misery one learns the technique of self-control. So *kṛcchrasādhana* has a positive role but it is only a secondary role. Sense-organs have attachment towards objects but that does not mean that our ideal should be complete severing the connection between sense-organs and objects. The ideal of *saṁnyāsa* as preached in the Upaniṣads is that sense connection with objects requires to be controlled.

In *Vasiṣṭha Saṁhitā* about a religious mendicant (*parivrājaka*) it has been said that a religious mendicant is expected to promise safety to all creatures from injury. The ascetic should live on alms, for it is better than fasting. An ascetic is required to be compassionate towards everybody. Freedom from rebirths is certain for him who always lives in the forest, who has conquered the sense-organs, who has renounced all sensual gratification, whose mind is devoted to the meditation of the supreme self and who is perfectly indifferent. There is no freedom for him who is addicted to the study of the science of words, nor for him who is given to the acceptance of presents in this world, nor for him who is fond of eating and clothing, nor for him who likes beautiful residence. One shall not seek alms by ominous speeches, nor by skill in astrology and palmistry, nor by casuistry. He shall not be dejected when he gets nothing nor glad when he receives something. Renouncing all attachment for earthly possessions he shall seek only as much as needed to sustain life. He alone is the foremost among those who are on the road to emancipation caring neither for a hut, nor for water, nor for clothes, nor for the three *puṣkaras* (the sacred talks at the holy shrines of Puṣkara), nor for a dwelling house, nor for a seat, nor for food.

An elaborate treatment about dos and don'ts of a *yati* or a mendicant is provided in *Śaṅkha Saṁhitā*. A careful observation would reveal some aspects of this *āśrama-dharma*. This stage of life is called *brahmāśrama*. From the third stage of life (*vānaprastha*) to the domain of *brahmāśrama* is not without any action. Through the performance of religious sacrifices (*homas*), the *brāhmaṇa* enters into a *brahmāśrama*. A *brahmāśrama* is mainly supposed to thrive upon begging alms from the householder. They are not supposed to go for alms at any time night or day simply. The *yati* is supposed to stay companionless. Here reference is only to male *yatis*, and he may leave his wife with his sons. The *yati*s are to shun luxury of dresss. He would wear only a girdle cloth to cover his nudity. The *yati* should put his foot-steps purified by sight (*dṛṣṭipuṭam*) carefully observing that he does not tread on any animate being. While drinking water he should drink purified water, should speak words purified with truth (*satyapuṭam vadet vākyam*) and should act as he thinks (*manaḥpuṭam samācaret*). The *yati* should not be bothered by whether good (*kalyāṇa*) or bad (*akalyāṇa*) occurs to him. He should not be bothered whether his body is besmeared with sandal paste or be spattered with clay and ashes. The *yati* is described as one who promotes the well-being of everyone (*sarvabhūtahitakārī*) and is friendly to everyone (*maitraḥ*). The *yati* looks upon gold, stone, brickbat as of same value, and remains absorbed in the contemplation of the infinite and acquires the highest bliss.

Śaṅkha Saṁhitā provides a description of brāhmaṇa as follows: A brāhmaṇa is one who is from his birth apathetic to life considering it to be a series of mental and physical sorrows and sufferings to be borne with the greatest unconcern. Some idea is derived from this description about the person who bears the capacity for being liberated. It has been said that one who views body as a reservoir of excrement, and looks upon the worldly life, and body as the sources of all sorts of disappointment, gets liberation. Further *yati* is advised to keep his body pure by the regular exercises like *prāṇāyāma*. The *pratyāhāra* consists in withdrawing the senses from their objects. The *yogī* has been advised to exhaust *doṣa*s (bodily diseases) with the help of *prāṇāyāma*. The concentration of the mind or controlling of the mind is called *dhāraṇā*, and *dhāraṇā* is also another important quality for the *yati*s. *Dhyāna* (act of profound meditation) enables to see god of gods. These three acts, viz. *dhāraṇā, pratyāhāra* and *dhyāna* are to be practised by the *yati*. It has been stated in *Śaṅkha Saṁhitā* that the *yati* is the person who is griefless (*vītaśoka*), whose soul is purified, beholds the glory of the supreme soul, which is subtler than the subtlest (*aṇoranīyan*), and larger than the largest things (*mahato mahīyan*).

In general, the core of all duties (*dharma*), whether it is *varṇa-dharma* or *āśrama-dharma*, each individual should perform those actions which are according to his *varṇa* and *āśrama*. The observance of *svadharma* has always been encouraged. Thus in the concluding portion of *Hārīta Saṁhitā* it is said:

> . . . there are four *varṇa*s, and four *āśrama*s. Those who abide by their own duties, come by the most excellent result.[66]

The admission of four stages of life and also respective duties suitable for different stages of life are also one of the integral aspects of the Vaidika Dharma-Ethics. To the Vaidika viewpoint the whole human existence is typically moral existence. The ideology of *āśrama-dharma* is the peculiarity of the Vaidika Dharma-Ethics. The Jainas use the term *saṅgha* (community) embracing four orders of monks (*sādhu*s), nuns (*sādhvī*s), laymen (*śrāvaka*s) and laywomen (*śrāvikā*s). Asceticism and renunciation are very prominent among the Jainas. The Buddhist tradition speaks of two orders of *bhikkhu* and *gahapati*. But in the Buddhist tradition the interplay between *bhikkhu* and *gahapati* is discernible. The *gahapati* has to maintain the *bhikkhu*. The *gahapati* for the Buddhist is the source of charity (*dāna*), which in turn maintains the *saṅgha*. The Buddhist and Jaina views do not speak very much about the necessity of *gṛhastha*, i.e. family stage of human beings. In their effort to prioritize the trend of renunciation, the great influence of Buddha who in contrast to the Brāhmanic tradition, followed the śramaṇic vision of life, is discernible. Some argued for abstaining from the stage of *gṛhastha* for giving more attention and effort towards renunciation. The authors of Dharmasūtras, on the other hand, were emphatic on regarding *gṛhasthāśrama* as a pre-condition for renunciation for going through family life, made more difficult and challanging to renounce worldly life.[67] The

---

66 *Hārīta Saṁhitā, The Dharmaśāstra*, vol. 1, p. 187.
varṇaścatvāro . . . catvāraścāpi cāśramāḥ |
svadharme ye tu tiṣṭhanti te yānti paramaṁ gatiṁ || – 7.18

67 Baudhāyana II.10.17.2-5; Āpastamba II.9.21 cited in Romila Thapar, 2003, *Cultural Pasts*, p. 922.

Dharma-Ethics tradition, represented by sub-groups, how far differed and agreed is a debatable matter and requires a separate investigation. From the present discussion on *āśrama-dharma*, we derive two distinct corollaries of the Vaidika Dharma-Ethics:

1. In the Vaidika Dharma-Ethics tradition emphasis on social obligation of an individual is quite obvious. The logic behind making *saṁnyāsa*, or recluse the final stage in the life cycle is to vindicate that for an embodied social being performance of social obligations is not less important than renunciation.
2. The four *āśrama*s are theoretical preconditions to the concept of *puruṣārtha* (fourfold objectives) of human existence.[68]

[68] In the next chapter the fourfold *puruṣārtha*s are being discussed.

4

The Fourfold Scheme of Puruṣārthas
Dharma, Artha, Kāma and Mokṣa

In the Vedic scheme of human life and existence the concept of *puruṣārtha* (objective of human beings) is one of the primary concepts. Grammatically speaking, the Sanskrit expression *puruṣārtha* is a compound expression consisting of *puruṣa* and *artha*. *Puruṣa* signifies human individual, not in its literal sense, male person. The other constituting expression *artha* of the compound expression *puruṣārtha* has various senses such as aim or purpose, motive or reason, thing or object, object of the senses and wealth or property. The concept of *puruṣārtha* has been analysed as *puruṣasya artha* (objects of desire of human individuals). This analysis brings out the descriptive meaning of *puruṣārtha*, and thus no doubt brings out broadly speaking, psychology of human nature. However, questions may arise as to if Indian theory of *puruṣārtha* is only a description of what human beings psychologically desire, and does not have any value or normative component in its meaning, how far the discussion of *puruṣārtha* would be relevant in the context of Dharma-Ethics. Does the theory of *puruṣārtha* contain an evaluative aspect as well? Does the theory of *puruṣārtha* convey anything about what a human being ought to desire or aim at? It may be most pertinently asked, what human does value should or ought to be valued?

In the present chapter, in the first place, an attempt has been made to discuss about each of the *puruṣārtha*s spoken of in the scheme of the fourfold *puruṣārtha*s and second, to discuss about the nature of each of the *puruṣārtha*s in relation to one another. In the final part of this chapter an attempt will be made to provide answer to the query as to whether the recognition of *puruṣārtha*s entails any prescriptive code.

The *puruṣārthas* as have already been pointed out are enumerated to be four and these are *dharma* (morality), *artha* (wealth), *kāma* (desire) and *mokṣa* (liberation). These four *puruṣārthas* are closely interrelated with one another. However, there is some controversy as to whether there were originally three (*trivarga*) or four (*caturvarga*) *puruṣārthas*, the *trivargas* consisting of *dharma, artha* and *kāma,* the fourth *puruṣārtha mokṣa* being a latter addition. In fact, Cārvāka philosophers consider *kāma* as the only goal of life (*kāma evaikaḥ puruṣārthaḥ*) and *artha* as the means or instrument for attaining *kāma*. From this point of view, *dharma* and *artha* have only been accorded instrumental value. In order to form some idea about the Vedic scheme of morality, a proper understanding about these objectives is very much important. No single text, however, is sufficient to present all the details about these four *puruṣārthas*. Nor can we depend upon any particular school of philosophy to get a complete idea about the theory of *puruṣārthas*. In this connection we may refer to the epics *Rāmāyaṇa* and *Mahābhārata,* different Dharmaśāstras and *Arthaśāstra*. From the Indian viewpoint, both *Rāmāyaṇa* and *Mahābhārata* are often considered as *itihāsa* (history). The notion of *itihāsa,* broadly speaking, embodies specifications regarding morals, wealth, desire and liberation through investigations into the events of the past.

> *dharmārthakāmamokṣāṇām upadeśa samanvitam* ।
> *pūrvavṛttam kathāyuktamitihāsaḥ prakṣyete* ॥[1]

One of the frequently debated issues as to whether, in Indian culture, no importance has been assigned to human life and worldly existence, may also be addressed in course of this discussion. We may be able to throw some light on the role of the Vedic viewpoint in generating optimism and encouragement to human existence. It is important to deliberate on the Indian concept of man, i.e. how do Indian philosophers understand the essence of man. Without entering into any detailed discussions about the nature

---

1 Kaliprasanna Sinha (tr.), 2001, *Mahābhārata*, vol. 1, 55.

of man, with reference to different Indian viewpoints separately, it suffices to mention, following two central beliefs in general, of *āstika*-minded Indian philosophers: one is man's aspect of spiritual immortality and the other is its aspect of mortality, struggling with daily chores of human existence. Of the four objectives of human life (*puruṣārthas*) recognized by the Hindu belief system, three objectives, viz. *dharma, artha* and *kāma,* mainly cater to this worldly existence; on the other hand, the last one, *mokṣa* is indicative of trans-world existence. We may begin to analyse the concept of *dharma* from the perspective of *Mahābhārata;* the fundamental questions about *dharma* are really the questions[2] posed by Yudhiṣṭhira to Bhīṣma. He asks:

1. What is *dharma*? (*ko 'yam dharma*?)
2. Why and wherefore is *dharma*? (*kuto dharma*?)
3. Do the fruits of *karma* bear result in this world, or in the other world? Or in both the worlds? (*dharmastvayamihārthaḥ*? *kimamutropi vā bhavet*? *ubhoyārtho hi va dharmastanme brūhi pitāmaha*?)

In the Vedic literature, as we have already found, the expression *dharma* has been used in different senses and it is difficult to decide which particular sense would be the most suitable one. It has been pointed out that it is also difficult to translate the expression *dharma* in English. We may once again recapitulate some of the senses of *dharma*. In one important sense of the term *dharma,* it is taken to mean *karma*. Performance or non-performance of actions, which are duties, is believed to result in *puṇya* (merit) or *pāpa* (demerit) which are also referred to as *dharma* and *adharma*. We come across discussion about five types of *dharma,* in the sense of duties, which are *varṇa-dharma, āśrama-dharma, nitya-dharma, naimittika-dharma* and *guṇa-dharma* in *Rāmāyaṇa, Mahābhārata, Manusmṛti* and other literatures on the Dharmaśāstras. There are three authoritative sources of *dharma*: these are Śruti, Smṛti and Śiṣṭācāra. Śruti is the Veda, and it is considered as a

---

[2] Haridas Bhattacharya, *Mahābhārata*, Śāntiparva, vol. 37, p. 2567.

separate and independent *pramāṇa* or source of valid belief by some schools of Indian philosophers. There is a vast body of Smṛti literatures which is supposed to document various deliberations on the basis of memory, regarding the meaning of Vedic sentences. Śiṣṭācāra stands for *ācāra* (practices) of well-disciplined persons, sometimes taken to mean specially those practices of Vedic branches, which are no longer read or known by the people of present generation. These activities are known as *śiṣṭācāra* and have their source in the Vedas. In this connection, an important question may be raised as to who may be called *śiṣṭa* (disciplined or cultured)? We may recapitulate the characteristics of a disciplined person from the description of a disciplined or cultured person as given by Bhīṣma to Yudhiṣṭhira:

> Those who are not afraid of rebirth or hell, those who consider the pleasant and the unpleasant are similar, those who are never attracted towards any object of enjoyment, those who are disciplined in their actions, those who have control over their sense-organs and stick to the truth, those who are not moved by happiness or pain, those who are very much compassionate, liberally disposed, mild in temperament, and aware of all virtues, those who do not take any gift from others, those who always with great devotion honour ancestors, gods and guests, and do not hesitate to give his own life for the sake of others and those who are not perturbed by anybody.[3]

In some other passages of *Mahābhārata*, we come across other characteristics of well-mannered persons: of such persons it has been further stated that

> . . . they do not embrace *dharma* out of greed for wealth or fame, they follow the path of righteousness considering it to be a necessary duty as taking of food is absolutely necessary for the maintenance of the body.[4]

In *Gautamasūtra*, it has been stated that along with the Vedas, and

---

3 Sinha, 2001, 2nd vol., Śāntiparva, 158 adhyāya, p. 645.

4 Ibid.

tradition, and the practice of those who know all these are to be considered as authority on the subject. The Vedas and traditional texts suffice as source of *dharma* generally, but when these do not address any issue, the practice of a cultured person is considered to be decisive.

The vast body of literatures conveys to us what is to be accepted as *dharma* and what is to be rejected as *adharma*. Śāstric injunctions regarding performance of some actions or their prohibitions regarding abstentions from certain actions may not be known to everybody, but there are disciplined or cultured people who know meaning of all these injunctions and prohibitions, hence it is required to follow their practices to determine what is *dharma* and *adharma*. The people who are of demonic or satanic nature do not know what is virtue and what is vice, nor do they know about any textual injunctions or prohibitions as determining the nature of virtue or vice, nor do they care for any advices by *śiṣṭajana* (disciplined people). In *Śrīmadbhagavadgītā*, a person with satanic nature (*āsurivr̥tti*) is described as follows:

> *yaḥ śāstravidhimutsr̥jya vartate kāmakārataḥ* | *na sa siddhimvāpnoti na sukham na param gatim* ||[5]

It has been stated that one, who disregards injunctions of authoritative texts and goes on doing actions according to his own impulse, is not fit for obtaining the goal of human life, nor does he enjoy worldly happiness nor liberation-like ultimate bliss. *Dharma*-compendium does not only consist of *vidhivākyas* (imperative statements) enjoining duties, nor only *vidhivākyas* are to be regarded as Śāstra alone. *Vidhivākyas* are determiners of *dharma*, and statements of Vedānta are determiners of *brahma*.

Another important expression other than *dharma* is *daṇḍa* which has often been observed as a close ally to *dharma*; now, the question may be raised as to whether the concept of *dharma* is the same as the concept of *daṇḍa*? Or, do the uses of the concept of *dharma* and that of *daṇḍa* overlap one another? We have discussed about

---

[5] Nalinikanta Brahma (ed.), 1986, *Śrīmadbhagavadgītā*, 16.23, p. 1033.

Dharmaśāstra and also about its object of concern. In the classical Indian philosophical tradition, among the four types of *vidyā* (studies) recognized, *daṇḍanīti* is one. *Daṇḍanīti* proclaims its objective is to study *naya* (justice) and *anaya* (injustice). In many discussions *daṇḍanīti,* Arthaśāstra and *rājanīti* are understood in more or less synonymous senses. But in some cases the interpreters of Śāstra differ from this standpoint. In the commentary named *Mitākṣarā* on *Yājñavalkyasmṛti,* it has been said that the object of pursuit for Arthaśāstra is *artha,* meaning thereby agriculture, rearing of animals, trade, etc. for acquiring wealth. But how far this sort of characterization is acceptable has been questioned. In the Indian taxonomy on subjects of study, there is a clear-cut admission of Vārtāśāstra. The work of agriculture, animal rearing, trade, etc. are objectives of Vārtāśāstra and gold, silver, copper, animals, iron – these are all called *vārtā*. If *dhana* (wealth) is taken to be the meaning of *artha,* Arthaśāstra, and Vārtāśāstra and Dhanaśāstra all come to acquire the same meaning. But when types of *vidyā* (studies) are named, we find separate mention of Daṇḍanītiśāstra and Vārtāśāstra.

Recently pursued subject like economics has close affinity with Vārtāśāstra of ancient India. What is called Arthaśāstra is different because its objective has been stated differently: The requirement for the Arthaśāstra has been stated to obtain the land that has not been possessed, to look after the land that is in possession, to develop the land that has been possessed and to give the developed land to a right person – thus understood, this discipline is closer to *daṇḍanīti.* From some quarters apprehensively it has been said that, "If *daṇḍanīti* is not properly understood, then that will necessarily lead to the total annihilation of a state, and if a state is annihilated there will be no prosperity or liberation." The *Nirukta* of Yāska, has given different senses to the expression *daṇḍa*. One of the senses of *daṇḍa* is to sustain apart from its other senses like that of "to repress" or "to punish". Commonly, the expression *daṇḍa* signifies the stick that was used by the farmer to drive away cow or other animals from eating the paddy from the field. Thus from the extension of this commonsensical meaning of *daṇḍa,* the sense of *daṇḍa* turns out to be the basis of protection (*rakṣākāraṇam*). The householder protects his wealth with the help of *daṇḍa*. Arjuna said:

> *daṇḍa sāsti prajāḥ sarva daṇḍa evabhirakṣati* ।
> *daṇḍa supteṣu jāgarti daṇḍam dharmam vidurbudhāḥ* ।।[6]

Thus, *daṇḍa* is spoken of as the controller and protector of the subjects. When everybody is asleep, *daṇḍa* remains awake. The power of restraint is called *daṇḍa*. Manu and Yājñavalkya have mentioned that *dharma* and *daṇḍa* are the same. To quote from *Manusmr̥ti*, *daṇḍam dharmam* (*daṇḍa* is *dharma*). It has been stated in *Mahābhārata* that all persons follow the path of truth in the fear of *daṇḍa*.[7] Though all beings of the world are related by the relation, of being an eatable and being an eater, the application of *daṇḍa* enables to fulfil the purpose of everyone. It has been remarked by some that *daṇḍa* has been created by God to protect the world.[8] Thus the role of *daṇḍa* is to sustain all beings in their respective roles. Hence in that sense Daṇḍanītiśāstra may be considered helpful in making rooms for individuals to attain objectives of their life.[9] In *Mahābhārata*, Bhīṣma maintained that the principle of *daṇḍa* in association with the principle of justice protects the world.

Dharma is worthy of pursuit, that *dharma* is superior to other *puruṣārtha*s, it has been mentioned in different literatures. In *Manu Saṁhitā*, it has been said that *dharma* is the true friend of an individual because it moves with the individual even after his death. Friends abandon the dead body as wood and iron on the earth, and go away, but *dharma* follows the person.[10]

---

6 Haridas Bhattacharya, *Mahābhārata*, Śāntiparva, *Pañcadaśo 'dhyāya*, 2, 1400 BS, p. 114.

7 *daṇḍasyaiva bhāyadete manuṣyā vartmāni sthitāḥ* । – Ibid., 15.12, p. 117

8 *daṇḍo vidhātra vihito dharmārthau bhūvi rakṣitam* । – Ibid., 15.35, p. 123

9 *daṇḍonityam praṇītāyām sarve siddhanti upakramaḥ* । – Ibid., 15.28, p. 121

10 *Manu Saṁhitā* 8.17, p. 202.
eka eva suhr̥ddharmo nidhane 'pyanujāti yaḥ ।
śarīrena samamnāśam sarvamanyadhigacchati ।।

In the Vedic tradition, *dharma* has been considered to be an object of practice or *sādhanā*. In the traditional literatures suggestions are found about various ways for the attainment of *dharma*. The perusal of *dharma* has never been unproductive. The question has often arisen as to whether Dharma-Ethics model provides an absolute sense of *dharma* or not. Bhīṣma's deliberations on *dharma* through dialogues with Yudhiṣṭhira and others in the Śāntiparva of the *Mahābhārata* provided clue about various aspects of *dharma*.

Generally by duties are understood *varṇa-dharma*, *āśrama-dharma*, *nityanaimittika-dharma* or *guṇa-dharma*-like duties. Whenever we begin to discuss about *varṇa-dharma*, the question of brāhmaṇa's *varṇa-dharma*, kṣatriya's *varṇa-dharma*, vaiśya's *varṇa-dharma*, or śūdra's *varṇa-dharma* come to the forefront. Similarly, in any discussion about *āśrama-dharma*, the discussion about fourfold *āśrama*s as *brahmacarya*, *gārhasthya*, *vānaprastha* and *saṁnyāsa* will come up. In general discussion about *dharma*s, it may seem that it is based upon rigid and unsurmountable distinctions. The theory of *svadharma* may be supposed to be the ground for giving rise to this sort of perception about *dharma* in the context of Hindu ethics. But if we do not turn a blind eye to the actual situation, the question will definitely come to our mind as to whether commitment to *dharma* is to be understood as independent of situation and time? This sort of rigidity does not seem to be the feature of Dharma-Ethics, especially in *Mahābhārata*. In the third chapter entitled Prāyaścitta in Prakaraṇa Āpaddharma, an elaborate discussion about the performance of *dharma* in times of contingencies has been done. Does the sense of *dharma* change with the change of time? In fact, in *Mahābhārata*, it has been admitted that what was recognized as *dharma* during the first of the four ages of creation of the world, the golden age, called *satyayuga*, was not accepted as *dharma* during the second age of the world (Tretā-yuga), and what was accepted as *dharma* during this period was not accepted as *dharma* during the third stage of the world, the brazen age (Dvāpara-yuga) and finally what was accepted as *dharma* during this age is not accepted as *dharma* in the fourth age of creation of the world known as Kali-yuga. However, question may be raised as to whether this implies a change in the sense of *dharma* or a change in the application of *dharma* to concrete situations? Further it may be asked if the notion of *dharma* is relative, how would we accommodate Kr̥ṣṇa's announcement that whenever there would be decline of *dharma*, Śrī Kr̥ṣṇa would appear?[11] Thus, in the context of Dharma-Ethics, the discussion about the notion of *dharma* as absolute and also as relative is relevant.

Yudhiṣṭhira had expressed his allegiance to *dharma* on many occasions. He had expressed that without any expectation for a consequence he would stick to the path of *dharma*. But in *Mahābhārata* we come across various instances where we observe deviations from *dharma*. Yudiṣṭhira who is considered to be the epitome of *dharma* had also violated norms of *dharma*. Śrī Kr̥ṣṇa himself had told Bhīma that in a just war, he would not be able to defeat Duryodhana. Hence Śrī Kr̥ṣṇa himself advised Bhīma to take recourse to some pretext to defeat Duryodhana. When Bhīma killed an elephant by the name Aśvatthāmā, Yudhiṣṭhira uttered loudly *aśvatthāmā hata* (Aśvatthāmā is killed) and softly *iti kuñjaraḥ* (thus named elephant). Requested by Bhīma Yudhiṣṭhira uttered a sentence like this to protect them in the war. Some have argued that in some cases *mithyā* (falsity) dominates over the truth. Some other cases, where telling of lies has been approved, are to a lover, in marriage and to protect brāhmaṇa and cow.

In *Rāmāyaṇa* also, we come across some instances where the role of *dharma* has been doubted. At one point of time, when Rāma was fighting he was informed that his wife Sītā had died, and hearing that news grief-stricken Rāma became unconscious. Lakṣmaṇa, his younger brother while consoling Rāma said to him that though he is always following the path of truth, he has control over his sense-organs, yet *dharma* could not protect him from this undesirable situation. To disheartened Lakṣmaṇa, it seemed that

[11] *Srimadbhagavadgītā*, 4.7.

dharma has no meaning at all.[12] To quote from Yuddhakāṇḍa, we may refer to another incident from the epic, *Rāmāyaṇa* where again disillusionment about *dharma* surfaces: when Hanumān informed Rāma that before their eyes wailing Sītā, had been killed, Rāma became very sad, and Lakṣmaṇa too became extremely sad seeing Rāma's sadness and began to praise worthiness of *artha* and not of *dharma*: Lakṣmaṇa said that one who has wealth (*artha*) has relatives, friends, one who has wealth is regarded as great among men, as courageous, as intelligent and wise. One who has wealth is regarded as very fortunate and exceptionally qualified.[13]

As the second object of pursuit, the Hindu ethics cites *artha*. In the Vedic ethics, discussions are found about the meaning of *artha* and its usefulness in human life. Broadly speaking, *artha* as *puruṣārtha* has been corroborated as means for acquiring wealth, property, and other economic means of subsistence for a man's material life in general. Without wealth, it is not possible for human beings to sustain and maintain their existence in the material world. In this model knowledge (*vidyā*), land (*bhūmi*), gold (*hiraṇya*), animals (*paśu*), material objects (*bhāṇḍopaskāra*), friends (*mitra*) and their proliferation are all included under *artha*. Knowledge which is recognized as *artha* has four divisions such as *trayī*, including three Vedas *Ṛg*, *Yajur* and *Sāma*, Ānvīkṣikī (*yukti-vidyā*), *daṇḍanīti* and *vārtā*. Manu has included *ātma-vidyā* as another sort of *vidyā*. The land (*bhūmi*) which has been referred to as *artha* (wealth) does stand for both cultivated land and uncultivated land as well. *Suvarṇa* (gold) means thereby all other metals like silver and copper. Again *paśu* as a general term taken to stand for various species of animals including elephants, horses and others. Again *dhānya* (grain) is also not restrictive in its use and it stands for all varieties of corns like *vrīhi* (a type of grains of rice), *śāli* (another type of grains of rice) or any grain similar to rice. *Bhāṇḍopaskāra*

---

12 Yuddhakāṇḍa 83.14:

śubhe vartmani tiṣṭhantam tvāmārya vijitendriyam |
anarthebhyo na śaknoti trātuṁ dharmo nirarthakaḥ ||

13 Yuddhakāṇḍa 83.35-36.

stands for all sorts of functional and useful articles required by a householder. The expression, *mitra* stands for friends, clothes and ornaments. From this list of items that complete the range of *artha*, it is quite clear that regular daily lives and their requirements were never overlooked in Hindu culture.

Vātsyāyana has prescribed four means for acquiring wealth, *artha*. For the maintenance of life, the necessity of *artha* is undisputable, but it has been pointed out that with a view to earn *artha*, a person must proceed according to his own capacity.[14] First, *pratigraha* (taking as a gift or taking possession) of something has been accepted as one of the ways for earning *artha*s. After the end of the *āśrama* period of a *brahmacārī*, the brāhmaṇa may earn *artha* by receiving gifts from others by performing various rituals on behalf of others. Thus we find that the *dāna* (act of giving or donating) has been upheld as one of the ways of procuring *artha*. Through the ways of *dāna*, *artha* is transmitted from one hand to another. The role of a donor has always been praised and it has been said that wealth of a donor is never decreased by his act of donation, rather a miserly person has been rebuked for not performing any act of giving to others. A miserly person does not find anybody at the time of his distress. Second, earning of *artha* is possible by conquering, i.e. by forcibly acquiring the country that belonged to another king. This way of earning wealth is suitable for a kṣatriya. The wealth that a kṣatriya possesses by conquering other territories is his income. In *Mahābhārata*, Bhīṣma has quite categorically maintained that a king's duty lies in maintaining the treasury of the kingdom and spending money with due consideration. While discussing about the duties of a king, Bhīṣma remarks that if a king's treasury is bereft of money, then the king is not respected by his subjects.[15] The third way for acquiring or earning *artha* is through trade and commerce. Whatever is earned by a vaiśya (trader) is his earning. Fourth, by

---

14 Ganga Charan Vedanta Vidyasagar (tr.), 1313, *Kāmasūtra of Vātsyāyana*, p. 11.

15 Sinha, 2001, 2nd vol., p. 614.

getting wages for the service rendered is the earning of the śūdra. The money that a śūdra earns in exchange of his physical labour is his *artha*. To maintain a happy and comfortable life, *artha* is very much required. To put it in brief, *artha* obtained by a brāhmaṇa as donation, *artha* obtained by a king by conquering a land, *artha* acquired by a vaiśya by trading, *artha* earned by a śūdra by his physical labour – all, even if not much in amount – are recognized to be conducive to *dharma*. Thus we find that in the ethics of the Hindus, though requirement of wealth has been admitted, always emphasis has been upon possessing wealth in the rightful way. In different texts we come across lots of discussions about the rightful earning and rightful spending of *artha*. It has been encouraged to consider *artha* rather as a means for attaining a higher end, instead of considering *artha* as the end in itself. The worth of wealth is increased by the proper use of it and by preventing unnecessary wastage of *artha*. In general, in the context of acquiring *artha*, the main emphasize has been laid upon a person's effort (*utthāna*). In *Mahābhārata*, it has been maintained that through *utthāna*, Indra and other gods obtained *svargaloka*.[16] *Arthaśāstra* speaks categorically about one's effort in the acquisition of material wealth. It has further cautioned about the destruction of what has already been acquired or what will be acquired in the future in the absence of effort. To quote *Arthaśāstra* (1.19.36):

> *anutthāne dhruvo nāśaḥ prāptasyanāgatasya ca* ।
> *prāpyate phalamutthānālabhate cārthasampadām* ।।[17]

Whatever be the necessity for *artha* for maintaining material prosperity, always it has been reiterated that wealth is to be procured by honest and fair means. In *Manusmṛti* the concept of *arthadūṣaṇam* (tainted or polluted wealth) has been discussed. A person should earn *artha* only by such activity which does not violate the norm of *dharma*. Since to cause harm to others, to

---

16 *Mahābhārata* 112.58.14, cited in Y. Krishnan, 1992, "The Meaning of the Puruṣārthas in the Mahābhārata", in *Moral Dilemmas in the Mahābhārata*.

17 Quoted from Krishnan, 1992, op. cit., p. 66.

deceive or cheat others, to intend unlawful gain for oneself and loss to another are all considered to be the cases of violation of the norm of *dharma*.

Mahābhārata strongly dissuades one to resort to the means of *adharma* (illicit means) for acquiring wealth. The inherent normative tone of *puruṣārtha* justifies *Mahābhārata*'s warning to a person who forsakes *dharma*, and runs after wealth out of greed. The act of giving (*dāna*), and the performance of sacrificial rites (*yajña*) are to be done only by wealth acquired through right means. In *Mahābhārata*, there are various passages, where from we learn about *Mahābhārata*'s strong warning against unlawful material possession. The property which has been acquired by just means and by the person himself by his effort were regarded as worthy of the act of giving. The expressions such as *nyāyapāttena* (acquired by just means) *yathā nyāyena sañcita* (saved by rightful means) and *nyāyenānnopārjitam* (grains acquired by fair means) quite clearly establish primacy of *dharma* over *artha*.

Let us now turn to the third objective of *puruṣārtha*, i.e. *kāma*. The word *kāma* has many senses. The pleasure that is derived by a man through the enjoyment of colour (*rūpa*), taste (*rasa*), smell (*gandha*), touch (*sparśa*) and sound (*śabda*) through the instrumentality of visual sense-organs, gustatory sense-organ, olfactory sense-organs, tactile sense-organs and auditory sense-organs is known as *kāma*. In *Kāmasūtra*, this sense of *kāma*, meaning thereby the experience of pleasure that is derived from the enjoyment due to sense-organs is regarded as the primary sense of *kāma*. The experience of pleasure or enjoyment is caused because of the inclination of each of the sense-organs like visual, tactile, auditory, olfactory and gustatory towards its objects. This inclination of sense-organs induced by the desire for enjoyment, is also regarded as *kāma*, and that is the secondary sense of *kāma*. Thus, in a general sense, *kāma* is of two sorts according to ground (*hetu*) and consequence (*phala*).[18] In *Kāmasūtra*, the sense of *kāma* has a special sense, which also admits of a primary sense and a

[18] Vidyasagar, 1313, op. cit.

secondary sense. From the following verse from Vanaparva of *Mahābhārata,* we obtain an idea of *kāma* in two different senses, both general and special:

> *dravyārthasparśasaṁyoge yā prītirūpajāyate* ।
> *sa kāmaścittasaṁkalpaḥ śarīram nāsya dr̥śyate* ॥[19]

> The desire for the pleasure that arises from the touch of a woman or the acquiring of wealth is *kāma,* no material form of *kāma* is visible.

In *Kaṭhopaniṣad,* in the earlier sections, through the dialogue in the form of questions and answers between Naciketā and Yama, a full description is found about objects that are desired by men in their worldly existence. Yama, to examine whether Naciketā is truly fit for acquiring self-knowledge, was trying to lure him by worldly objects; Yama said to Naciketā:

> You ask for sons and grandsons with long lives, you ask for many cows, elephants, horses, gold and huge portion of land in this world; moreover, as long as you like to remain alive, you remain so. . . . Or if you want to ask for any other boon similar to it, you ask for it. You may ask for a long life, gold and jewels. I will give you all energy to enjoy all desirable objects, both worldly and other-worldly.[20]

Thus from the list of things Yama proposes to give to Naciketā, hundred years of life, sons, grandsons, animals, gold everything that comes under *artha* is included. We know Naciketā did not succumb to this sort of allurement for all these sorts of worldly objects of desire. His story is a story of refusal of fame, wealth and worldly establishment. But no doubt from the angle of an ordinary person these are all highly desirable. Ordinary people's

---

19 Bhattacharya, 1400, op. cit., p. 309.

20 *Kaṭhopaniṣad* 1.1.23-24:

śatāyuṣaḥ putrapautrānvr̥ṇīṣva vahūnpaśūn hastihiraṇyamasvān ।
bhūmairmahadāyatanam vr̥ṇīṣva svayam ca jīva śarado yāvadicchasi ॥

etattulayam yadi manyase varam vr̥ṇīṣva vittam cirajīvakāṁ ca ।
mahābhūmau naciketstvamedhi kāmānām tvā kāmabhājam karomi ॥

inclination towards all these objects of pleasure is found to be natural. Now, it may seem that since desires are supposed to be one of the major factors for bondage, how can such phenomena as desire be promoted as the object of human effort (*puruṣārtha*) and object of pursuit (*artha*)? No doubt, it is one of the famous sayings that *kāma*s are not pacified through their enjoyment (*na jātu kāmaḥ kāmanām upabhogena na śāmyate*). *Kāma* grows by indulgence: the more one indulges in sense-enjoyment the more it whets the appetite of the senses. In fact, *kāma* when considered as a *puruṣārtha* it has been conferred with a specialized sense, thus it has definitely acquired some normativity and in that sense *kāma* has been distinguished from the expression *kāma* understood loosely in common parlance. *Kāma* in a specialized sense is not viewed as an alternative for *bhoga.*

In the epics *Rāmāyaṇa* and *Mahābhārata,* considerable importance has been attached to these *trivarga*s, i.e. *dharma, artha* and *kāma*. In Kiṣkindhākāṇḍa of *Rāmāyaṇa,* Rāma was telling to Sugrīva, the king of the monkeys, that a king who enjoys fruits of *dharma, kāma* and *artha* is related to *dharma.*[21] In Ayodhyākāṇḍa, when Rāma was enquiring from Bharata about his way of administering his kingdom, he asked Bharata whether he was able to prevent the presence of any sort of obstacle by *artha* to the course of *dharma,* or the obstacle of *dharma* to the course of *artha* or the obstacle of *kāma* to the course of *artha* or *dharma*. Rāma had advised his younger brother Bharata to give equal importance to *dharma, artha* and *kāma* and to deal with these three as separate.[22] In *Mahābhārata* also we find that the author Vyāsadeva is also emphasizing upon the practice of *artha* acquisition and enjoyment of *kāma* be done in a virtuous way.[23]

---

21 Kiṣkindhākāṇḍa 38.23.

22 *kaccid arthena vā dharm amarthaṁ dharmeṇa vā punaḥ* ।
ubhau vā pratilobhena kāmena ca na vibādhase ।।

kaccidarthaṁ ca kāmaṁ ca dharmaṁ ca jayatāṁ vara ।
bibhajya kāle kālajña sarvān varada sevase ।। – Ayodhyākāṇḍa 100.62-63

23 *Mahābhāratam*, Svargārohaṇaparva, 5.62: *dharmāt arthaśca kāmaśca sa dharma kim na sevyate* ।

Thus we find that from the perspective of the Hindu view of life, these three, i.e. *dharma, artha* and *kāma* are considered to be indispensable. But questions may still be asked as to how these three – *dharma, artha* and *kāma* – are to be graded in the scale of indispensability? No doubt, opinions vary on this issue. According to some:

> *Dharma* is superior for under the influence of *dharma* sages have been able to cross the world. . . . Gods have been able to develop themselves with the power of *dharma,* and *artha* is subservient to *dharma.*[24]

In Śāntiparva of *Mahābhārata,* Arjuna has argued vehemently in favour of *artha* (wealth) as the best among these three objectives of human existence. *Artha* has been argued to be the most important one for *artha* is the main ground for the sustenance of agriculture, trade, rearing of animals, and art and craft. Without *artha,* there is no possibility for attaining *dharma* or *kāma*. A wealthy person can easily practise *dharma* and can enjoy those objects of desire which are difficult to get. *Dharma* and *kāma* are like parts of *artha*. If wealth is established, then these two *dharma* and *kāma* are properly practicable.[25] After the end of the terrible war in Kurukṣetra, grieved Yudhiṣṭhira expressed his desire to relinquish his kingdom to Arjuna and to retire in the forest, Arjuna kept on convincing Yudhiṣṭhira about the utility of wealth, especially for a king. Arjuna argued that a person who tries to maintain his livelihood through collecting alms and does not work to earn wealth, that person is not famous in society and cannot possess any relatives or animals.[26] Arjuna drew an analogy between a hill from which all rivers ascend and *artha,* earned from various

---

24 Sinha, 2001, op. cit., p. 652.

25 Ibid.

26 *yo hyjijīviṣedbhaikṣyam karmanā naiva kenocit* |
samārambhān būbhūkṣeta hatasvastirakiñcanaḥ ||
sarvalokeṣu vikhyāto na putrapaśusaṁhitaḥ |
– *Mahābhārata,* Śāntiparva, 8th *adhyāya*, p. 52

quarters by which all sorts of works are sustained.[27] Arjuna's comment regarding *artha* seems quite acceptable and applicable for all ages. Nakula and Sahadeva, two other Pāṇḍava brothers, also upheld the case for *artha* as the important and utilitarian among the three conditions of human existence. Nakula and Sahadeva said:

> Whether a man sleeps, sits or walks he will under all circumstances by adopting different means would try to acquire wealth. *Artha* is the dearest to all and very much difficult to possess. If one possesses *artha* then he is able to fulfil all his desires in this world. Wealth compounded with *dharma* and *dharma* compounded with *artha* are charming like honey compounded with nectar. The person who does not have money cannot fulfil any of his desires, and for one, who is not virtuous, it is very much difficult to possess money.[28]

Nakula and Sahadeva gave importance to *artha* no doubt, but also reserved important place for *dharma*. They commented further that people should engage primarily to the practice of *dharma*, and without violating *dharma* should earn *artha* and then would engage themselves for the gratification of their sensual inclinations.[29]

Again there are some who would give primacy to *kāma* among all these three conditions of human life. Among the Pāṇḍava brothers, Bhīma may be considered as the representative of this viewpoint which contradicts the viewpoints stated earlier.

> The person, who is devoid of desires (*kāmanā-śūnya*), can never desire for *dharma*, *artha* and *kāma*. *Kāma* is of the first order among three *varga*s (objectives) for human existence. Great sages who live on vegetables (*tṛṇabhojī*), live on air (*vāyubhojī*), have control over sense-organs, have knowledge of Vedas and Vedānta and study Vedas regularly being motivated by *kāma* (desire) take on performing sacrificial rites and charity, living on alms and

27 *Mahābhārata*, Śāntiparva, 8th *adhyāya*, pp. 55-56.

28 Sinha, 2001, op. cit., p. 653.

29 Ibid.: 654.

> meditation. The traders, agriculturalists, artists and craftsmen – all motivated by *kāma* (desire) are engaged in their own occupation . . . thus, humans pursue different professions motivated by *kāma*.[30]

There are others who would argue for *mokṣa* and would say that *mokṣa* is *parama,* i.e. the ultimate among the *puruṣārtha*s.

Yudhiṣṭhira's question to Bhīṣma as to why do men strive towards *trivarga* and how does the relentless pursuit of these three *varga*s, viz. *dharma, artha* and *kāma* bear on *mokṣa,* is no doubt a very pertinent question. These three *varga*s go through two states, one is their state of interconnections (*saṁsṛṣṭa*) and the other is their state of separateness (*asaṁsṛṣṭa*). *Dharma, artha* and *kāma* treated as *puruṣārtha*s of human life, if pursued simultaneously, that is called the state of interconnectedness of *trivarga. Artha* as an objective of life, if pursued in the way of *dharma,* from *dharma* does originate *artha*; again *artha* has been considered to be helpful in maintaining *dharma*. In *Mahābhārata,* when Duryodhana expressed his jealousy seeing the prosperity of the Pāṇḍavas, Dhṛtarāṣṭra told him that prosperity comes to one, who has a good character. The interconnectedness of *dharma, artha* and *kāma* of *trivarga* is the state of good character. In Hindu ethics through the practice of *trivarga,* formation of a good character has been emphasized. In order to obtain *mokṣa,* performance of good *karma* is no less important than acquiring knowledge. It has been said that *nivṛtti,* i.e. cessation from *trivarga* is *mokṣa.*

> In the context of *dharma,* desire for consequence is considered to be like a blemish, In the context of *artha,* refusal of donation and renouncing enjoyment are considered to be like blemishes, in the context *kāma,* abstention from delight is considered to be like a blemish. When *trivarga*s are free from all these blemishes, they acquire the capability of producing bliss as in *Brahman* as a consequence.[31]

---

30 Sinha, 2001, op. cit., p. 654.

31 Ibid., p. 606.

The concept of *mokṣa* or *mukti* is the unique contribution of Indian philosophy, excepting the Cārvākas, the materialist school of thinkers. According to the different schools of philosophy, the same concept of *mokṣa* has been named as *apavarga*, *nirvāṇa*, *kaivalya* and others. Most of the schools of Indian philosophy, whether they owe their allegiance to the Vedas or not, they agree in holding that liberation is the ultimate goal of human existence. Among the schools of Indian philosophy, there is, however, a lot of differences of opinion regarding the nature of the state of liberation and the method to be followed for attaining that state of liberation. According to some Indian philosophers, *mokṣa* is a state of bliss, according to some it is a state of absolute cessation of all pains, according to some in this state one attains absorption into the divine essence. According to some schools of Indian philosophers, liberation is possible in this worldly life (*jīvanmukti*). But some are of the opinion that liberation means *videhamukti* (disembodied liberation). In general, three *mārga*s (paths) of knowledge (*jñāna-mārga*), of devotion (*bhakti-mārga*) and of action (*karma-mārga*) have been proposed for the attainment of liberation. Schools of Indian philosophers bear differences among themselves as to how many paths are to be chosen, i.e. one, two or more; they also differ among themselves as to the importance of the path/paths to be followed. All the schools have accepted the importance of *dharma*, broadly speaking, in the sense of *karma*, in the attainment of liberation. But it would be a hasty generalization to infer from that all the schools are unanimous in giving similar importance to *dharma*/*karma* in the attainment of liberation. Rather we find that schools are divided as to whether *dharma*/*karma* is a direct path towards liberation or an indirect one. Thus, in whatever way the state of liberation is discussed, liberation ultimately signifies final release from the state of birth and rebirth, sorrows and pain. In this section, it will be not possible to address all the issues relating to liberation. Some of the important viewpoints on liberation will be touched upon in this section.

In the chapter entitled Daivāsurasampadvibhāga-yoga of

Śrīmadbhagavadgītā[32] a distinction is maintained between a man possessed of *daivī-sampad* and one possessed of *āsurī-sampad* and it has been claimed that the possession of *daivī-sampad* enables a person to obtain liberation. In *Bhagavadgītā*, Śrī Kṛṣṇa tells Arjuna that possession of *daivī-sampad* is the cause of *mokṣa* and *āsurī-sampad* is the ground for bondage: *daivī sampad vimokṣāya nibandhāyāsurī matā* |[33] We have already discussed about *varṇa-dharma* and *āśrama-dharma*. The agent when performs his *varṇa-dharma*, i.e. duties relating to his *varṇa* and *āśrama-dharma*, i.e. duties relating to his station without any desire for consequences, just because these are his duties, his action is considered as *sāttvika* action according to the Hindu texts and such an agent is characterized by divinely fulfilment (*daivī-sampad*). On the other hand, when an agent performs those actions with desire for some consequences or guided by selfish motives, such actions are called *rājasī*, i.e. relating or belonging to the quality of *rajas*, as such actions are endowed with passion and *tāmasī*, i.e. appertaining to or affected by the quality of *tamas*, i.e. ignorance respectively. Those *rājasī* actions and *tāmasī* actions are possessed of devilish feat (*āsurī-sampad*). The attainment of divinely fulfilment paves the way for release from the worldly existence, whereas involvement in devilish feat drags to the cycle of bondage and to its necessary consequences. In the different Purāṇas also we find admission of *caturvarga* and arguments supporting their statements.

1. *dharmārthakāmamokṣa ca puruṣārtha udāhṛtaḥ*, i.e. *dharma*, *artha*, *kāma* and *mokṣa* are examples of four *puruṣārthas*.[34]
2. *dharmārthakāmamokṣākhyāḥ puruṣārthāḥ sanātanāḥ*, i.e. the eternal objectives of humans are called *dharma, artha, kāma* and *mokṣa*.[35]

The Buddha taught two things primarily: (a) there is *duḥkha*

---

[32] *Gītā* XVI.5

[33] *Gītā* V.16

[34] *Viṣṇu Purāṇa* 1.18.

[35] *Nārada Purāṇa* 1.4.1312.

(pain and suffering), and (b) there is release from *duḥkha* and this state of non-arising of *duḥkha* for the Buddha is *nibbāna*. *Nirvāṇa*, called *nibbāna* in Pāli literatures, is the ultimate purpose of human existence. It is a state of purification (*pariśuddhi*) or the highest good (*parama-kuśala*). The literal meaning of *nirvāṇa* is "to make cool by blowing". In the Pāli canon *nirvāṇa* is defined as the complete extinction of three utterly unwholesome roots of greed, hate and delusion. In the Buddhist literatures, the state of *mukti* or *nirvāṇa* has been variously described as a state marked by the absence of a fall (from the divine existence for rebirth as a man) (*acyuta*), immortality (*amṛta*) and calmness (*śānti*).[36] In *Buddhacarita* of Aśvaghoṣa, the Buddha's state of *nirvāṇa* has been described as a state which is markedly devoid of old age (*jarā*), devoid of fear, devoid of diseases, devoid of birth, devoid of upward and downward movement, devoid of space and devoid of frequent movement.[37] The Buddha himself has narrated the state of *nirvāṇa* as free from birth-cycles, old age, diseases, death, suffering and pain.[38] The Buddha sometimes said that there are two types of *nirvāṇa*, one is restricted or limited by some conditions and the other is unconditional *nirvāṇa*. Again sometimes the Buddha had said that there is no difference among *nirvāṇa*s as there is no difference in the fire caused by different kinds of wood pieces. In the Buddhist philosophy, people who are on the path of *nirvāṇa* have been grouped into four orders as follows:

1. *Srotāpanna* – Literally speaking, these are the people who entered into the river (*srota*) leading to *nirvāṇa*. The *srotāpanna*s are always proceeding towards the goal of enlightenment and have never come backward.
2. *Sakṛdagāmī* – This is the second order of *nirvāṇa*, referring to those who have already born seven times in this world, and would return or reborn only once again in this world.

---

36 *Suttanipāta*, 204 (*Vijayasutta* 12), cf. Vidyāraṇya, 1984: 169.

37 *Buddhacarita*, Aśvaghoṣa, 11.56; Vidyāraṇya 1984.

38 Vidyāraṇya 1984: 213.

3. *Anāgāmī* – This is the third order of *nirvāṇa*, referring to those who after their death in this world are not subject to return.
4. *Arhat* – This is the highest rank in the Buddhist hierarchy, it refers to a Buddha who is still a candidate for *nirvāṇa*.[39]

In the Buddhist literatures there are lots of different opinions as to actually what is meant by *nirvāṇa*. However, all these details are not part of the present discussion.

Tattvārthasūtra is based on the premise that the goal of human life is *kaivalya* (liberation) and the author Umāsvāti begins his text by mentioning that enlightened world-view, enlightened knowledge and enlightened conduct[40] are the path to liberation.

In the Jaina philosophy eight types of *karma*s are mentioned such as:

1. Knowledge-covering (*jñānāvaraṇīya*),
2. intuition-covering (*darśānāvaraṇīya*),
3. sensation-producing (*vedanīya*),
4. deluding (*mohanīya*),
5. lifespan determining (*āyu*),
6. body-making (*nāma*),
7. status-determining (*gotra*), and
8. obstructive (*antarāya*).[41]

These are the *karma*s that cause changes in the nature of the soul and on account of which soul gets involved in bondage. According to the Jaina philosophers, *jīva* has potential for obtaining *kaivalya*. At the state of *kaivalya*, *jīva*, acquires *ananta catuṣṭaya*, i.e. four eternal requisites for being liberated; these are *ananta darśana* (infinite faith), *ananta jñāna* (infinite knowledge), *ananta vīrya* (infinite strength) and *ananta sukha* (infinite bliss). According to

---

[39] Monier-Williams, 1986, op. cit., p. 93.

[40] *samyagdarśanajñāna caritrāṇi mokṣamārgaḥ* | – 1.1

[41] Umāsvāti, 1994, *Tattvarthasūtra*, p. 33.

the Jaina view, a liberated soul (*kevalī*) is a *jīvanmukta*.

According to the Nyāya philosophers liberation (*apavarga*) is a state of absolute release of soul from rebirth.[42] This state of liberation has often been described as *niravāṇamukti* and has been described as a state marked by fearlessness (*abhayam*), non-decadence (*ajaram*), immortality (*amṛtyupadam*), and tranquillity like attaining Brahma (*brahmakṣemaprāpti*).[43] The state of liberation has been characterized as a state of freedom from fear for once reached that state, there is no fear of rebirth and bondage to worldly existence. The state of liberation has no possibility of reversal, hence that state is said to be imperishable. Once the individual-soul is liberated, the question of birth or death becomes irrelevant. The individual-soul is liberated when all the qualities of the soul such as knowledge, pleasure, pain, desire, aversion, conation, *dharma*, *adharma* and *saṁskāra* are completely annihilated. According to the Nyāya philosophy at the state of liberation there is absolute cessation of all sorts pains. In the Nyāya philosophy twenty-one sorts of pains have been enumerated, instances of which are six sense-organs, six types of objects to be accepted by respective sense-organs, six types of perceptual knowledge resulting from such acceptance by sense-organs, body (*śarīra*), pleasure (*sukha*) and pain (*duḥkha*) in the primary sense. The individual-soul, when desirous of release, considers *sukha* also as *duḥkha*. According to these philosophers, absolute cessation of pain is also absolute cessation of pleasure, hence they define the state of liberation negatively as the state of absolute cessation of pain. In their opinion, pleasure is always tainted by pain. To make the sense of liberation more vivid, in the Nyāya literature, the state of dreamless sleep (*suṣupti*) has been cited as an example to compare with the state of liberation. At the state of dreamless sleep, the person concerned does not see any dreams and no knowledge or aversion do originate.[44]

---

42 *tadatyantarvimokṣopavargaḥ* I – *Nyāyasūtra* 1.1.22

43 *tadabhayamajaramamṛtyupadam brahmakṣemaprāptiriti* – Vātsyāyana, *Nyāya Bhāṣya* in *Nyāyadarśana*, p. 234

44 *suṣuptasya svapnadarśane kleśābhāvād apavargaḥ* I – *Nyāyasūtra* 4.1.63

The Naiyāyikas do not accept the theory that *apavarga* consists in the manifestation of soul's happiness. The Nyāya account of *mukti* bears an ideological difference from the Advaita Vedānta account of *mukti* on another important aspect also: according to the Nyāya viewpoint, liberation of the individual-soul is the attainment of the unattained (*aprāptasya prāpti*). For in this view, during worldly existence, the individual-soul being in a state of bondage is deprived of its existence in its own essence, but liberation enables the individual-soul to attain to its own essence. According to the Advaita Vedānta, though it is said that in the state of release, the soul realizes its own essence, the soul really is in its essence. Thus for the Vedāntins, liberation is attaining to what has always been attained (*prāptasya prāpti*).

According to the Advaita Vedānta, liberation is a state of absolute cessation of all pains, and with the disappearance of pains, the nature of soul as unmixed bliss manifests. The freed soul assumes the form of his true self (*svātmanyavasthānam*). Thus, for Śaṅkarācārya, liberation is like finding out the forgotten necklace in the neck that is already worn in the neck. According to the Advaita Vedānta, performance of duties without viewing any consequence, but just considering these as duties, in other words, as *niṣkāma-karma*, generates desire for knowledge (*vividiśā*) and that finally leads to the realization of *Brahman*.

The idea of liberation that we find from Rāmānuja is different from that of Śaṅkarācārya. According to Rāmānuja, knowledge in relation to *karma* is able to provide release from this worldly existence. The released soul attains the nature of God, though not an identity with God.[45] Rāmānuja has explained five types of liberation:

1. Being in the same sphere or *loka* (*sālokya*).
2. Being in the same proximity in space and time (*sāmīpya*).
3. Being in the same form of identity of appearance, resemblance (*sārūpya*).

---

45 *brahmaṇo bhāvaḥ na tu svarūpapaikyam* – 1.1.1

4. Being equal in rank or power or condition (*sārṣṭi*) with God.
5. Being in intimate union or communion with God (*sāyujya*).

There are many things to discuss about these types. According to Rāmānuja, there are three classes of *jīvas*: eternal (*nitya*) those who dwell in *vaikuṇṭha*, enjoying bliss and free from *karma* and *prakṛti*; the freed (*mukta*), or those who attain liberation by knowledge, *karma* and devotion; and the bound (*baddha*) or those who are in bondage through ignorance. Rāmānuja does not accept *jīvanmukti*. Briefly speaking, all these sorts of liberation are desirable states of existence for the individual souls. These five types of liberation indicate some sort of development in individual souls. According to Rāmānuja, *sālokya*, *sāmīpya*, etc. states of liberation are more like states of existence at *vaikuṇṭha*. According to Rāmānuja, *sāyujya* is the primary sense of the term *mukti* and the remaining others are secondary sense of the expression *mukti*.

The Sāṁkhya school of philosophers speak of three types of sufferings which are *ādhyātmika* (arising from the psycho-physical nature of man), *ādhibhautika* (arising from the external world) and *ādhidaivika* (arising from the supernatural agencies). According to the Sāṁkhya philosophers bondage belongs to *prakṛti* and is attributed to *puruṣa*. Bondage arises through the conjunction of *prakṛti* with *puruṣa*; *puruṣa*, according to Sāṁkhya philosophers, is eternally free and enlightened. Non-discrimination (*aviveka*) is the cause of bondage, freedom is brought about by knowledge, which results from the practice of virtue and *yoga*, etc. The Sāṁkhya thinkers find that *viparyaya* (wrong knowledge), *asmitā* (egoism), *rāga* (desire), *dveṣa* (hatred) and *abhiniveśa* (fear) are the causes of bondage.

Thus how all these Indian philosophers have viewed the nature of ultimate objective for existence (*parama puruṣārtha*) is a matter of long discussion and deliberation. It is needless to add how deeply Indian thinkers dealt with these concepts is beyond imagination. In this regard, the Cārvāka school of thinkers are the only exception in not admitting liberation as the final *puruṣārtha*. The Cārvākas maintain that *sukha* is the only *puruṣārtha* or the objective of human existence.[46] However, even among the Cārvākas, it has been found that they did not stick only to the concept of sentient pleasure. They themselves have raised questions about the nature of pleasure and that had led to divisions among the Cārvākas. Is self-centred egoistic pleasure, pleasure arising out of embracing females, is the only sort of pleasure? Or some refined feeling, pleasure which is shareable is *sukha*? There are Cārvākas who are known as learned (*śikṣita*) Cārvākas; they searched for something higher as *sukha*. It has been recorded that some refined and enlightened Cārvākas had commented that: *nālpe sukhamasti, bhūmātveva vijijñāsitavya.*

From the perspective of Indian ethics what is the ultimate goal of human life, in other words, what is the main conclusion about the discussion on *caturvarga* has been very succinctly expressed by Bhīṣma in his dialogue with Yudhiṣṭhira, Bhīṣma says:

> As birds which move on water, do not get bogged by it, so intelligent persons moving through worldly lives do not get stuck in worldly affairs.[47]

Now, coming back to the previous question as to whether the discussion on *puruṣārtha* is at all relevant in the scheme of the Vaidika Dharma-Ethics? Among the recent interpreters of Indian ethics, Shyam Ranganathan writes:

> A better translation, thus of the term *puruṣārtha* is "values of persons" because what it stands for are distinct value-theoretic spheres.

In his enumeration of different senses of the expression *artha* he has enumerated value as one of its senses. He cites Swāmī Ādidevānanda's translation of *Gītā* XVIII.32 wherein *artha* has been rendered as value:

---

46 *kāma evaika puruṣārthaḥ* I – Sastri, 1982, *Cārvāka Darśana*, p. 147.

47 Sinha, 2001, op. cit., p. 679.

adharmaṁ dharmam iti yā manyate tamasāvr̥tā |
sarvārthān viparītāṁś ca buddhiḥ sā pārtha tāmasī ||

That *buddhi*, O Arjuna, which enveloped in darkness, regards *adharma* as *dharma* and which reverses every value [*artha*], is *tāmasika*.[48]

Rajendra Prasad[49] also argues for the in-built evaluative component of the theory of *puruṣārtha*. In his defence, Prasad has focused upon the concept of desire as one of the senses of the expression *artha*. He shows that a desire has built into it an attitude of favour, a sense of considering what is desired is worthwhile; that is an evaluating attitude and is a natural constituent of the concept of desiring to do it or to have something. To desire to do or to have something is, thus to value doing or having it. Thus for, what has been stated, it is clear that the theory of *puruṣārtha* is also a normative theory. This brings out that from this angle the theory of *puruṣārtha* has two components: it is a normative theory in the sense of corroborating that for anything to be *puruṣārtha* is to be something desirable and valuable and not merely a positive theory stating what is desired or valued. The question, however, still remains, if the theory of *puruṣārtha* is interpreted as the theory of human values, does it necessarily reduce itself to the theory of human ethical values? In this connection, throughout this discussion an answer has already been suggested. In discussing especially the three *puruṣārthas*, such as *dharma*, *artha* and *kāma* that very much govern mundane existence, we have found they bear peculiar relation with one another. *Dharma*, *artha* and *kāma* are regarded as three *varga*s, but these are not of equal importance in the scheme of *puruṣārtha*. We have already seen that the regulation of *artha* and *kāma* by *dharma* has given very much importance. To attain goals of *artha* and *kāma*, to be worthy of their purpose, must always follow moral means. The role of *dharma*,

---

48 Swāmi Ādidevānanda, 2007, *The Puruṣārtha Explanation of Indian Ethics*, p. 181.

49 Prasad 2008b: chap. 8.

of moral value, has been essential in this fourfold scheme of *puruṣārtha*. In the enumeration of *puruṣārtha*s also that may be the primary reason for placing *dharma* first followed by *artha* and *kāma*. In the order of enumeration of the *trivarga*, in *Mahābhārata* the *dharma* is the foremost followed by *artha* and *kāma*. The old adage of *Mahābhārata* is *jātasdharma tato jaya* (wherever there is *dharma*, there is victory). The *Mahābhārata* proclaims, 12.123.4 that *dharma* is the root (*dharma mūlastu*), *artha* is the body or trunk (*dehosṛtaḥ*) and *kāma* is the fruit of *artha* (*kāma artha phalam*). But there are also instances where we find that the importance of *artha* has also been asserted. In one such passage of *Mahābhārata*, it has been said that *artha* is an essential constituent (*avayava*) of *dharma* and *kāma*. It has also been stated that *artha* is primary in the sense that without *artha* the scope of performing *dharma* in the shape of different *karma*s gets trenched. The perspective from which *artha* has been given more importance, however, does not lessen the importance of *dharma* as such in the smooth-functioning of a society. *Artha* requires to be attained by adhering to the norm of *dharma*. The same is true also about *kāma*, otherwise uncontrolled *kāma* would only deter the process of release from the shackles of piled up *sañcita-karma*s. This necessitates that *kāma* be regulated by *dharma*. From this account of *dharma*, the moral dimension in the theory of *puruṣārtha* can well be accommodated and explained. We need to be cautious about our way of characterizing *dharma* as primary in comparison to other two *puruṣārtha*s – *artha* and *kāma*. The question of primacy of one *puruṣārtha* over the others has not been determined absolutely, nor do they provide or attempt to provide any such criterion for determination. We can easily find passages in the same *Mahābhārata* or other *dharma* literatures where *artha* has been regarded as the *mūla* of *dharma*. From the parameter of *Arthaśāstra*, *puruṣārtha*s have been graded differently for *Arthaśāstra* 9.7.61 directs that *artha* to be followed by *dharma* and *kāma*. Thus contexts are different, hence the importance may vary from context to context.

Again some critics have found the concept of *mokṣa* as *puruṣārtha* quite an odd one out among the rest of the three *vargas*. Prasad commented:

> The addition of *mokṣa* does not seem to full in or improve upon the theory of *trivarga* from the point of view of offering a descriptive-cum-prescriptive picture of how best social life should be organized and regulated.[50]

Dharma-Ethics, as it has already been discussed, is an indispensable part and parcel of Indian philosophy excepting the Cārvāka philosophy. Hence trying to understand Dharma-Ethics by dissociating it from its umbilical chord is just to kill it. R.N. Dandekar has said:

> The whole theory of *puruṣārtha*s suffers from the lack of a logically argued and analytically defended treatment.[51]

Dandekar also says:

> *Mokṣa* falls outside the orbit of the social-functional theory of the *puruṣārtha*s that there is conceptual disparity and discontinuity between *trivarga* and *mokṣa* . . . *mokṣa* is personalistic not social . . . while *dharma* aims at the maintenance of the world order, *mokṣa* deliberately rejects it. The purport of *mokṣa* is the negation of *dharma*.[52]

These objections seem to be rather unsympathetic to the point of view of Dharma-Ethics. Dharma-Ethics is not life-denying. But that does not imply that its goal of transcendence does not match with its social objectives.

---

50 Rajendra Prasad, 1981, "Theory of Puruṣārthas: Revaluation and Reconstruction", *Journal of Indian Philosophy*, 9(1): 66

51 R.N. Dandekar, 1987, "The Theory of Puruṣārthas: A Re-Thinking", *Annals, BORI*, 1(XVIII): 667-68.

52 Ibid., pp. 664-67. These two have been cited in Krishnan 1992.

5

The Nature of Human Motivation and Agency

THE notions of agency and autonomy are two universally acknowledged domains in any ethical discourse whatsoever. Dharma-Ethics is no exception to it. In the present chapter, I would offer reflections upon the nature of agency, particularly moral agency as has been advocated in Dharma-Ethics. In this meta-ethical enquiry into Dharma-Ethics some metaphysical and psychological deliberations about the very nature of an autonomous agent is incontrovertible. To provide a conceptual analysis about the notion of agency, no attempt has been made to trace the history of the uses of this idea within the fold of Dharma-Ethics as a whole. In this chapter, an attempt has been made to dwell primarily upon the concept of will or conation (*pravṛtti*) and its related concept, viz. "the desire to do" (*cikīrṣā*) as two defining marks of moral agency. In Indian philosophical literatures, there are lots of equivocations about the notion of *pravṛtti*.

The expression *prayatna* (impulse) comes quite closer to the notion of *pravṛtti* and in some, cases used synonymously with it. According to some, *prayatna* may be of two sorts; accordingly as impulse or drive towards automatic or reflexive activities or as impetus towards voluntary activities caused by desire (*icchā*) and aversion (*dveṣa*). In the former instance, such drives are explained as necessary for the preservation of the life of the being. This sort of impulses has been designated as *jīvanpūrvaka-prayatna*, for this secures the drive for the preservation of life. The Naiyāyikas have called such impulse as *jīvanyoni-prayatna* on the same ground. The latter sort of impulse or drive which is caused by *icchā* and *dveṣa* are designated as *icchā-dveṣa-pūrvaka-prayatna*, keeping in focus the sources of such impulses. The impulse prompted by desire leads to action, and this may be called the positive sense of will (*prayatna*). The opposite happens when the impulse induced by aversion desists from action and this may be called the negative sense of *prayatna*. In a broad sense the notion of *prayatna* may include both the varieties, including drive or impulse for self-preservation and drive towards voluntary acts. But understood in its narrow sense, the notion of *prayatna* covers will or conation as impulse towards voluntary acts both in its positive and negative senses. Dinakara, one of the distinguished Naiyāyikas, has focused upon the notion of freedom as a necessary condition for volition and has distinguished between a sense of *prayatna* as impulse towards voluntary activity from the other sense of *prayatna* as impulse towards life preserving activities. The subtle distinction between the conscious choice and the consciousness that the choice has been free, has also been realized by Dinakara.[1] An attempt has been made to analyse and explicate the notion of conation or will (*prayatna/pravṛtti*) to find out the causes of its origination. In this connection, mainly after *Siddhāntamuktāvalī* of Viśvanātha the enquiry has been carried out. To mark off the Dharma-Ethics perspective as different from the perspective of the adherents of the doctrine that matter is consciousness or Bhūtacaitanyavāda interesting deliberations have been offered in *Nyāyasūtra* and its other commentaries regarding the nature of *prayatna* which are also being considered in this chapter.

The discussions about the nature of human motivation are plenty across different philosophical and psychological traditions. The materialistic determinists assume that all thoughts, values, volitions, decisions and acts are the products of physical, chemical or physiological processes going on in the body. The Cārvākas or the Indian materialists also argue in a similar vein. This is indeed, one alternative model from which the nature of human volition and motivation has been understood. The Freudian would come up with his theory of *eros* and *thanatos*, the life instinct and death

---

[1] Sushil Kumar Maitra, 1963, *The Ethics of the Hindus*, p. 28.

instinct, to account for our conscious behaviour. None of these approaches has anything in common with the account of motivation as given by Indian philosophers, both of the Āstika and Nāstika traditions, except the Cārvākas. To explain why does a person move to perform an action and why does one refrain from performing an action are to explain the "what" and "why" of voluntary action. My objective is to present a model that shuns altogether the pan-physicalism of the previously-stated materialistic model. The Nyāya-Vaiśeṣika thinkers and the Prābhākara Mīmāṁsā thinkers were engaged in extensive discussions about the nature of human volition.

No one should harbour the wrong idea that everything that is materialistic is Western, and everything non-materialistic or for that matter spiritualistic, is Indian. The Nyāya-Vaiśeṣika model of volition, however, requires to be introduced as one of the models to explain and understand human volition in a non-materialistic pattern. Aristotle made a careful analysis of that aspect of human nature that is involved in acting and accepting moral responsibility. To ascribe moral responsibility to an agent for the performance of an action, according to Aristotle, is to leave open for the agent to act voluntarily. In the Aristotelian ethics, we find clear-cut statements about two distinct conditions under which human actions are involuntary. An agent is not responsible for actions that are produced by some external force. Thus, if someone grabs my hand and uses it to strike a third person, then I cannot be morally blamed for this action. If someone at a gunpoint made me kill a third person, then I am not to be blamed for what I have done. To the list of involuntary actions, according to Aristotle, is to be included actions performed out of ignorance. Thus, according to Aristotle, such actions are deemed to be moral which are within the capacity of the agent to perform or to avoid.

In Indian philosophy, the Nyāya-Vaiśeṣika thinkers like Praśastapāda, Viśvanātha and many others have provided elaborate account of volition. Śālikanāth Miśra in his *Prakaraṇapañcikā* elaborates the position of the Prābhākara

Mīmāṁsakas about the nature of volition. The discussion about volition, as distinguished from automatic or reflex actions, will throw some light on the nature of human individual as a person. According to Gautama, the founder of the Nyāya school of philosophy, one of the reasons put forwarded for his arguing about the existence of self, is on basis of his admission of the episode called *pravṛtti* (volition). His viewpoint will be addressed in detail. Broadly speaking, all activities performed by human beings are of two sorts: in one case, in the performance or the non-performance of an act, the desire or aversion of the agent, who thus engages himself in the act, has some decisive role to play; but in another sort of action the agent's desire and aversion are non-starters. Various types of organic actions and automatic actions have their suitable effects and also serve some specific ends for the organisms. But these actions do not fall within the domain of actions that presuppose either the desire or the aversion of the agent concerned.

Now voluntary actions are there to serve certain ends, viz. the selection of the good and the rejection of the bad. *Pravṛtti* is a technical term in the Nyāya philosophy and admits of at least two different senses, meaning thereby either particular kind of activity (*kriyā-viśeṣa*) or particular kind of conation (*prayatna-viśeṣa*). These two senses of *pravṛtti* are not like disjointed segments, but are very closely related concepts. The general framework, as we shall subsequently expound, may be viewed as a causal chain consisting of knowledge (*jñāna*), desire (*cikīrṣā*), will to do (*pravṛtti*) and motor effort (*pravṛtti* or *ceṣṭā*). Gautama in his *Nyāyasūtra*[2] in course of enumeration of twelve *prameya*s (objects of knowledge), knowledge of which has been considered to be essential for the attainment of liberation or the highest good, begins with the mention of *ātmā* (self or soul) and continues mentioning body (*śarīra*), sense-organs (*indriya*), objects of those sense-organs (*artha*), cognition (*buddhi*), mind (*manas*), action (*pravṛtti*), defects (*doṣa*),

---

2 *Nyāyasūtra*, 1.1.2 in *Nyāyadarśana*.

the beginningless series of birth and death (*pretyabhāva*), results (*phala*), suffering (*duḥkha*) and concludes by mentioning liberation (*apavarga*). Thus in *Nyāyasūtra* 1.1.9, among those all important *prameyas*, *pravr̥tti* has been included as one. In *Nyāyasūtra* 1.1.9 and 1.1.17, *pravr̥tti* stands for *kriyā-viśeṣa*.[3]

In *Nyāyasūtra* 1.1.17, the *pravr̥tti* which is one of the objects for true cognition, i.e. *prameya* has been introduced. *Nyāyasūtra* 1.1.17 runs as follows: *pravr̥ttirvāgbuddhiśarīrāmbhaḥ*. The expression *ārambha*, literally means beginning. Vācaspati Miśra has pointed out that *ārambha* signifies *karma*. Thus, here the intention of the *sūtrakāra* Gautama is to refer to three types of *karma* or *ārambha*:

1. *Vāgārambha*, i.e. action produced by words.
2. *Buddhyārambha*, i.e. the action produced by the mind. The expression *buddhi* has different senses, in this context *buddhi* means *manas*. The word *buddhi* when understood as a *kāraṇa* (cause), it signifies *manas*. In this context, the word *buddhi* is derived as a means for cogitation, i.e. in the sense of a *kāraṇa*.
3. *Śarīrārambha*, the action produced by the body.

In the first place, a person is motivated to act if he has a desire to perform that act. Broadly speaking, desire is defined as the yearning for the unattained. Desires are sometimes, self-centred, egoistic and sometimes all-involving, altruistic. In the Nyāya literature, a long list of various desires is given, ranging from sexual desire, desire for food and drink, desire to remove the suffering of others, desire to renounce the world, desire to deceive others, and finally desire for action. There is also another sort of classification of desire depending on the principle as to whether the desire is guided towards an end or consequence that is good or whether it relates itself to the means or the method for achieving a certain end; thus desire (*icchā*) may be of two kinds:

1. Desire disposed towards or focused upon fruits or results (*phalaviṣayaka icchā*).

---

[3] See Phaṇibhūṣaṇa Bhattacharya Tarkbagisa 1981.

2. Desire disposed towards or focused upon means by which one arrives at his aim (*upāyaviṣayaka icchā*).

Desire when focused upon a result, that result is nothing other than a desirable result (*iṣṭa*) which is pleasure (*sukha*), or in other words, absence of pain (*duḥkhābhāva*). Desires are born out of knowledge, hence in the absence of knowledge no desire can arise. Since from the knowledge of the result (to be attained), the desire for that result arises, it may also be stated that from the knowledge of a desirable result, i.e. *sukha* does desire originate, and desire disposed towards pleasure (*sukha*) or absence of pain (*duḥkhābhāva*), as we have already pointed out, is characterized as desire directed towards a desirable consequence, i.e. *phalaviṣayiṇī icchā*. It may be maintained, therefore, that knowledge of pleasure (*sukha*) or absence of pain (*duḥkhābhāva*) is causally related to the origin of such desire that are called as *phalaviṣayiṇī icchā*. In the Nyāya philosophy, the expression *svataḥ-puruṣārtha* has been introduced to account for pleasure and absence of pain. The definition of *svataḥ-puruṣārtha* is as follows: "The category which, when known becomes the object of desire through such inducement as "may it be mine".[4] To prevent this definition from being flawed by the fallacy of too wide definition (*ativyāpti-doṣa*), the intended meaning of the expression has further been clarified by stating that the desire spoken of as *svataḥ-puruṣārtha,* is such a desire, as is not itself dependent upon another desire as object of desire.[5] It is common among all livings beings including man to seek pleasure and avoid pain. The desire for pleasure is not subordinate to any other desire. But the second sort of desire, the desire for stratagem (*upāya*) to accomplish some end, cannot be said to be not dependent on any other desire as its object. To put it straightforwardly, the so-called *upāyecchā* (desire for means) is subservient to the desire for a desirable consequence. The notion of desire for the means is

---

[4] To put it Sanskrit; *jaj jñātam sat, savavṛttitayeṣyate sa svatapuruṣārtha iti* – Pañcānan Bhattacharya, 1377 BS, *Muktāvli Saṁgraha: Bhāṣāpariccheda, Nyāya-Sidhāntamuktāvali Ṭīkā Sahita*, p. 555.

[5] *itarecchānadhīnecchā viṣayatvam phalito 'rthaḥ* । – ibid.

important in relation to the motive (*pravṛtti*). The desire which is operative as the cause of *pravṛtti* (motivation) is called *upāyecchā*, the desire for the means for attaining the end. Thus from the above discussion, it is clear that desires are of two sorts:

a. desire for an end (*phalaviṣayaka icchā*), and

b. desire for the means (*upāyaviṣayaka icchā*).

The motivation to act (*pravṛtti*) is produced by the desire for the means (*upāyaviṣayaka icchā*), which unlike the desire for an end (*phalaviṣayaka icchā*) is dependent upon certain conditions. Thus, the desire to perform (*cikīrṣā*) is the desire for the means (*upāyaviṣayaka icchā*) for reaching the desirable consequence (*iṣṭa*). In *Siddhāntamuktāvalī*, *cikīrṣā* has been explained as *kṛtisādhyatvaprakārakecchā*[6] of the motivated agent. The consciousness or belief about some means as capable of being performed by the agent concerned (*kṛtisādhyatā jñāna*) gives rise to desire to accomplish an end by that means. Such desire which is the desire to do or accomplish, technically known as *cikīrṣā*. This desire to do (*cikīrṣā*) is directed towards an action which is capable of being accomplished (*kṛtisādhya viṣaya*), thus, this type of desire is characterized in terms of the property of being accomplished.

The awareness or belief that a certain act can be performed implies some sort of credence in one's own competence. To desire to perform an act, the act must not be such, which is not within the ability of the agent to accomplish. As an agent, one cannot desire to perform an act for which one's ability to perform is lacking. The consciousnes about an act as capable of being accomplished by an individual is the necessary condition for the individual concerned to have desire to act. The Naiyāyikas point out that mere consciousness that some act is fit to be done by an individual is not sufficient to arouse desire in the individual concerned to perform the act. The Naiyāyikas elaborate the following conditions to account for the desire to perform an action:

---

[6] Bhattacharya 1377 BS; op. cit., p. 555.

1. Consciousness about an act as fit for being performed by an agent (*kṛtisādhyatā jñāna*).
2. Consciousness that the performance of this act is conducive to a desirable consequence (for that agent) (*iṣṭasādhanatā jñāna*).
3. Consciousness that the benefit is unaccompanied by any stronger evil (*balavadaniṣṭhānanubandhitva jñāna*).

It has been made clear by the Naiyāyikas that if there is no consciousness that the performance of the act is beneficial for the agent, then there would be no volition from the side of the agent towards the performance of such an act. The Naiyāyikas are consequentialists and they account for the motivation in terms of a preconceived beneficial end or consequence. Thus according to the Naiyāyikas, the second necessary condition for motivation towards the performance of an act, is the consciousness that the performance of the act is conducive to a desirable end. Without the consciousness about any desirable consequence to result from the performance of an act, nobody is motivated to perform that act. That is one of the reasons to account for why people are not motivated to perform such acts which are not known to produce any desirable consequences. But, of course, it should not be supposed that according to the Naiyāyikas, knowledge that act would lead to desirable consequence is alone sufficient to motivate towards its performance. One may have knowledge or consciousness about some action as leading to a desirable consequence; say namely, the action of bringing down the moon from the sky. In spite of having consciousness about effecting a desirable consequence (*iṣṭasādhanatā jñāna*) with regard to an act such as bringing down the moon (*candrānayana kriyā*) from the sky, no individual under normal circumstances would be motivated to perform such an act. This is because of the simple reason that the person concerned does not have consciousness about the act of bringing down the moon from the sky as having efficiency of being accomplished (*kṛtisādhyatā jñāna*) by him. In this connection, it may be asked, how can we justify a motive for suicide from the perspective of the Naiyāyikas? The agent concerned who proceeds to commit suicide also has a consciousness that the performance of the act is beneficial. The actor has definitely a consciousness, but no doubt an erroneous one, that the performance of the act of suicide is not a greater evil. Another important thing about the awareness of an act as beneficial is that it must be understood as relative to the time and circumstances; for, it may be argued what is good in one circumstance at one time, may not be so for an agent in another time and circumstance. What one desires to perform in one situation may desire to avoid in another situation in life. Are these two conditions – the consciousness that the performance of the act would lead to desirable consequence, and consciousnesses that the act is performable – sufficient to motivate an agent to perform an act? If we take as an example of an act, the act of eating rice mixed with poison, a person who is very hungry and has the consciousness that the performance of the act of eating rice mixed with poison would lead to the desirable consequence of removing his hunger, and also has the consciousness that act is capable of being accomplished by him, then also we will find the person is not motivated to perform the act of eating rice mixed with poison. Hence, this clearly establishes that something else is required.

Now, so far what has been pointed out by the Naiyāyikas in accounting for causal conditions for the origination of volition needs further supplementation.[7] The Naiyāyikas definitely have something very important to add in this connection to make their account about the causal conditions for volition exhaustive, but the concept that has been introduced is a matter of considerable debate even among the Naiyāyikas themselves. It may also be doubted whether something else the Naiyāyikas speaks of is to be considered as the amplification of already specified conditions or to be treated as a third independent condition. The clause expressing this condition may be stated after the orthodox Nyāya as "*balavadanistanubandhi* . . ." which has turned out to be a very

[7] Maitra, 1963, op. cit.

difficult and complex notion. According to one interpretation as offered by some leading Naiyāyikas, it is the consciousness of the absence of evil or undesirable consequences. On the other hand, according to others including Viśvanātha, the author of *Siddhāntamuktāvalī*, this condition is a negative one as it implies the absence of consciousness about an act (towards which the agent is motivated) being productive of evil consequences. In defence of negative interpretation, Viśvanātha brings in certain empirical considerations in favour of it. There are evidences of actual situations in which an agent has volition towards an action in spite of his not having any positive consciousness about the absence of evil with regard to the performance of such an action. However, Viśvanātha did not offer any supportive clues for the denial of the claim that in other cases there may be positive consciousness of the absence of evil immediately preceding volition as a condition. The Naiyāyikas who do not favour negative interpretation, maintain that to admit the absence of consciousness of evil as a condition is to accept psychologically unintelligible something as a condition of willing.[8]

From the above discussion about the conditioning factors of volition, the other aspect of volition when it gets thwarted comes out to be equally important. In this regard the Naiyāyikas reflect upon the nature of the deterrent elaborately. In this section, I would like to touch upon main observations of the Naiyāyikas without entering into many details, to bring to light the role of some other factors recognized by the Naiyāyikas in accounting for foundering of volition in spite of all causal conditions being present for its occurrence. Two alternative explanations are possible in this case: according to one view, the consciousness of evil consequences that acts counter-productively is the subjective feeling of aversion of the agent; in another view, it may be said that there is some object, which is of evil nature that gives rise to the subjective feeling of aversion. Of these two possible

8 Indrani Sanyal, 2003, "The Nature of Human Motivation", in *On Mind and Consciousness*, pp. 118-128.

interpretations, some Naiyāyikas favour the first one, according to which it is the subjective feeling of aversion that acts as the deterrent. Thus for some Naiyāyikas, it is the subjective state of the agent that is important. The feeling that restrains volition is relative to the person, time and circumstances: hence it can never be held to be absolute. The Nyāya account of volition thus presupposes as its condition certain complex entities comprising of cognitive, conative and affective aspects.

The Naiyāyikas do not admit causal relationship between the consciousness of good with respect to an action and the cognition that action has to be done. The object concerning which the consciousness of good is directed is the same object regarding which the consciousness of duty has arisen. The Naiyāyikas here do not like to postulate two psychoses, one conditioning the other, but only one psychic compound with two features, one is consciousness of good and the other is cognition of duty with regard to the action. In other words, the Naiyāyikas do not bring in any *niyāmaka* relation, i.e. conditioning relation between these two psychoses. From the above discussion, it also clearly emerges that nothing is good or beneficial, except in relation to a subject. In this analysis, proper significance is attached to the subject of volition that determines his own values. This account in no way leads any support to a mechanical determination. The Naiyāyikas provide what may be called an account of motivation situating upon an embodied soul. We may refer to another version of this sort of account of motivation centring an embodied soul obtained from the Prābhākara Mīmāṁsakas.

This account of volition in terms of the psychology of the human mind has some significant metaphysical presuppositions. In Gautama's *Nyāyasūtra*, it has been categorically asserted that desire, aversion, volition, pleasure, pain and cognition are the marks of the self. Thus desire, which is one of the factors conditioning volition, is accepted as the characteristic feature of the self. Nothing else can possess it. Further the Naiyāyikas argue that desire, etc. also prove the existence of an immaterial substance. This view goes against the views of the materialist Cārvākas. This view of the self also goes against the views of the Buddhists who believe in the doctrine of universal flux. The Buddha, however, had made the statement that the willed or volitional act is ethically significant. Buddhists also maintain that will is the distinctive endowment of human beings by virtue of which humans are moral beings. The Naiyāyikas urge that the Buddhist doctrine of universal flux leaves no room for voluntary activity. The main argument here is that since all voluntary activity is inspired by some conscious end which the agent seeks to attain, the doctrine of universal flux fails to account for any active endeavour of a conscious being. Hence unlike the Buddhists, the Naiyāyikas urge that there is some definite error in the supposition that the belief in the existence of a psychical continuum is a construction or the result of abstraction. Rather, the Naiyāyikas enforce the existence of a permanent self as a distinct category. This is, however, just a very brief resumé of a very long story.

The Prābhākara Account of Volition

The Prābhākara Mīmāṁsakas do not agree with the Naiyāyika's account of origination of volition. The Prābhākara Mīmāṁsakas maintain that *svaviśeṣaṇavattā pratisandhānajanya kāryatā jñāna* is the cause for volition. To state preliminarily, according to the Prābhākara Mīmāṁsakas, *kāryatā jñāna* is the cause for volition. Now, what actually is meant by the Sanskrit expression *kāryatā jñāna*? The two expressions, viz. *kāryatā jñāna* and *kṛtisādhyatā jñāna,* are used as synonymous expressions by some thinkers, whereas according to some these two expressions are different in senses. We have already discussed the viewpoint of Naiyāyikas and for them *kṛtisādhyatā jñāna* and *kāryatā jñāna* are not distinct instances of knowledge. *Kṛtisādhyatā jñāna* (the knowledge that an act is capable of being performed) is one of the necessary conditions for volition according to the Naiyāyikas. The Prābhākara's notion of *kāryatā jñāna* implies something more than the Nyāya conception of *kṛtisādhyatā jñāna*. *Kāryatā jñāna* is not merely consciousness that an act can be accomplished, but it implies the consciousness that an act must be done. Understood from the Prābhākara position, the cognition about an act as must be done is inclusive of the cognition that it is capable of being done. The Prābhākara notion of *kāryatā jñāna* (cognition of duty) is thus a wider notion than the notion of *kr̥tisādhyatā jñāna*. Hence in their view *kāryatā jñāna* leads to *pravr̥tti* (will) through *cikīrṣā*. Unlike the Naiyāyikas, the Prābhākaras do not acknowledge that the consciousness about an act as conducive to desirable consequence (*iṣṭasādhanatā jñāna*) is an indispensable condition for all instances of volitional action. The other important difference from the Naiyāyika's viewpoint is Prābhākara's emphasis on self-reference in all motives. The clause, *svaviśeṣaṇavattā pratisandhāna* meaning thereby the representation of a certain act as *viśeṣaṇa* (specific determination) of the acting agent or the *pravartamāna puruṣa,* is a necessary requisite for giving rise to cognition of duty (*kāryatā jñāna*). Thus here, from the point of the view of the Prābhākara Mīmāṁsakas, there is also emphasis on the subjective consciousness about such capacity or competency on the part of the acting agent. The admission of *kāryatā jñāna* enables the Prābhākara Mīmāṁsakas to provide uniform account of volition both in the case of *kāmya-karma* (conditional duties) and *nitya-naimittika-karma*s (unconditional duties). According to one principle of classification of duties, some duties are said to be *kāmya-karma* because in these cases the agent's choice of the end or consequence is taken to be very crucial. There are some ends which are by themselves not morally authoritative but whoever chooses these ends is also under specific obligations to seek for their implementation in the proper manner. Generally, *kāmya-karma*s are scriptural injunctions that are authoritative only when there is a desire for a particular end. The *nitya-karma*s are categorized as such duties which are obligatory for all time and *naimittika-karma*s are categorized as such duties which are conditionally obligatory provided *nimitta*s (special) occasions arise for their performance. Thus *nitya-karma*s, so to speak, with respect to *āśramī*s, i.e. those who belong to one of the four stages of religious life are *niyatanimittaprāpta,* i.e. invariably or necessarily found to be obligatory. Thus for the twice-born (*dvijas*), the performance of evening prayers (*sandhyāvandanādi*) is considered to be invariably obligatory duties. In contrast to this sort of duties, as we have already pointed out are *naimittika-karmas* (occasional or periodical ceremonial rites) as in the case of birth of a child (*jāteṣṭi kriyā*), i.e. oblation given at the occasion of the birth of a child. The *karma*, known as *prāyaścitta* (atonement or expiation), instead of being considered as a distinct variety of obligatory act, is considered by many as an instance of *naimittika-karma*, for it is obligatory depending upon the occasion for its performance. What we see clearly that what are classified as *kāmya-karmas* are very much related to the consequence or the result of such actions. Thus desires for obtaining heaven, villages, sons, territories as ends or consequences, often act as motivating factors for actions which are called *kāmya-karmas*. Therefore, those who are desirous of attaining those objectives or ends may naturally proceed to perform such actions. But one who does not have any desire for such ends or consequences may skip the performance of such sacrificial rites and rituals. According to some Mīmāṁsakas, the non-performance of unconditional duties leads to the contrary course of sinful (*pratyavāya*). But regarding the non-performance of the conditional duties there is no Vedic stricture for its non-performance as leading to sin; or something else, for the performance of conditional duties is optional.

These are duties and performance of these duties presupposes motivational impelling on the part of the acting agent. According to the Nyāya, as we have already discussed, the consciousness about a desirable consequence, i.e. *iṣṭasādhanatā jñāna*, is necessarily involved in all volition. The Prābhākaras, however, join issue with the Naiyāyikas in denying consciousness of desirable consequence as a necessary cause to volition. According to the Prābhākaras, as we have already discussed what is required for volition to originate is the representation of an act as the specific determinant of the self, but not necessarily the knowledge of desirable consequence. The reason for not admitting knowledge of desirable consequences of volition as one of the necessary conditions for volition is not far to seek. The Prābhākaras are not short-sighted to have overlooked the role of the condition, viz. *iṣṭasādhanatā jñāna* in giving rise to volitional activities. They have admitted in some empirical actions (*kāmya-karma*s) material motives of personal profit or gain do have important roles to play. But the Prābhākara Mīmāṁsakas also have noticed that with regard to unconditional duties (*nitya-naimittika-karma*s), since these are necessarily binding upon the agent, the knowledge of desirable consequence in the shape of personal profit or gain is not present.

The Prābhākaras have pointed out that the Nyāya account of volition, especially in terms of its admission as one of the necessary conditions, *iṣṭasādhanatā jñāna*, i.e. knowledge of being conducive to desirable consequences for volition, is not necessary to explain the motivational drive of the agent towards *nitya-naimittika-karma*. Both the conditional and unconditional duties are such regarding which agents are incited to actions. We need to account for the volitional impulse of the acting agent no doubt, but in all cases of volitional activity, "the knowledge of a desirable consequence"as necessary condition cannot be accounted for. The Prābhākara Mīmāṁsakas maintain that *nitya-naimittika-karma*s are similar to *kāmya-karma*s in the sense that individual agents are motivated to perform such actions. But if *iṣṭasādhanatā jñāna* is supposed to be a necessary condition for the origination of volition, then because of the absence of cause, the absence of effect has to be admitted, and then in that case there has to be absence of volition towards *nitya-naimittika-karma*. But the Prābhākara Mīmāṁsakas would point out that in those cases the origin of *pravr̥tti* is there, but it is not without cause, and *iṣṭasādhanatā jñāna* is not its cause. Then what else needs to be postulated to account for volition towards unconditional duties? The Prābhākara Mīmāṁsakas would urge that it is *kāryatā jñāna*.

In the analysis derived both from the Naiyāyikas and the Prābhākaras, much significance has been attached to the agent of volitional actions, who determines his own values. These two view points have agreement in lending no support to mechanical determination. The Naiyāyikas give what may be called, in a broad sense, an account of motivation presupposing an embodied self. The Prābhākara Mīmāṁsakas also agree with the Naiyāyikas in this respect in proposing an account of motivation in this direction. These schools of philosophers dealt elaborately on the psychological aspects of human volition. But there are some major points of disagreement between the Naiyāyikas and the Prābhākaras in the way they developed their total theory on volition. The Prābhākaras, unlike the Naiyāyikas are not consequentialists and they do not consider the consciousness that the act is conducive to good or beneficial result as one of the conditions for volition.[9] The Prābhākaras reject the claim that the real cause for volition is anything external; rather the Prābhākaras projecting the self assert consciousness about self itself as qualified by or specified by some act which is to be done, is necessary cause for volition. Thus, according to them the agent, prior to his actually being motivated to activity, must have knowledge of himself as one who is qualified by the capability to perform that particular act. Criticizing the Nyāya approach, the Prābhākaras claim superiority of their theory of volition over the Nyāya model. The merit of the Prābhākaras position lies in their outright rejection of any consequentialist perspective on morality. The advantage of the Prābhākara position is quite obvious for this theory of volition can account for all instances of motive towards action, whether it has some preconceived end or consequences in view or not. However, it should not be supposed that Prābhākaras deny that empirical acts lead to certain ends or consequences, but they do deny knowledge about some end or consequences is required to be admitted as one of the motivating factors. The knowledge about some desirable end or consequence is not the real cause for volitional activity. The Prābhākaras are not dreamers, oblivious of real empirical situations. For Prābhākaras would not deny that empirical acts lead to certain ends or consequences and in these cases some belief about the end as beneficial is there; but

[9] Sanyal, 2003, op. cit., pp. 125-26.

they would also assert that is not a real motive that moves us. In empirical cases also this desire for attaining an end moves the will not independently, but as specifying the self or as appropriated by it. Hence they maintain that in all cases of volition we have two distinct psychoses, one leading to the other, and thus having a kind of determining relation as that of the cause of the ground (premise) and the ground (conclusion). The Naiyāyikas, as we have discussed, do not recognize any causal relationship between the consciousness of good regarding an act and the cognition that is to be done. From the Nyāya perspective, the object, which is the object of consciousness of good, is the same as the object of consciousness of duty. The Naiyāyikas, here, do not like to postulate two psychoses, one conditioning the other. The Nyāya explanation of volition rests on the postulation of one compound cognitive state consisting of conjunction of cognitions.

6

Decoding Prescriptions for Work

The Analysis of Vidhivākya

THE Indian philosophers, who owe their allegiance to the Vedas, are known as the *āstika* thinkers, and for them the role of Śruti is very important in their philosophical orientation. Among the *āstika* thinkers, there are lots of differences of opinion as to the question whether God is the author of the Vedas or not, but each of them accept the authority of the Vedas without question. The Vedas are classified into *vidhi-mantra-nāmadheya-arthavāda-niṣedha* according to their contents. The section of Vedas that deal with *vidhivākya*s (obligatory statements) are important in the context of discussions about Dharma-Ethics. The *āstika* thinkers have raised many questions about the nature and implication of *vidhivākya*s and have also tried to provide solutions to these questions from their perspectives. The meaning of *vidhi* has been variously discussed by the Indian philosophers. The *nyāyasūtrakāra* Gautama writes, *vidhir vidhāyaka*[1] (the precept enjoins or prescribes to act), and the later interpreters of the text say that statements that direct or impel are *vidhi*. *Vidhi* is taken to mean *vidhivākya*s (imperative sentences) that urge or impel to perform certain rites. Now there are sentences which positively impel to perform certain acts, but there are certain sentences which convey a sense of negative impulsion, by prohibiting performance of certain acts. In one sense of the term *vidhivākya*s, only affirmative imperative sentences are regarded as *vidhivākya*s as distinguished from negative sentences which prohibit, and known as *niṣedhavākya*s. Thus, the Vedic imperative statements or *vidhivākya*s are sometimes taken to mean

---

[1] *Nyāyasūtra* 2.1.63 in Tarkavagisa 1984, p. 327.

both the sentences which impel to perform certain acts (*pravartanā vidhāyaka vidhivākya*) and sentences which prohibit the performance of certain acts (*nivartanā vidhāyaka vidhivākya*). In general, in grammars of language, the syntactical rules governing the formation of an imperative sentence have some distinctive features. In Sanskrit grammar specially, the mark for finding out an imperative sentence is determined by reference to the verbal phrase occurring in a sentence. According to the Sanskrit grammar a class of suffixes known as injunctive suffixes, in Sanskrit as *vidhiliṅ* or in short as *liṅ*. According to the syntactical rules of Sanskrit grammar, there are ten varieties of verbal suffixes, such as *laṭ, liṭ, loṭ, liṅ*, etc. which are conjoined with verbal roots (i.e. the basic element (*dhātu*) from which a verb grows) such as *kṛ* (to do), *gam* (to go) *pac* (to cook), etc. There are ten sorts of verbal suffixes in Sanskrit grammar for determining six tenses and four moods, known as *daśalakārah*. These suffixes, over and above determining tense and moods of all verbs, also determine the type and number of person or persons engaged in an action. In a verb, according to Sanskrit grammar, there are two parts: (i) one is its part of verbal root or (*prakṛti*); and (ii) the other is its part of suffixes (*pratyaya*). The main difference between a descriptive sentence and an imperative sentence lies embedded in the verbal expression, which commonly happens to be one of the constituent-expressions of the sentence. The verbal expression has an inflected verbal base or so-called *tiṅanta pratyaya*. In the *Vaiyākaraṇabhūṣaṇasāra*, it has been stated that a verbal expression conveying any direction, invitation (courteous), inquiry, order and request are formed by attaching a class of verbal suffixes, known as injunctive or optative suffixes, in Sanskrit grammar known as *vidhiliṅ* or in short as *liṅ*-suffix with the verbal roots.[2] The injunctive suffix is assigned with the following six meanings by Pāṇini:

a. *Vidhi*, i.e. prompting a person to act.

b. *Nimantraṇa*, i.e. prompting a person to act pointing out the adverse effect if he does not act.

---

[2] *vidhinimantraṇāmantraṇādhīṣṭhā sampraśna prārthaneṣu liṅ* (6.2.131).

c. *Āmantraṇa,* i.e. prompting to undertake the act or not to undertake as per the option.

d. *Adhiṣṭham,* i.e. prompting a superior person to undertake the act with respect.

e. *Sampraśna,* i.e. asking whether one likes to undertake the act.

f. *Prārthanā,* i.e. appeal to undertake the act.

Thus, the *liṅ lakāraḥ* is used in case of *vidhi, nimantraṇa, āmantraṇa, adhiṣṭha, sampraśna* and *prārthanā.*[3] The sense of *vidhi* is to impel to, to urge to, to incite to activity (*preraṇā*).

Now the person who hears an imperative statement, how does that command, direction or incitement contained in the statement reaches to him? How does the hearer understand the meaning of the uttered sentence? When a person is being ordered and said, "Go, rope the cow". The person who has been ordered, experiences to be urged on, or to be incited: *ayam mām pravartayati,* i.e. the person concerned impels me (to perform the act). This sort of explanation may be given with respect to ordinary empirical statements. But the question may be raised as to what is in the imperative statements (*vidhivākya*s) like, "The person desirous of heaven ought to perform Viśvajit sacrifice" (*svarga kāmo viśvajita yajeta*), or "The person desirous of animals ought perform *citra* sacrifice" (*paśukāmo citrayā yajeta*), or "The person desirous of rain, ought to perform the *kāriri* sacrifice" (*kārīrya vr̥ṣṭikāmo yajeta*), that incites a person to act? To find an answer to this question, to get some idea about the nature of the causative factor that determines the process of being impelled or incited to act, we need to concentrate upon the verbal constituent of that sentence, both upon its part of verbal root (*prakr̥ti*) and its part of suffix (*pratyaya*). In the discussion of Indian ethics, the meaning of sentence that is being conveyed by these *vidhivākya*s, is important. It cannot be denied that these *vidhivākya*s convey a

---

[3] K.T. Pandurangi (ed.), 2006, *Purvamimamsa from an Interdisciplinary Point of View*, p. 163.

sort of incitement (*preraṇā*), which is also known as *pravartanā* (motivation). It is acknowledged that some sort of *preraṇā* or *pravartanā* is communicated. People proceed to perform activities as enjoined by Vedic sentences, for the feature of urging to perform is there in the *vidhivākya*s.

In Indian philosophy different schools like the Grammarians, Naiyāyikas and Mīmāṁsakas including Bhāṭṭa Mīmāṁsakas and Prābhākara Mīmāṁsakas have elaborately discussed this issue. In this connection, lots of differences of opinion among these schools of thinkers are observed. Indian philosophers have offered different analysis of Vedic sentences. Apparently, the discussion about the analysis of *vidhivākya*s as have been done by different Indian philosophers does not have any direct implication on their views on Dharma-Ethics. But a deeper consideration would show how intimately these issues relating to the nature of *vidhivākya*s have determined the nature of Dharma-Ethics as such. In the context of Indian philosophy, this discussion is very much relevant because of its admitting the Vedas as the source of Dharma-Ethics. Truly speaking, the Vedas are the embodiment of language, heard, spoken or written. It is utterly mysterious, what was heard, said and written in the Vedas as obligatory has been comprehended by the mundane beings and are obligated to work accordingly. The Indian schools of philosophers, who owed their allegiance to the Vedas, however, did not leave the mystery unattended through downright dejection. The domain of Dharma-Ethics is not confined only to the empirical. The Dharma-Ethics spans the complete being of the moral agent which is eternal self in its essence. What are regarded as *codanā* (Vedic imperative statements) are not to be treated as on par with ordinary empirical imperative statements. The question as to what is special mark of a Vedic injunction has been discussed in various philosophical literatures. In *Śābarabhāṣya* on *Jaiminisūtra* it has been stated that the Vedic imperative statements also referred to as the Śāstric injunctions have evidential value and validity in regard not only to the present but also the past, the future, the supersensuous, the remote and the mediate.[4] Thus, the most difficult question is: How is such a *codanā* (Vedic prescription) empirically known? Sushil Kumar Maitra has very succinctly formulated the question as follows: How is the authority of a scriptural imperative revealed to the moral agent?[5] Through the study of these analyses, we get different alternative interpretations about the Dharma-Ethics also. The discussion about the nature of *vidhivākyas* forms a part of a very specialized and technical area of research in the domain of *śabda-pramāṇa*, which is often treated as the domain of Indian philosophy of language. In the present chapter only the viewpoints of some of the major schools of Indian philosophy like that of the Grammarians, the Bhāṭṭa Mīmāṁsakas, the Naiyāyikas and the Prābhākara Mīmāṁsakas have been minimally touched upon to delineate their link with the beliefs of Dharma-Ethics. The speculation as to whether Dharma-Ethics has any rational or argumentative foundation may also be addressed through these discussions of different philosophical schools tracing from their distinctive perspectives the link between the empirical and the transcendental to account for the origin of impulsion in the mundane consciousness through the causative process of Vedic injunctions.

I

According to the Grammarians, in understanding the meaning of a sentence, the meaning of the verb occupies the primary position. According to the Sanskrit grammar, the sentence *caitraḥ pacati* (Caitra is cooking) the inflected verbal base *pacati*, has two parts:

1. *pac*.
2. *ti*.

Of these, the first one is (*prakṛti*) and the second one is the verbal-suffix or *pratyaya*. Now, what do these verbal root and

---

4 *codanā bhūtam bhavantam bhaviṣyam sūkṣam vyavahitam viprakṛṣṭam ityevam jātiyam artham śaknoti adhigamayitum, na anyat kiñcana indriyam – Jaiminīsūtra, Śābarabhāṣya*.

5 Sushil Kumar Maitra, 1963, *The Ethics of the Hindus*, p. 112.

suffix signify? According to the Grammarians, we may draw the following diagram to show what are being signified by the verbal root (*dhātu*) and the suffix (*pratyaya*):

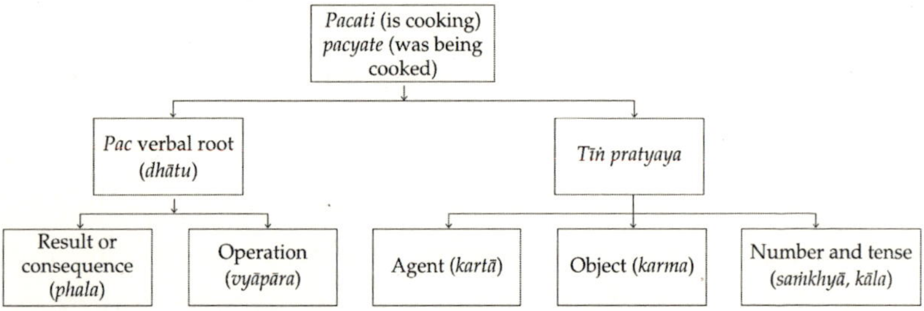

From the above diagram, it is evident that the verbal root is supposed to signify the result or consequence (*phala*) and operation (*vyāpāra*); and the verbal suffix, in this instance, *tiṅg pratyaya* denotes the person or the thing in which any quality or article is inherent (*āśraya*). This referent of *tiṅ pratyaya* is the agent (*kartā*) as the locus wherein operation (*vyāpāra*) is retained, and the referent of *tiṅ pratyaya* is the object (*karma*) as the locus wherein result or consequence (*phala*) is inherent. The referent of *tiṅ pratyaya* or *akhyāta* (suffix) in the active voice of the inflected verbal base is the agent; in the passive voice of the inflected verbal base, *pacyate,* the referent is *karma* (object). Apart from agent and object, *tiṅ* suffixes are indicative of the number of the subject, as to whether it is in singular number or dual number or plural number, indicative of the person of the subject as to whether in the first person, second person or third person and also indicative of the tense and mood of the action.

According to the Grammarians, among *phala* and *vyāpāra,* which are signified by the expression with the inflected verbal base with *tiṅ,* in a verbal understanding of a sentence (*śābdabodha*), *vyāpāra* is given more importance than the result or consequence (*phala*). There are differences of opinion among the grammarians as to whether *tiṅ*-verbal suffix is to be taken as signifying both consequence and the operation as different things or as the operation qualified by the consequence (*phala-viśiṣṭa vyāpāra*), thus taking it as one. But Kauṇḍa Bhaṭṭa, the author of *Vaiyākaraṇabhūṣaṇasāra,* thinks that the denotation of the verbal root is not *vyāpāra* as qualified by the result (*phala*), but rather both the operation (*vyāpāra*) and *phala*. What is meant by *phala* has not yet been addressed here. In a simplistic manner it may be said that the goal or purpose for the attainment of which, the action is being performed that purpose is to be considered as the primary result or consequence (*phala*). Thus understood, it may be said that the purpose for the fulfilment of which the cooking activity is performed is the main *phala* of that cooking activity. If it is maintained that for getting rid of hunger, the activity of cooking is performed, then we may admit that the removal of hunger (*kṣudhānivṛtti*) is the result of the cooking activity. Similarly, if it is maintained that the sacrificial rites (*yāgakriyā*) are performed with the purpose of attaining the heaven and not for obtaining some other substances, it has to be said that *phala* of the performance of *yāgakriyā* is the attainment of heaven (*svargaprāpti*).

This easy and simple account of the notion of *phala,* however has not been accepted. There are some difficulties in accepting the notion of *phala* in this way. Technically speaking, of the two referents of a verbal root, viz. *phala* and *vyāpāra, phala* has been accounted for as caused by *vyāpāra*.[6] Generally speaking, *vyāpāra* is the operative process; *vyāpāra* is instrumental in bringing/producing the final effect. According to this definition *phala,* the result which is being signified by the verbal root *pac,* is in this case, called in Sanskrit *viklitti,* meaning thereby becoming softer, moist through some peculiar conjunction or disjunction of its parts. The other question is: what is meant by the notion of *vyāpāra*? Generally, *vyāpāra*s that are being signified by the verbal root *pac* are puffing or blowing of the fire or lighting fire from the below. According to the Grammarians, *vyāpāra* is also known as *bhāvanā*. *Bhāvanā,* which is also called, *abhidhā,* is the operation which causes

---

[6] The technically the notion of *phala* has been introduced as follows: *taddhātvartha janyate sati taddhātujanyopasthitiviṣayatvam taddhātvārthatvam vā – Vaiyākaraṇabhūsaṇasāra,* p. 11

the origination of *phala* to-be-done.[7] From the point of view of the Grammarians, a sentence consists of words that refer to items that are already accomplished (*siddha*) and the items yet to be accomplished (*sādhya*). They say that the syntactic-semantic items (*kāraka*s) of a sentence are representative of things which are accomplished (*siddha*s), and the verbal expressions of a sentence are representative of actions as *sādhya*. In the sentence "He brings the cow" (*sa gām ānayati*), the subject expression "He" and the object "cow" signify such items which are accomplished, whereas, the action of bringing the cow, is the item yet to be accomplished. According to this analysis of sentence, action is viewed as *sādhya* (to be accomplished), hence this has been given the primacy; whereas *kāraka*s as representatives of such items called as subject, object and instrument, which are already accomplished (*siddha*) are secondary for their contribution towards the accomplishment of an action.[8] Thus, according to these Grammarians, the sentence consists of words that refer to what is *siddha* and what is *sādhya*.

According to the Grammarians both *phala* and *vyāpāra* are designates of a verbal root. We have already discussed, according to the Grammarian viewpoint, that the designates of *ākhyāta* are both agent and object. The point here is to stress that when suffixes are conjoined with verbal roots we have the knowledge of agent and objects.

II

According to the Bhāṭṭa Mīmāṁsakas, in understanding the meaning of a sentence, *vyāpāra* which is of the nature of *bhāvanā* (*bhāvanā rūpa*) is primary. In this connection, we need to clarify the notion of *bhāvanā* as understood by the Mīmāṁsakas. We must keep in mind that the *bhāvanā* as understood by the Vaiyākaraṇas are signified by the verb roots, whereas for the Mīmāṁsakas, *bhāvanā* is signified by the inflected verbal base (*akhyāta*). In Indian

7 Thus in *Vaiyākaraṇabhūsaṇasāra* it has been stated clearly, *vyyāpārastu bhāvanābhidhā sādhyatvenābhidhīyamāna kriyā.*

8 V.P. Bhatta, 2001, *Navya-Nyāya Theory of Verbal Cognition*, chap. IV.

philosophy of language, the sentence meaning or verbal cognition is dependent upon the syntactical and semantical relations among word-meaning. Indian philosophers of language presenting alternative interpretations in their analysis of relation between the syntax and the semantics, propounded three divergent theories depending on their respective answers to the question as to which part of speech occupies the central position in the determination of meaning of a sentence. Looking at from this perspective, the difference between the viewpoints of the Grammarians and the Bhāṭṭa Mīmāṁsakas become obvious in the context of the verbal comprehension (*śābdabodha*): according to the Vaiyākaraṇa School represented by Kauṇḍa Bhaṭṭa, the verb as one of the parts of speech in a language occupies the central position in accounting for the meaning of a sentence. The verb plays a significant role in the sentence in which it occurs, and thus the meaning of the sentence would, to a large extent, depend on the meaning of the verb too. According to them, the action that is expressed by the verb (predicate) is the most crucial factor; hence from their viewpoint, the verb in its verbal root aspect, which designates action, is the principal element.

The Mīmāṁsā school of philosophy analysed sentence meaning from their interest in interpreting rituals and sacrificial acts prescribed by the Vedas. Second, they were interested in evaluating efficacy of *vidhivākya*s in terms of their "efficiency" or "potency" towards accomplishing a particular goal or purpose. Hence according to the Bhāṭṭa Mīmāṁsakas, a sentence has to have a verb (*akhyāta*) that expresses *bhāvanā* or the efficient means for actualizing the purpose as its principal element (*viśeṣa*). Hence in this view the primary element is *bhāvanā* as designated by the verbal suffix (*pratyaya*).

According to the Bhāṭṭa Mīmāṁsākas, there is no author of the Vedas, so the Vedas are *apauruṣeyaḥ*. The Bhāṭṭa Mīmāṁsakas also maintain that in the case of the Vedic imperative statements (*vidhivākya*) such as "one who wishes for heaven ought to make sacrifice", induces an "urge" or incitement towards a particular act for the attainment of an object or end. If the Vedas were supposed to have any author, and God was postulated as the author of Vedas, one possible explanation could have been provided regarding the authoritativeness of the Vedic imperative statements in generating the urge in the embodied individuals towards an action directed to some particular goal. As the Bhāṭṭa Mīmāṁsakas do not admit any author of the Vedas, according to them, this urge or prompting to act towards a particular end does not come from God. Hence it is important for the Bhāṭṭa Mīmāṁsakas to explain how do the Vedic imperative statements get revealed in the consciousness of the agents who realize the motivational force from such statements as urging men to act accordingly to attain some end. In other words, how does the impelling force or the obligatoriness of the Vedic imperative statements relate to the motive of the moral agent? The Bhāṭṭa Mīmāṁsakas would maintain that hearing the sentence, "The person desirous of attaining the heaven do perform sacrificial rites" (*svargakāmo yajeta*), the urge to act towards the end is derived from the clause, "do perform sacrificial rites", for which the corresponding Sanskrit expression with inflected verbal base is *yajeta*. In this view, one of the constituent expressions of the Vaidika *vidhivākya*, has been posited as the originator or *bhāvayita* (*utpādana kartā*) of the urge towards action to attain a particular end and this stimulation or urge does not come from any person. The Bhāṭṭa Mīmāṁsakas have offered uniform explanation to account for the nature and stimulating force or the incitement to actions as conveyed by imperative statements directed towards some end – whether transcendental (*alaukika/vaidika*) or empirical (*laukika*). In the above-mentioned Vedic imperative statement (*vidhivākya*), the expression *yajeta*, if analysed further, there are two parts of this expression: (i) the part that constitutes the verbal root *yaj* expressing the nature of the act, viz. sacrifice; and (ii) the suffix-ending-*ta*- in optative mood *liṅ*. The second part consisting of the suffix-ending-*ta*- in optative mood *liṅ* is determined by two sorts of properties:

a. The property *akhyātatva* which is common to all ten suffixes of tense and mood, known as *daśa lakāraḥ.*

b. The property *liṅtva*, which is its specific property.

Thus from the above analysis, it is quite obvious that the inflected verbal suffix, in this case, the *liṅ pratyaya* has both a common property (*sādhāraṇa-dharma*) and also a specific property (*asādhāraṇa-dharma*). Thus it can be said that the verbal suffix ending with *ta* (*liṅ pratyaya*) is determined by two properties: one is the *akhyātatva* property and the other is the *liṅtva* property. According to the Bhāṭṭa Mīmāṁsakas these expressions that have suffix-ending-*ta*- in optative *liṅ* instances are embedded with operational efficiency (*bhāvanā*) in two forms: as *śābdibhāvanā* and *ārthibhāvanā*. Now let us try to comprehend the technicalities behind the concept of the *śābdibhāvanā*. The *śābdibhāvanā* may be presented through the following diagram:

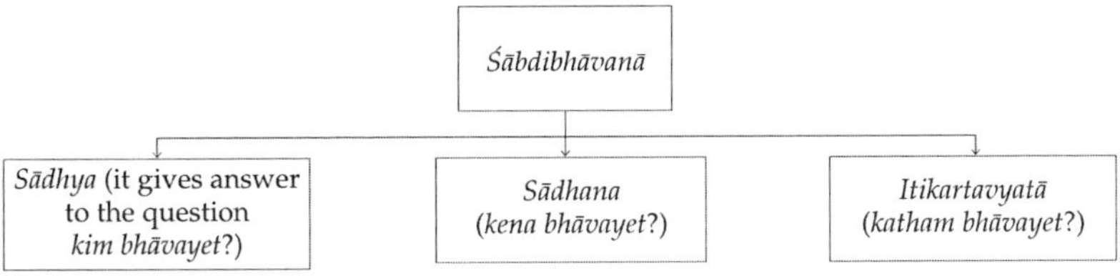

The concept of the operational process or operational efficacy (*bhāvanā*), as understood by the Bhāṭṭa Mīmāṁsakas, technically speaking in the philosophical terminology, is a *vyāpāra*, meaning thereby an intermediate cause. The concept of *bhāvanā* has been defined as a sort of intermediate cause (*vyāpāra viśeṣa*) favourable for bringing forth of something which is going to be produced by the producer (*prayojaka*). Thus *bhāvanā* is of two sorts depending upon the nature of that which is prompting to bring forth (*prayojaka*) which ought to become or to be (*bhavitṛ*). *Śābdibhāvanā*, literally speaking is the operation or process of the imperative statement, and *ārthibhāvanā*, literally speaking, is the operation or process of the will. According to the Bhāṭṭa Mīmāṁsakas, these two processes together constitute the mode of operation of imperative statements. The Bhāṭṭa Mīmāṁsakas conceive that these two operational processes together constitute the mode of transporting the obligatoriness of the Vedic imperative statements to the consciousness of the moral agent. The operative agency of the Vedic imperative statements (*śābdibhāvanā*) is inherently implicated in such statements. *Śābdibhāvanā* or the prompting to bring forth resides in the words (*śabdagata*) and in the case of *ārthibhāvanā*, it resides in the individual person (*puruṣaniṣṭha*). This prompting force residing in the words (*śābdibhāvanā*), itself has been analysed as a complex consisting of three parts: *sādhya* or to be accomplished *sādhana* or means for accomplishment and manner for such accomplishment (*itikartavyatā*).

The Bhāṭṭa Mīmāṁsakas project *śābdibhāvanā* as containing within its complex unit answers to three questions: thus in answer to the question, what sort of action (*karma*) would think of accomplishing?, is that *aṁśatrayavatim ārthibhāvanām bhāvayet*. To the question as to how this *bhāvanā* is to be done, the answer is through the knowledge of the inflected verbal base or *liṅ prataya* (*liṅgādijñānena bhāvayet*). The third part entitled *itikartavyatā* provides answer to the question, as to in what manner that is to be effected? The answer is that it is to be effected accompanied by praiseworthy words for such action. *Śābdibhāvanā* is the verbal efficiency in respect of the action. *Ārthibhāvanā* is the objective efficiency in respect of the end-goal, indicated by the optative or the imperative form of the verbal element. Thus according to the Bhāṭṭa Mīmāṁsakas, *śābdibāvanā* is inherent in the expression *ta*-in-*liṅ*-suffix. The second, *ārthibhāvanā* is inherent in the individual, i.e. disposition inherent in a person during some objective or goal. The expression *artha* of the compound expression *ārthibhāvanā* requires explanation. In one sense, *artha* is indicative of end-goal or result (*phala*). By which *phala* is strived to obtain or "asked for", i.e. *arthyate prārthate phalamyena iti arthaḥ*. There is another sense of the expression *artha* by which is meant desire, wish, and *arthin*, one who wants or desires anything. *Artha* may also signify an individual desirous of some end-goal. This *bhāvanā*, that causes or effects, is called *ārthibhāvanā*, an inherent disposition of an individual (*puruṣaniṣṭha*). This *ārthibhāvanā* is also a composite including its parts of *sādhya*, *sādhana* and *itikartavyatā*, i.e. what is to be accomplished? How that is to be accomplished? And by which manner that is to be accomplished?

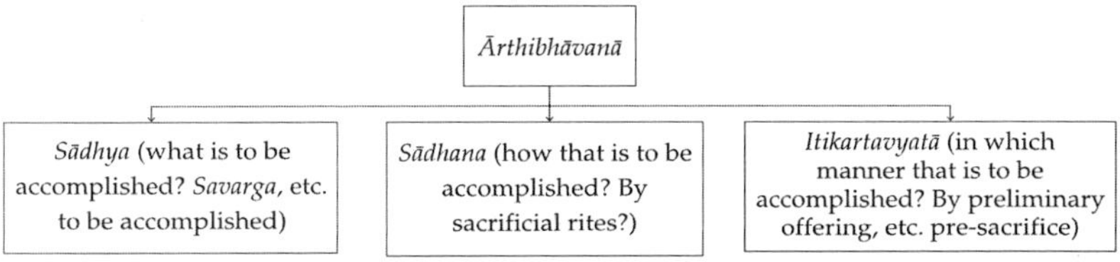

The first type of instigation or prompting efficiency coming from the word motivates an individual person about what ought to be accomplished. The *ārthibhāvanā* inherent in the individual person, which is brought forth by *śābdibhāvanā*. Thus *ārthibhāvanā* which is caused by *śābdibhāvanā*, motivates individual person towards the goal of heaven. From the Mīmāṁsā viewpoint, the heaven has not been considered as a place whatsoever, rather it is viewed as of the nature of joy (*prīti-svarūpa*), a sort of unmixed joy, and not pleasure mixed with pain. This pleasure is without any diminution, without any end, because it has no destruction and is not mixed up with any future pain; and because it is obtained just by desire, it is not mixed with any sorrows of the past. Now, it may be asked as to why sacrificial rites (*yāga*) are not accepted as the object (*karma*) of activity of the *ārthibhāvanā*. (This question has been raised because we know that according to the Grammarians the *vyāpāra* is *bhāvanā*.) The word *yajeta*, occurring in the imperative statement, has two parts, viz. *yaj* verbal root and *ta liṅ* verbal suffix and since these two, that is *prakṛti* and *pratyaya* are closest to one another, why can it not be said that *bhāvanā* which is here taken to be signified by *ta* verbal suffix (*pratyaya*), has as its object to be accomplished or *karma* the *yaj dhātu* denoting *yāga*. In reply to this objection, it may be said that according to the Mīmāṁsā position the object denoted by the verbal suffix is *bhāvanā* does not have as its *sādhya* (to be accomplished) *yāga*.

According to Pāṇinian *sūtra, karturīpsitatamam karma* (1.4.47, p. 12) i.e. the most desired, immediately aimed at object of an action is *karma*. It has been said that the performance of sacrificial rites is very much laborious (*bahu-śramasādhya*) and expensive (*vittasādhya*), hence sacrifice can never be aimed at as the immediate object of action. According to the Mīmāṁsakas, it is heaven (*svarga*) that is the most desired, as *yāga*s are means (*sādhana*) for such attainment. For that reason the Bhāṭṭa Mīmāṁsakas are of the opinion that it is not *yāga*, but *svarga* is *bhāvya* or what ought to be effected by *ārthibhāvanā*.

The *vidhivākya*s, for example, *darśapūrṇamāsābhyām svargakāmo yajeta*, i.e. "One who is desirous of heaven ought to perform sacrificial offerings on the day when new moon and full moon become visible", *udbhidā paśukāmo yajeta*, i.e. "One who is desirous of possessing cattle ought to perform the sacrificial rite named as *udbhid*", *citrayā yajeta paśukāmo*, i.e. "One who is desirous of possessing cattle ought to perform sacrificial rite named as *citra*", clearly seek to inspire to perform different sacrificial rites to accomplish respective goals. For the completion of any activity, the primary means adopted for effecting or accomplishing the goal, is said to be *karaṇa*; the idea of *karaṇa* is expressed in Sanskrit language by using the expression signifying means in instrumental case.

Some conceptual difficulty, however, has arisen from the postulation of *yāga* as means for the attainment of heaven (*svarga*) or any other supposed goals: for *yāga* or sacrificial rite as an action like all other actions supposedly endures for a moment succeeding the moment of its origin and is extinguished in the next moment.

But just immediately after the performance of the sacrificial rite, its result does not show itself. The person who has performed the sacrificial rite obtains the result for such performance after a long period. Since a cause is supposed to be present immediately before the occurrence of the effect, how can the performance of a sacrificial rite be considered as a cause for obtaining *svarga*. On the other hand, if sacrificial rites as enjoined by the Vedas in the statement, *svargakāmo yajeta,* i.e. "one who is desirous of obtaining heaven ought to perform sacrificial rites" cannot be explained as the cause for the attainment of *svarga,* then validity of the Vedic statements will be doubted. Hence from the performance of sacrificial rites, which lasts for a moment, the origination of *svarga* as a consequence has to be accounted for. The Mīmāṁsakas have admitted a sort of valid knowledge (*pramāṇa*) known as *arthāpatti* (presumption) to account for the existence of something else intermediary between the performance of sacrificial rites and attainment of heaven as a result. That intermediate something is called *adṛṣṭa* (unseen) or *apūrva* (a potency).

There are lots of debates and doubts about the nature of *apūrva* among the philosophers. In the Mīmāṁsā literature *apūrva,* i.e. not having existed before has been explained as a sort of potency or power. Prior to the performance of the sacrificial rites by the *yajamāna* (sacrificer), it has to be assumed that the performer (*anuṣṭhātā-puruṣa*) and the sacrificial activities lack the potentiality or power for the attainment of *svarga*. If it is maintained that with the performance of sacrificial rites the heaven is attainable, then it has to be admitted that lack of power or incapability that was in activities like sacrificial rites and its ancillary activities has been removed; also the incapability or lack of power that was in the performer for attaining heaven before the performance of the sacrificial rites has been removed. Thus, it has to be admitted that the lack of potentiality for the attainment of heaven as a result, has been dispelled, otherwise, it has to be conceded that the attainment of heaven (*svarga*) as a goal has been accomplished by a person, even though the person was not fit for the attainment of heaven or by the performance of an act, even though the act was not suitable for obtaining heaven. According to the Bhāṭṭa Mīmāṁsakas prior to the performance of the primary sacrificial action, dearth of potentialities that were in the performing agent and in action as such for the attainment of heaven, requires to be removed. The potentiality or the power acquired by the agent from the performance of a sacrificial rite for obtaining the result thereof and by the action for leading to the goal, is referred to as *apūrva*[9] by the Bhāṭṭa Mīmāṁsakas.

The question may arise as to, if *apūrva* has to be admitted as a separate category, then why not accept *apūrva* as the cause for the attainment of heaven or *svarga*? If *apūrva* is accepted as the cause for the attainment of *svarga*, then *yāga* or the ceremonial actions need not be postulated as the cause for the attainment of *svarga*. To reply to this objection, it has been maintained by the Bhāṭṭa Mīmāṁsakas that it is *yāga* or the sacrificial rite that leads to the attainment of *svarga* through *apūrva* – the intermediary causal efficiency or *vyāpāra*. *Apūrva* itself originates from the performance of sacrificial rites, but it is a cause for the attainment of *svarga*, which again is due to the *yāga* or sacrificial rite. Hence according to the technicalities or *vyāpāra*, *apūrva* is really a *vyāpāra*. That an axe is the cause for the cutting asunder of the branches of a tree is not denied if it is admitted that by the operation of the raising and falling of an axe (*udyamana, nipātana*) that cutting asunder of the branches of a tree has been accomplished. One thing needs to be clarified in this context: it has never been suggested that by the performance of sacrificial rites that *svarga* originates, for *svarga* has already been admitted to be in existence. The person by performing sacrificial rites or *yāga*, attains thereby heaven or *svarga* as a result.

The doctrine of *bhāvanā* that is supported by the Bhāṭṭa Mīmāṁsakas has been questioned on some other grounds also. One of the crucial questions is how to account for the link between *śābdibhāvanā* and *ārthibhāvanā*? One striking thing has already been revealed in course of our analysis of the pivotal expression *yajeta* in the body of an imperative statement as determined by two properties, viz. *akhyātatva* and *liṅtva*. Both *śābdibhāvanā* and *ārthibhāvanā* are represented by the same *pratyaya ta*, hence both *bhāvanās* have the property of being named by the one and the

---

9 *karmabhyoḥ prāgayogyasya karmaṇoḥ puruṣasya vā yogyatā śāstragamyā yā parā sāpūrvamiṣyate* ।

–*Mīmāṁsādarśana, dvītīya adhyāya, prathama pāda*, p. 244

same verbal suffix *ta,* i.e. *ekapratayābhidheyatva*. It seems to be quite pertinent to raise the question, which of *bhāvanās* –, *śābdibhāvanā* or *ārthibhāvanā* – precede the other? Among the later Bhāṭṭa Mīmāṁsakas this question has been discussed and no unanimity among all Bhāṭṭa Mīmāṁsakas has been observed.

III

According to the Naiyāyikas, in the case of verbal comprehension, the word in nominative case occurs as the primary subject of predication. In *śābdabodha* of the sentence, "Caitra is cooking rice"(*caitrastandulapacati*) according to the Naiyāyikas, the word *caitra,* in the nominative case as per rules of Sanskrit grammar, occurs as the primary subject of predication. According to them, the verbal suffix-base ending with the conjugated form *ti,* etc. as in *pacati* and similar other verbal suffix – base signifies volition or *prayatna/kr̥ti,* which as qualifier of the subject, in this case of *caitra,* occurs in our understanding of the meaning of the sentence, *caitrastandula pacati.*

According to the Naiyāyikas, the viewpoints of both the Grammarians and Bhāṭṭa Mīmāṁsakas violate the law of parsimony. We have already discussed, according to the Grammarians, the agent (*kartā*), i.e. one who is possessed of volition (*kr̥timān*) is signified by the significatory power of the *akhyāta*. Understood thus, if *akhyāta* (verb) is taken to signify the agent (*kartā*), the determining property of the signified (*śakyatāvachhedaka dharma*) is nothing other than volition (*kr̥ti*). The Naiyāyikas do not accept this view, rather they maintain that volition (*kr̥ti*) is signified by *akhyāta*. In this case, the determining property of volition (*kr̥ti*) is the universal *kr̥titva*. The Naiyāyikas claimed their view to be better enough than other competing views for it satisfies the law of parsimony. In this connection, the Naiyāyikas have offered two arguments. The acceptance of the thesis that the explicit meaning (*śakya*) of *akhyāta* (verb) is volition or *kr̥ti,* no doubt implies multifarious instances of volition or *kr̥ti*. Though instances of volition or *kr̥ti* are many, there is no need to posit different determining properties (*avacchedaka dharma*), for as the determining property of volition (*kṛti*), there is only one universal property *kṛtitva* in all the multifarious loci of such property. On the other hand, according to the grammarians, the significatory power of the *akhyāta* signifies agent (*kartā*) in active voice or object (*karma*) in the passive voice. Now as there are many varied agents then in respect of different *puruṣa* (individual) their differentiating property *kṛti* has to be many. This argument of the Naiyāyikas does not seem to have any direct implication upon Dharma-Ethics as such. The Naiyāyikas as logicians seeking logical justification for their theory. It is almost universally acknowledged that a good theory requires to be neat and elegant and one of the requisites for satisfying it has been understood in terms of reducing needless multiplication of entities. However, from the Naiyāyikas' claim that their account of meaning of the conjugated verbal base (*akhyāta*) is volition, some grounds may as well be elicited for commending Dharma-Ethics.

In the previous chapter, we have already discussed that according to the Naiyāyikas, *prayatna* is a quality of self. As discussed in the Nyāya philosophy, obviously it seems that *prayatna* may be the property of a conscious being. There is no rule in the grammar of language that prescribes that verbs should be conjoined only with such nouns which signify conscious beings. In many cases, in ordinary uses of language, verbs are rather found to be conjoined with nouns which signify non-sentient, material objects. As in language there are sentences like "Caitra knows", "Caitra cooks", there are also sentences like "The chariot goes", "The horses run". Now, in the above examples, the word "chariot" is a word that designates a non-sentient being. If we stick to the Nyāya point of view, we have to say, in general, the meaning of *akhyāta* is volition (*yatna*). In the case of the sentence, "Devadatta is cooking" (*devadatta pacati*), the understanding of the meaning of the sentence roughly is as follows: Devadatta is the locus of volition agreeable to the act of cooking (*pākānukūla kṛtyāśrayaḥ devadatta*). In the case of the sentence, "the chariot is going" (*ratha *gacchati*) are we to say in the similar way that the understanding of the meaning of the sentence is as follows: "The chariot is the locus of volition agreeable to going?" Are we entitled to maintain that the non-sentient chariot (*ratha*) is the locus of volition (*kṛti*), etc.? Here objection may arise as to how can a non-sentient substance like the chariot be the locus of a sentient quality for volition (*kṛti, yatna*) is the quality of a sentient being.

Thus the opponents may argue against the Naiyāyikas that the verb (*akhyāta*) cannot be said to designate volition (*kṛti*). The question remains, if the view that the *akhyāta* signifies volition gets contradicted by the instance of an unconscious chariot, what is signified by *akhyāta*? The Grammarians urge that their viewpoint upholding that the verbal root signifies *vyāpāra* and the verbal suffix (or operative process) signifies the locus of causal efficiency, i.e. the agent or *kartā*, is more creditable.

In response to this objection, the Naiyāyikas have drawn a distinction between two sorts of uses of *akhyāta*, in its primary sense and in its secondary sense. This distinction is based upon the assumption that there are different modes of signification of the same word depending upon the kind of functional relation a word bears clearly between itself and the object signified. Indian theories of language are unanimous in attributing, at least two significatory capacity to words, viz. *śakti* or primary or direct signification and *lakṣaṇā* or the secondary or indirect signification. This enables to maintain a distinction between two sorts of meaning or significance, of which the primary meaning is variously called as *mukhyārtha, śakyārtha, abidhārtha*; and the secondary meaning is known as *lakṣyārtha*.

In the example such as, "The chariot is going", as it is difficult to explain natural order of connection between words "chariot" (*ratha*) and "going" (*gacchati*), they admit the secondary meaning of *akhyāta* (*gauṇārtha*).

There are no convincing arguments to refute the view that one and the same word may have two sorts of uses, in its primary sense (*mukhyārtha*) and in its secondary sense (*lakṣyārtha*). It has been insisted on that the meaning of the verbal root *kṛ* is volition. Now when the verbal root *kṛ* is conjoined with a noun which signifies a sentient being, then the meaning of the verbal root *kṛ* may be taken in its primary sense as volition. But when the verbal root *kṛ* is conjoined with a noun which signifies a non-sentient being then the primary meaning of the verbal root *kṛ* cannot be maintained. Thus when it is uttered, "The threads are making cloth", the subject expression "threads" (*tantavaḥ*) signifies non-sentient beings, so there cannot be any connection of words *tantvaḥ* and *kurvanti* if the meaning of verbal root *kṛ* is taken in its primary sense.

There are some who are not in favour of accepting two senses, one primary and the other secondary with regard to *akhyāta*. Their opinion seems to be like this: that if *yatna* (volition) were not taken as the meaning of *akhyāta*, then there would not have arisen any reason for drawing a distinction between the primary sense of *akhyāta* and the secondary sense of *akhyāta*. But this sort of argument is not at all convincing to overrule the distinction between the primary sense of *akhyāta* and the secondary sense of *akhyāta*. Rather, we can find many other instances where the distinction between the primary sense and the secondary sense of *akhyāta* has been adhered to.

The distinction between the primary sense and the secondary sense of *akhyāta* has been accepted in the case of the first person use of verbal suffix (*tiṅ pratyaya*) and the second person use of it (*tiṅ pratyaya*). When in a sentence, it is uttered, "You go", it is presumed that the person addressing whom this sentence has been uttered must be a sentient being. Similarly, when it is uttered, "I am going", it is presumed that the pronoun is a signifier of a sentient being. These are all instances of general use of *akhyāta*. Suppose pointing to a person's photograph, it is said, "you go", then that cannot be said to be the primary sense of the verbal-suffix. This is to be recognized as the secondary sense of *akhyāta* of the verbal suffix because the photograph of the person is not a sentient being. Similarly, by pointing towards the photograph of a person, not the person itself, it may be said, "He knows", "He goes". In all these instances the subject expression, which is agent here is not a sentient being. In all these instances the secondary sense of *akhyāta* has to be admitted.

To establish their viewpoint that volition, i.e. *kṛti* is the *artha* of *akhyāta*, the Naiyāyikas also have some other arguments to corroborate their thesis. According to the Nyāya view there are many ways for *śaktigraha* or obtaining knowledge about the relation between the word (the signifier) and the object (i.e. the signified), such as *vyākaraṇa* (grammar), *upamāna* (knowledge by analogy), *kośa* (dictionary), *āptavākya* (authoritative sentence), *vyavahāra* (uses of words by other persons), *vākyaśeṣa* and *vivaraṇa*. In this case, we need to concentrate upon the notion of *vivaraṇa*, which literally means some kind of uncovering or explanation. In roughly speaking, *vivaraṇa* consists in explaining the meaning of a word by its equivalent expression. In the case of *akhyāta*, its meaning can be explained by *vivaraṇa*. The explanation of the verbal expression, *pacati* (is cooking) is given by the expression *pākam karoti* (doing cooking). Similarly, in the case of *gacchati* is explained by the co-designative expression "doing the activity of going". Thus in all instances the meaning *tip*-suffix is explained by the verb *karati*. So the Naiyāyika maintains and establishes that the significant of *akhyāta* is volition.

To make it evident, that the expressions, *yatna* and *kṛti* are equivalent expressions, the Naiyāyikas refer to the idea of *kṛtatva-vyavahāra*: *kṛta* means accomplished and *kṛtatā* means the state of being accomplished or the state of being performed. The Naiyāyikas fix a criterion as *kṛtatva-vyavahāra*, i.e. with respect to which "the state of being performed" or "the state of being accomplished" such uses can be made. Thus in the case of the sentence, *kulāla ghaṭam karoti* (the wife of a potter is making a pot), a synonymous expression can be found of the form: *kulālena ghaṭam kṛtam* (pot has been made by the wife of a potter). This sort of instance of use of a verbal expression is called its *kṛtatā-vyavahāra*. This sort of *kṛtatā-vyavahāra* is not applicable to all cases of verbal usages. If we consider this particular instance, what we find is that the pot has been produced by the wife of a potter. In other words, this pot is *kulālajanya* (is due to the *kūlāla*). In this particular example, with reference to the uses of words, "the usage of being accomplished" and "is due to this" these two expressions go hand in hand. But from this it should not be jumped to the conclusion that wherever something is due to something else, a corresponding example of *kṛtatā-vyavahāra* can be supplemented for it. "The sprout is due to the seed", but from this it cannot be said that *bīja aṁkuram karoti* (the seed is making the sprout) or *bījena aṅkuram kṛtam* (the sprout has been done by the seed). The distinction between these two examples can be explained by taking into account the very nature of a *kartā*. According to the Naiyāyikas, a sentient being who takes effort or works with volition (*yatnavāna*) is an agent. In other words, in case of performing certain action, the performer of such action, i.e. agent has to be a sentient being who performs the act voluntarily. Thus the Naiyāyikas establish a close relation between instances of *kṛtatā-vyavahāra,* i.e. usages of expressions like being accomplished and cases where the action has been performed by a sentient being voluntarily. Thus from their angle *kṛtatā-vyavahāra* and knowledge of being performed voluntarily or with volition, i.e. *yatnapūrvakatva jñāna* correspond to one another. The Naiyāyikas further argue that wherever with regard to any activity, there is no knowledge of being performed voluntarily, i.e. *yatnapūrvakatva jñāna* there cannot be any corresponding usage of verbal expression as being done or performed (*kṛta*). In the case of sprout and seed (*bījāṅkuram*) though sprout is caused by *bīja*, it cannot be said that "the seed is doing sprout or 'the sprout has been done by the seed' " *bīja karoti aṅkuram, bījena aṅkuram kṛtam*. It has already been explained that, in the example of *bījāṅkuram*, there is a failure of *kṛtatā-vyavahāra*. Now, we get to know the reason why there is a failure of *kṛtatā-vyavahāra* in some instances of verbal expression. If agency is understood in terms of a sentient being who acts with volition (*cetana yatnavāna*), then only knowledge of performed by a sentient being with volition can be obtained. Thus, the Naiyāyikas would urge that *yatna* (volition) is *kṛti* and that is the meaning of *kṛ-* verbal root. Some have proposed that instead of positing *yatnapūrvakatva jñāna* as a condition for explaining the usage of being accomplished (*kṛtatā-vyavahāra*) why not suppose knowledge of some what possessed (*yatkiñcit*) of being conducive to the operation, i.e. *yatkiñcit anukūlavyāpārapūrvakatva jñāna*. Thus, from the above discussion, the important question comes up what is the peculiarity of agency? Who can really said to be an agent? We find that according to the Naiyāyikas the meaning (*artha*) of *akhyāta* in general is volition (*yatna* or *kṛti*). In this view, the locus of volition (*kṛti*), i.e. *kṛtyāśraya* is the agent or *kartā*.

IV

There are, however, differences of opinion between the old Naiyāyikas and the Neo-Naiyāyikas regarding the meaning of the conjugated verbal suffix placed in an imperative statement (*vidhipratyaya*). The verbal expression *yajeta* occurring in the imperative statement *svargakāmo yajeta* (one who is desirous of heaven ought to perform sacrificial rites), as has already been discussed, has *liṅ* suffix in particular. In order to account for causal factor behind the motivation to voluntary act, it has been admitted by the Naiyāyikas that desire to do (*cikīrṣā*) is the cause for volition; knowledge about the action as leading to good consequences, knowledge about the action as capable of being performed and knowledge about the absence of greater evil associated with that action are necessary conditions for the arising of desire to do (*cikīrṣā*), which finally leads to volition. But while determining the meaning (*artha*) of *vidhipratyaya*, there are some differences of opinion among the old Naiyāyikas and the Neo-Naiyāyikas. According to the old Naiyāyikas conduciveness to good consequences (*iṣṭasādhanatā*) is the meaning (*artha*) of *liṅ pratyaya*; thus understood, the fully expanded meaning of *vidhipratayaya* is the state of effecting good consequences (*iṣṭasādhanatā*) by the performance of an act, the possibility of accomplishing (*kṛtisādhyatā*) the act concerned and such act as being not associated with greater evils (*valavadaniṣṭananubandhitva*). To put it more idiomatically, it may be said that *valavadaniṣṭananubandhitvaviśiṣṭakr̥tisādhyatāviśiṣṭa iṣṭasādhanatā*. Udayanācārya, the author of *Nyāyakusumāñjali*, deviates from this old Nyāya position by his refusal to accept the state of effecting good consequences (*iṣṭasādhanatā*) as the meaning of *vidhipratyaya*. Udayanācārya does not disregard the role of knowledge about some act as effecting desirable consequences as one of the necessary factors in motivating an agent to a voluntary action by giving rise to a desire in him to perform that action. But he maintained a distinction between the causal factors necessitating origination of volition and the meaning of the conjugated verbal suffix occurring in a Vedic imperative statement. Udayanācārya has provided five reasons to show that *iṣṭasādhanatā* (state of effecting good consequences) cannot be the meaning of *vidhipratyaya*.[10]

The first reason is encapsulated in the clause *hetutvāt*. To explain the position of Udayanācārya we may refer to one Vedic imperative statement maintaining *agnikāmo daruṇī manthīyat*, i.e. "One who is desirous of (kindling) fire ought to produce it by mutually rubbing two pieces of wood (*araṇi*)". Hearing of this statement may give rise to the question in the mind of a hearer as to why he ought to rub mutually two pieces of wood? To reply to this question, the speaker may say that to kindle fire. Thus, the activity of mutually rubbing two pieces of wood produces the desirable consequence of kindling fire. From the above explanation, it is clear that the state of generating desirable consequence (*iṣṭasādhanatā*) is one of the necessitating factors behind a volitional activity, in this particular case, *manthanam* (mutually rubbing). But if the state of generating a favourable consequence (*iṣṭasādhanatā*) is postulated as the meaning of *vidhi-liṅ*-suffix and also as the ground for the volitional activity then that would lead to a

---

10 *hetutvādanumanācca madhyamādau viyogataiḥ* |
anyatra klaptasāmarthyānniṣedhanupapattitaḥ ||
– *Nyāyakusumāñjali, pañcama stabaka, sūtra* 14

Nyāyakusumāñjali, Udayanācārya, 1995, Srimohan Bhattacharya, West Bengal Book Board, Kolkata. Indrani Sanyal, *Vidhir artha viṣaye anunaitika paryālocanā*, 1998, pp. 240-42.

paradoxical situation. For to accept *iṣṭasādhanatā*, i.e. the state of effecting desirable consequence in both of these above-mentioned senses, amounts to holding the same *iṣṭasādhanatā* in the sense of *sādhya*, i.e. what is to be accomplished and in the sense of *sādhana*, i.e. what has been accomplished. If *iṣṭasādhanatā*, i.e. the state of effecting a desirable consequence is taken as the ground for the volitional activity like kindling of sacrificial fire then the state of effecting a desirable consequence has already been accepted as an accomplished fact, so in this case it is *sādhana*, i.e. has been accomplished. When a person has not yet rubbed mutually two pieces of wood, but he has been directed to do so, the desirable consequence of kindling sacrificial fire is a matter to be accomplished, i.e. *sādhya*. If *iṣṭasādhanatā* is admitted as the ground for volitional activity then *iṣṭasādhanatā* cannot be accepted as the meaning of *vidhi-liṅ*-suffix without being involved in a paradox.

The second ground for rejecting that the meaning of *vidhipratyaya* is *iṣṭasādhanatā* is contained in the clause *anumānāt*. In the Vedas there are some statements apart from the Vedic imperative statements (*vidhivākya*s), known as *arthavādavākya* the function of which is the explanation of Vedic rites and rituals with high praises and extols. On many cases from the explanation of Vedic rites obtained from *arthavādavākya*s, one comes to have knowledge of accomplishing desirable consequences by their performance. One such *arthavādavākya* such as *aśvamedhayajñena tarati mr̥tyum tarati brahmahatyām*, i.e. "One is able to cross death and cross (the vices of) killing of brāhmaṇas by the performance of Aśvamedha sacrificial rite". This *arthavādavākya* does convey knowledge about what is conducive to desirable consequence. In this case as there is no corresponding Vedic injunction directly enjoining performance of such action, so on the basis of that *arthavāidavākya* a Vedic imperative statement may be inferred such as *mr̥tyu-brahmahatyātaroṇakāmo 'śvamedhena yajeta*, i.e. "one who is desirous of crossing death and vices of killing brāhmaṇas ought to perform Aśvamedha sacrificial rite". In this case and similar other cases, on the basis of *arthavādavākya*, one has knowledge about an action as means to a favourable consequence; but again if it is maintained that the meaning of *vidhipratyaya* or *liṅ*-verbal suffix is also *iṣṭasādhanatā*, then it would be redundant to infer from the *arthavādavākya* another corresponding imperative statement. Because in both these cases of *arthavādavākya* and the corresponding imperative statement derived from it inferentially, if the same *iṣṭasādhanatā*, i.e. means to favourable consequence is being conveyed, the inference drawn later to match with the *arthavādavākya* turns out to be futile. It is, however, accepted by all *āstika* schools that if knowledge of *iṣṭasādhanatā*, i.e. means to favourable consequence is obtained from *arthavādavākya*, and no corresponding *vidhivākya* is found, in that case a corresponding *vidhivākya* may be inferred. It has been urged that to justify the merit of formulation of the inference, something else has to be assumed to be the meaning of *liṅ*-verbal suffix of the inferred imperative statement. According to Udayanācārya, the meaning of *vidhipratyaya* is the desire of the authoritative person, i.e. *āptāibhiprāya*.

To prove that *iṣṭasādhanatā* is not the meaning of *vidhipratyaya*, the third reason offered is *madhyamādauviyogatalḥ*, implying thereby that in none of the cases of first person use and second person use of *liṅ*-verbal suffix in imperative statements, viz. "I ought to do it", or "You ought to do it", expressing desire of speakers who utter those injunctions, the sense of imperatives is means for desirable consequences (*iṣṭasādhanatā*). Rather, in all these cases after the knowledge of being means for desirable consequence has been realized, this gives subsequently rise to desire to accomplish it. From this observation regarding the first person and second person use of *liṅ*-verbal suffix, the third person use of *liṅ*-verbal suffix requires to be explained as also serving the same purpose. So, it has been proposed that the meaning of *liṅ*-verbal suffix or *vidhipratyaya* is the intention of a credible or trustworthy person, or in other words, *āptābhiprāya*.

Different contexts specifically recorded for uses of *liṅ* verbal-suffix or *vidhipratyaya* are *ājñā* (command/order), *adhyeṣaṇā* (instruction given by a teacher solicited for it), *anujñā* (request/asking for permission), *sampraśna* (seeking an answer to a question/query), *āśaṅkā* (doubt/suspicion), *prārthanā* (prayer), etc. In all these instances it has been shown that the underlying core meaning (*artha*) of *liṅ-pratyaya* in all these different contexts is intention or *abhiprāya*.

In the case of *niṣedhavidhi*, i.e. the precepts of prohibition, what is the meaning of *liṅ-pratyaya* is a matter of much dispute and discussions among the schools of *āstika* thinkers. In this connection without entering into all these details, we may just refer to the solution suggested by Udayanācārya: according to him if the meaning of *liṅ* verbal-suffix is accepted to be *abhiprāya* (intention) that will be the proper approach in accounting for the meaning of *vidhipratyaya*. However, all these discussions are not within the purview of the present section. Thus, according to the Navya-Naiyāyikas, the meaning of *vidhipratyaya* is *abhiprāya* and not desire for consequence. The motivation (*preraṇā*), according to the Naiyāyikas is a quality of an individual (*puruṣa dharma*) who is the motivator (*prayojaka*), whose intention (*abhiprāya*) is the core meaning of *vidhipratyaya*. The Bhāṭṭa Mīmāṁsakas, however, would never concede to this explanation of meaning of *vidhipratyaya*, for according to them the Vedas have no author, hence *pravartanā* (motivational force) conveyed through the Vedic imperative statements cannot be supposed to convey any intention of the speaker. One thing, however, is quite clear that it is not easy to resolve the issues among the conflicting views about the meaning of *vidhipratyaya*. From our attempt to decode the meaning of Vedic imperative statements we may deduce the following observations: to grasp the meaning of *vidhipratyaya*, (1) the meaning of *dhātu*, (2) the meaning of *ākhyāta*, (3) the meaning of *liṅ* and similar verbal suffixes particularly, and (4) the meaning of agent need to be explained.

V

In the context of Indian ethics, we have already seen that the notion of *dharma* has been used in various senses. According to the Nyāya-Vaiśeṣikas, in one sense of the term *dharma* is quality of the soul (*ātmagata-guṇa*). Among other special (*viśeṣa*) qualities of the individual soul (*jīvātmā*), *dharma* and *adharma* in the sense of merits and demerits, are also known as *adṛṣṭa* which is a quality of the individual soul. According to the Bhāṭṭa Mīmāṁsakas, all activities enjoyed by the Vedas are known as *dharma*. In that sense, *dharma* has objective existence. The Prābhākara Mīmāṁsakas admit *apūrva*, which is also a kind of independent and real entity (*padārtha*). The Bhāṭṭa Mīmāṁsakas also admit *apūrva*, but their sense of *apūrva* is different from that of the Prābhākara Mīmāṁsakas. According to them, Vedic activities like the performance of sacrificial rites and their consequences, viz. the obtaining of *svarga*, etc. presuppose in between a connecting causal operational process (*vyāpāra*), and the Bhāṭṭa Mīmāṁsakas admit *apūrva* as the immediate connecting link between the performance of sacrificial rites and the attainment of heaven as an effect. The Prābhākara Mīmāṁsakas admit *apūrva* as the same as *dharma* and admit that Vedas are the only proof for the existence of *apūrva*. Prābhākara Miśra in his *Bṛhatīṭikā* has said that knowledge of such objects which cannot be connected with sense-organs (*asannikṛṣṭa viṣaya*) is obtained through words as *pramāṇa* (*śabda-pramāṇa*). Further the Vedas are considered as *śāstra* meaning thereby '*śāstra*', that through which instruction or direction (*preraṇā*) is known. Both the Bhāṭṭa Mīmāṁsakas and the Prābhākara Mīmāmsakas admit that *dharma* is the sole object for the demonstration and explanation of which the Vedas are the authority. *Vidhivākya*s contained in the Vedas incite us or motivate us to obtain *dharma* which is one of the objectives of humans.

The Vedic injunctions or *vidhivākya*s have the power to urge or to incite to actions. We have already discussed the viewpoint of the Naiyāyikas who maintain that *pravartanā* (incitement to activity) is a quality of a sentient being, hence at the root of *pravartanā* (incitement or drive to activity) there must be some desire (*abhiprāya*), which is a quality of a conscious being. The Naiyāyikas with their theistic framework would say that *vidhivākyas* are the expressions of the desire of God. For the Bhāṭṭa Mīmāṁsakas these explanations of the Naiyāyikas are not at all acceptable for they do not admit God as the author of the Vedas, hence the Vedas are *apauruṣeya*, i.e. no conscious being is the author of the Vedas. Hence, according to the Bhāṭṭa Mīmāṁsakas, no intention (*abhiprāya*) that is in a conscious being has to be admitted to account for the motivational force of the Vedic imperative statements. According to them the motivational force of Vedic injunctive sentences is in the very force of the words contained in those sentences. We have already explained that the notion of *śābdibhāvanā* inherent in the words is leading to *ārthibhāvanā* in the individual man. The Prābhākara Mīmāṁsakas do not admit the position of the Bhāṭṭa Mīmāṁsakas, for according to them the relation between two *bhāvanās* is not properly explainable. If the relation between *śābdibhāvanā* and *ārthibhāvanā* is explained as cause and effect, then *śābdibhāvanā* necessarily leads to *ārthibhāvanā*. This has to be maintained. Then there will be no scope for explaining freedom of the agent in his action. Then in that case, it may be objected that the distinction between *dharma* and *adharma* will collapse and the discussion about morality will turn out to be irrelevant.

In this section, mainly, an attempt will be made to account for the position of the Prābhākara Mīmāṁsakas. We have already discussed that the role of *śabda-pramāṇa* is very important in understanding the nature of morality and ethics as understood by the Indian philosophers. The Prābhākara Mīmāṁsakas maintain that if knowledge of an object is not obtainable by *pratyakṣa* (perception), *anumāna* (inference), *upamāna* (analogy) or *arthāpatti* (postulation), then knowledge of that object may be obtained by verbal testimony (*śabda-pramāṇa*). The Prābhākaras, however, do not admit *laukika* (empirical) *śabda* (verbal testimony) with respect to empirical objects as *pramāṇa* (valid source of knowledge) for they think that such objects are knowable by other acceptable *pramāṇas*. Hence the Prābhākara Mīmāṁsakas when they talk about *śabda-pramāṇas*, they talk about Vedic sentences.

It is quite known that even among the thinkers who admit *śabda* as a *pramāṇa*, there are lots of differences of opinion as to the meaning (*vākyārtha*) of *śabda*. According to one trend, there are thinkers who admit *kārya*, broadly speaking as the meaning of *śabda*, and they are known as the supporters of the thesis that the meaning of *vākya* is *kārya*, i.e. *kāryavākyārthavāda*. Needless to add that the notion of *kārya* is a very technical notion and has been variously interpreted even by the philosophers who admit it. The Grammarians, the Bhāṭṭa Mīmāṁsakas and the Prābhākara Mīmāṁsakas – all are said to be the supporters of *kāryavākyārthavāda*, but they differ from one another as to the sense of the expression *kārya*. According to the Grammarians the meaning of *kārya* is *kriyā*, i.e. action (the general idea expressed by any verb) and according to them in determining the meaning of a sentence, the verbal expression contained in a sentence plays the primary role. The Bhāṭṭa Mīmāṁsakas, however, object to this account of *kārya* as offered by the Vaiyākaraṇas, and we have already discussed their theory of *bhāvanā* as *vākyārtha*. According to the Prābhākaras, in their scheme for the explanation of the meaning of a sentence, we have already hinted at that the notion of *kārya* is primordial. According to the Prābhākaras, the meaning of *vākya*, i.e. *vākyārtha*, is *kārya*, or *apūrva*, or *niyoga*. In *Vākyārthamātṛkāvṛtti*[11] Śālikanātha writes; *apūrvam kāryam vedavākyānāmartheti sādhayitumkāmaḥ . . .* ; here the author is expressing his intention to establish that *apūrva* or *kārya* is the meaning of Vedic sentences.

Among the Indian philosophers, broadly speaking, two theories are well-received about the verbal cognition or understanding of the meaning of a sentence (*vākyārthabodha*). Sentence meaning or verbal cognition is held to be indivisible (*akhaṇḍa*) and divisible (*sakhaṇḍa*),[12] and accordingly we have theories of *akhaṇḍa-śābdabodha* from Bhartṛhari (*Vākyapadīya* I) and *sakhaṇḍa-śābdabodha* from the Grammarians, Mīmāṁsakas – the

[11] Śālikanātha Miśra, *Prakaraṇapañcikā*, 2nd pariccheda, p. 67.

[12] B.K. Matilal, 1990, *The Word and the World*.

Bhāṭṭas and the Prābhākaras – and the Naiyāyikas. Among the supporters of *sakhaṇḍa-śābdabodha*, two major theories are Abhihitānvayavāda or the theory of the cognition of the relation between the meanings expressed by words (parts of speech) and (Anvitābhidhānavāda) or theory of the cognition of the expressed word-meanings that are already connected. However, in the production of sentence-meaning (verbal cognition) one of the most crucial auxiliary factors is the knowledge of the word-relations or word-functions (*vṛtti*). The hearer must have the correct understanding of what word has what functional relation (*vṛtti-jñāna*) with what word-meaning. Thus these thinkers admit prior to *vākyārthabodha*, the meaning of all the constituent words (*saṅketagraha*) be known. According to the Prābhākara Mīmāṁsakas from hearing of the Vedic injunctive sentences, which are causes of incitement to action, the apprehension of sentence-meaning does occur. The Prābhākara Mīmāṁsakas admit two types of sentences:

(a) Sentences which have as constituents *liṅ*-verbal suffixes connected to verbal roots.

(b) Sentences which are devoid of *liṅ*-verbal suffix as their constituents.

According to the Prābhākaras, the sentences which are devoid of *liṅ* or verbal suffixes of similar category ascertain what has been already accomplished or established (*siddhārthaka*). According to the Prābhākaras such sentences which are ascertaining what has been accomplished are not regarded as means to verbal cognition (*śabda-pramāṇa*). According to the Prābhākaras, we have already pointed out that the Vedic sentences are *śabda-pramāṇa* but *laukika vākya*s or non-Vedic, or so-called secular sentences, are not to be considered as *śabda-pramāṇa*. But the problem is that there are Vedic sentences such as *satyam jñānam anantam* which are not expressive of any action; are we then to question the validity of these Vedic sentences? The Prābhākaras have suggested that in cases mentioned above or similar cases, if no verbal expressions are explicitly contained in the sentence, and attempt may be made to furnish a supplementary verbal expression to enable such sentences to convey *kāryatābodha* explicitly.

According to the Naiyāyikas, we have already discussed there are various ways of grasping the relation between a word and its meaning. Thus the Naiyāyikas urge that through Vyākaraṇa (grammar), knowledge by analogy, etc. the relation between a word and a thing is grasped. The Naiyāyikas maintain that the usage of the senior persons (*vṛddha-vyavahāra*) is not the only way for the apprehension of the meaning of a word or a sentence. The Prābhākara Mīmāṁsakas however maintain that the only way of apprehending the relation between a word and a thing denoted by it is through the observation of the usages of the elderly persons. According to the Prābhākara Mīmāṁsakas there is a *svābhāvika* (natural) and eternal (*nitya*) relation between a *pada* (word) and a *padārtha* (a thing denoted by it). According to the Prābhākaras, the words do not denote pure (*śuddha*) or unrelated *padārtha,* but the words denote entities in their relatedness with other entities. According to the Prābhākaras, as we have already explained how through the observance of the usages of a word by an elderly person, the knowledge of *śakti* (denotative power) of a word are obtained. The learner child observes how hearing the utterance of an elderly person, the other middle-aged person proceeds towards some activity. The younger child, who is for the first time learning the use of words, understands that the meaning of the sentence is *kārya*, i.e. action.

According to the Prābhākara Mīmāṁsakas, the meaning of *liṅ*-verbal suffix is *kārya*. Now it has been already said that according to the Prābhākara Mīmāṁsakas, in all instances, the word stands for an object as related to *kārya* or activity (*kāryānvitārtha*). But if it is also maintained that according to the Prābhākaras, the referent of *liṅ*-verbal suffix is *kārya*, then are we to say that the referent of *liṅ*-verbal suffix is activity as related to activity and no pure unrelated *kārya*? Now, question may be raised as to whether there are other *kārya*s as distinct from the meaning of *liṅ*, etc. verbal-suffixes? There is no ground for the Prābhākaras to admit any *kārya* other than *liṅ*, etc. verbal-suffix denoted *kārya*.

It has been explained that to say that *artha* of a *pada* has denotative function (*śakti*) in *kāryānvitārtha*, i.e. object in connection with activity, means that *artha* of *liṅ*-verbal suffix is in a connected relation which is in connection with *kārya*.

The Prābhākara Mīmāṁsakas maintain that from *liṅ*-verbal suffixes we derive knowledge of *kāryatā* (being action to be done). Hence it can be said words like *liṅ* verbal suffixes designate action. If we find a person proceeds to perform certain action, then we can infer that his action is preceded by his knowledge of the action to be done. The Prābhākaras maintain that by *liṅ* sentences, *kārya* is being known. Knowledge of *kāryatā* being an action to be done is the immediate cause of *pravṛtti*. The desire (*icchā*) may be admitted as the cause of volition, but desire cannot be accepted as the *vācya* of *liṅ*-verbal suffix.

We may take up the instance of the observant boy who was witness to the volitional activity of the middle-aged person after hearing the utterance of an imperative statement containing *liṅ* or similar verbal suffix from a senior person. The boy infers that the volitional activity of the middle-aged person is due to some knowledge for this is what he experiences in case of his own volitional activities. Now, in this case knowledge that leads to volition is a sentence, so question arises as to what is the referent of the sentence. The Prābhākara Mīmāṁsakas determining from their viewpoint what is being referred to or meant by (*abhidheya*) the sentence is *kārya*, which is cause of volition (*pravṛttihetubhūta*), elaborately discuss all the proposed alternatives. The Prābhākara notion of *kārya* is a technical notion and in order to grasp the true sense of *kārya* we need to consider the distinction between *kārya* and *kriyā*. Śālikānāth Miśra categorically denied the following four alternatives as not acceptable:

1. Knowledge of *kriyā* gives rise to volition.
2. Knowledge of result due to a *kriyā* gives rise to volition.
3. Knowledge of mutual connection between result (*phala*) and *kriyā* gives rise to volition.

4. Knowledge of mutual connection between result and *kriyā* understood in terms of *sādhya–sādhana* relation gives rise to volition.

The person who has been motivated to volitional activity, prior to his motivation, has knowledge about an action that "it is my *kārya*". Thus it can be said that *kāryatājñānam* is cause for volition. To quote from Sālikanātha: *kāryatām budhhvā pravr̥tto 'ham, mamedam kāryamiti pratītya aham sarvatra pravr̥ttaḥ.*[13]

Naturally, a question arises as to what is implied by *kāryatājñāna*? The author of *Brahmasiddhi*, Maṇḍana Miśra took *kāryatājñāna* and *iṣṭasādhanatā jñāna* as equivalent for according to him what is meant by *kāryatājñāna* is nothing other than cognition of a desirable consequence. There cannot be any cognition other than cognition of leading to a desirable consequence (*iṣṭasādhanatājñāna*) that motivates a person to volition. Once cognized some action as suitable for producing some desirable consequence, the person considers the action to be his *kārya* (duty) and proceeds to act. Maṇḍana Miśra in *Vidhiviveka* has also argued that *kāryatā* and *iṣṭasāhanatā* are the same. To quote from *Vidhiviveka*:

> *puṁso neṣṭabhyupāyatvāt kriyāsvanyaḥ provartaka* ।
> *pravr̥ttihetum dharmam ca prabadanti provartanam* ।।[14]

The noted Vedāntin Citsukhācārya also does not accept the explanation offered by the Prābhākara Mīmāṁsakas. According to Citsukhācārya, generally any action is considered to be the source of suffering or sorrow – *svabhāvena hi karmāṇi duḥkhotpādahetubhūtāni*. How to account for *kāryatā* (obligatoriness) towards such actions which are painful by nature? In reply to this question, it has been suggested by Citsukha that the result or consequence of an action that is desirable for an agent is obtained by the performance of that action. So, an action is obligatory

---

13 *Vākyārthāmātr̥kāvr̥tti, Dvitīya parichheda*, Sālikanātha, Delhi: Indu Prakasan, p. 75.

14 *Vidhiviveka* 27, *Prathamakhaṇḍa*, Sri Mohan Bhattacharya, Calcutta: Sanskrit College, 1982.

because of its being meant to a desirable consequence. So an action that is conducive to *sukha* or pleasure (*sukhosādhana*) has to be considered as *kārya* (duty).

In *Vākyārthāmātr̥kāvr̥tti*, it has been stated that *phalasādhanatā* and *kāryatā* are not the same:

> *phalasādhanatā nāma vā so naiva ca kāryatā* |[15]

The Sanskrit expressions *kāryatā* and *phalasādhanatā* (or *iṣṭasādhanatā*) are abstract notions derived from the *taddhita* termination *tāl* suffixed to expressions *kārya* and *phalasādhanā* (or *iṣṭasādhanā*) which designate acts but in different senses – in the technical Prābhākara sense of what ought to be done and in the sense of means for effecting any result respectively. *Kāryatā* grammatically speaking may be analysed as the state of being what ought to-be-done or to-be-accomplished and *phalasādhanatā* as the state of being means for effecting any result or fruit. The notion of *kāryatā* has been explained as that state which requires to be accomplished by volition (*kr̥tisādhya*); whereas *phalasādhanatā* points to the state of being means for effectuating the result. The agent may have the cognition of means for effecting desirable consequences (*iṣṭasādhanatā jñāna*) with regard to actions already performed in the past or with regard to actions that are being performed at the present. But the question may be raised as to if an agent has cognition with regard to an action as what ought to be accomplished or done, or in other words, the agent has cognition of *sādhyatā* or *kāryatā*, then how can that agent would be said to have cognition of *phalasādhanatā* with regard to such an action as had not already been performed or is not being performed, but which ought to be performed or done? The agent may have cognition of *phalasādhanatā*, i.e. being means for fruition or means for producing a desirable consequence with regard to such an action as had been performed in the past, or is being performed at the present. This is one of the arguments adduced in favour of their viewpoint by the Prābhākara Mīmāṁsakas who insisted upon

---

15 *Vākyārthāmātr̥kāvr̥tti*, p. 76.

drawing a distinction between *iṣṭasādhānatā jñāna* and *kāryatā jñāna*. The other argument that has been provided by the opponents in support of the claim that *iṣṭasādhanatā jñāna* and *kāryatā jñāna* are the same is that *iṣṭasādhanatā* and *kāryatā* – these two properties inhere in the same locus (*ekādhikaraṇaniṣṭhā*). The Prābhākara Mīmāṁsakas do not deny that these two properties inhere in the same locus, but for that reason these two properties are the same – this has not been accepted by the Prābhākara Mīmāṁsakas. To quote from Śālikānāth: *yadyapi ekavastuniveśita dvayaḥ tathāpi svarpabheda 'styeva*. Thus, the Prābhākaras have tried to establish an essential difference between *kāryatā* and *phalasādhanatā*.

How to explain the nature of *kārya*? It has been further asked as to whether *kārya* is the same as *kriyā*? In Indian philosophy, generally, the relation between a word and its designatum, i.e. *pada-padārtha-sambandha*, or in other words *bodhya-bodhaka-bhāva* (state of being signifier and signified) is established through the relation of agreement in presence and agreement in absence between these two. It may be maintained by some that the *liṅ*-verbal suffix designates order, command (*praiṣa*). Thus it has been maintained that there is the relation of being the signified and the signifier between the command or the urge (*praiṣa*) and the signifier, in this case, the *liṅ*-verbal suffix. Thus expressions, such as *praiṣa* and *niyoga* are taken to be synonymous. Jayanta Bhaṭṭa, the author of *Nyāyamañjarī*, while explaining the position of the Prābhākara Mīmāṁsakas had commented that through such sentences containing words with *liṅ*-verbal suffixes, the relation between the acts of ordering and the order is made known. The nature of *niyoga* (order/command) or *kārya*, however, may be of various levels depending upon the mutual relation based on the seniority and juniority of the commander and the person who is being commanded. When a senior person urges another person to perform same activity, then the *liṅ*-verbal suffix occurring in the utterance of the person who is making the order is taken to signify the motivating urge (*pariṣa*), that is said to be *ājñā*, *ādeśa* (order or command).[16] Second, the person who is inciting or setting somebody to action (*pravartaka*), and the person who is being set to act (*pravṛttya puruṣa*) are of the same age, then *kārya* or *praiṣa*, expressed by the *liṅ*-verbal suffix, is said to be *āmantraṇa* or *parāmarśa*.[17] The relation here is between *āmaṇtrayitṛ*, the person who is inviting or asking, and *āmaṇtrya*, i.e. the person who is being called for or asked to perform certain act.[18] On the other hand, when the person, who is *pravartaka puruṣa*, i.e. one who is effecting someone to move, is inferior or weaker than the person who is being effected to act (*pravaṛttya puruṣa*), then the *liṅ*-verbal suffix contained in his utterance is said to express *kārya* of the nature *adhyeṣaṇā*, *kāmanā* or *prārthanā*. To put it in English, in this case, somebody is asking for instruction from a teacher. The meaning of *adhyeṣaṇā* is solicitation or asking for instruction. In the case of *prārthanā* as forming part of the worship of gods, the relation is between the *prārthayitṛ*, one who wishes for or asks and the *prārthya*, i.e. one who is desired or wished for. To quote, *hīnena adhyeṣaṇam iti*. The Prābhākaras, thus, provide an exhaustive domain for the application/employment of the *liṇ*-verbal suffix in general, taking into account three sorts of broad specificities. Thus here we may admit that from the point of view of the Prābhākaras, *praiṣa*, *āmantraṇa* and *adhyeṣaṇā* are the three sub-species of *kārya* or *niyoga* or *apūrva* or *adṛṣṭa*. Something there is little bit of equivocation is observed in their use of the expression *praiṣa*. When *praiṣa* is taken to mean as *artha* (designnatum) of *liṅ*-verbal suffix of any sort of enjoining or calling upon action, through the utterance of an injunctive statement, it may be said to have been used as a broad categorical concept. In the narrow sense of the term, *praiṣa* it is taken to exclude other varieties of *kārya* (to be done), like *āmantraṇa* and *adhyeṣaṇā*.

Now the question may be raised as to the nature of *niyojya*,

---

[16] *pravaṛttya puruṣāpekṣāyā jyāyaṣa vaktāpratipādyamānam kāryam praiṣā it vyapadiśyate* I –*Vākyārthamātṛkāvṛttiḥ*, p. 78

[17] *Vākyārthamātṛkāvṛtti*, p. 78.

[18] *samena āmaṇtraṇam* – Ibid.

i.e. the person who is being set to action. It has been maintained by the Prābhākaras that *niyojya* is the person who by himself understands that it is his duty to do an act. Thus it has been stated: *niyojya sa ca kāryam yaḥ svakīyatvena buddhyate.*[19] To put it more explicitly, the person who has been directed towards the performance of an act (*niyojya*) awakened by consciousness about that act as to be done by him, is said to be a *niyojya*. The individual man who understands the work or action that has been enjoined by *vidhivākyas* of the Vedas, as his work or action to be done, then that person is said to be a *niyojya*. In this connection, the important distinction between *kārya* and *kriyā* has been discussed by the Prābhākara Mīmāṁsakas. In one of the very common usages, the expression *kriyā* is taken to mean action expressed by any verb in general, conjoined by any *tiṅ* (*lakāra*) verbal suffixes. Hence it is quite clear that for the Prābhākaras *kārya* is signifying an action to be done, or *kārya* is synonymous with *niyoga*, i.e. action enjoined by awakening of consciousness as one's duty.

The person who has been incited to perform certain actions (*pravartaka puruṣa*) has some grounds for such incitement to activity. There are, however, lots of differences of opinion among the Naiyāyikas and the Prābhākaras in specifying reasons behind such actions. However, these philosophers unanimously maintained the difference between a volitional activity and a non-volitional action. This has already been discussed while accounting for the nature of volition. The Prābhākaras as we have already seen specified *svaviśeṣaṇavattā pratisandhānjanya kāryatājñāna*, i.e. knowledge of the thing to be done, caused by recognizing oneself as qualified by the capability for the performance of that action.

From the above discussion it is clear that for the Prābhākaras, the sentences of Vedas, which do not have any author, express independently (*svataḥ*) *niyoga* or *kārya*. To an individual man *niyoga* or duty is revealed as a sort of conscious awareness. The individual man proceeds to perform that act for he considers that act to be his duty.

---

19 *Vākyārthamātṛkāvṛtti*, p. 78.

Thus we also find lots of differences between the Prābhākaras and Bhāṭṭas as to the nature of the motivational force of the *vidhivākyas*. According to the Prābhākaras, *artha* of *vidhi*-verbal suffix is *niyoga* which is a state of consciousness and as such it is a quality of *ātmā*. Like the Bhāṭṭa Mīmāṁsakas, they do not propose the two-tier theory of *bhāvanā* (causal operational processes), primarily one existing in *śabda* causing the other in the individual man (*puruṣaniṣṭha*). There are some difficulties in accounting for the relation between these two *bhāvanās*, *śābdibhāvanā* and *ārthibhāvanā*, as to whether these two *bhāvanās* are simultaneous or successive. In general texts these are taken to be successively related as cause and effect. According to the Prābhākaras, there is some difficulty in accepting the position of the Bhāṭṭa Mīmāṁsakas in explaining the freedom or independence of the agent in performing an action. Because causal relation entails a sort of necessity and so there is no scope for the individual man to avoid the performance of the action. But according to the Prābhākara Mīmāṁsakas, if one has awareness that some action ought to be done by him, he is not necessarily led to the performance of that action. This also explains why in spite of knowing what is *dharma* or *adharma*, one is not incited to perform such actions?

VI

On the basis of the discussions that are already made in the previous sections, some important observations are to be made about Dharma-Ethics as such. Some of the Āstika schools whose viewpoints have been elaborated in this chapter are, broadly speaking, engaged in the analysis of the meaning of the Vaidika imperative statements or *vidhivākya* with a view to determine how does the objective prescription of duty relate with the subjective obligation to carry on these duties. The philosophical schools, that have shown much interest in explaining how does it happen in taking up the onus of obligation in the embodied consciousness from the transcendental source of objective obligation, are the Bhāṭṭa Mīmāṁsakas, Prābhākara Mīmāṁsakas and Naiyāyikas, including both the old Naiyāyikas and neo-Naiyāyikas. But our brief discussion about their views on the subject has shown that these philosophers very much differ from one another in their explanation. One thing has already been pointed out that, truly speaking, it would be an unrealistic imagination to try to delineate one neat and closed, unified theory as representing Dharma-Ethics. From the very beginning one should guard oneself from towing the mistaken idea of delineating the grand master plan of one universal viewpoint in India which may be characterized as the Indian view about morality. This is very much corroborated by the discussion about their analysis of the nature of the Vedic imperative statements.

In the introduction, it has already been pointed that the Pūrva-Mīmāṁsā school of philosophy puts much emphasis upon the ritualistic interpretation of the Vedas. The Mīmāṁsakas believe in the impersonal authority of the Vedas in giving directions for the performance of sacrifice. To them the sole purpose of the Vedas consists in directing rituals. There are many Vedic statements which apparently do not tell anything about action and which appear to lack any plausible meaning. According to the Mīmāṁsakas, any part of the Vedas which does not contain such direction would be useless, unless these statements can be shown at least to serve the purpose of persuading the persons to follow the injunctions for performing rituals. The Mīmāṁsā, which does not believe in any creator or destroyer of the world, believes that the Vedas are not the work of any person, human or divine. Hence with elaborate arguments the Mīmāṁsakas defend their position that the Vedas are impersonal. To them the Vedas are eternal because words are eternal. The Mimāṁsakas propound that the theory of *śabda* is not really the perceived sounds. The sounds produced by the speaker and perceived by the hearer are only the revealers of the words, but words themselves are not produced. Words are really the letters which are partless and uncaused. So the words as letters are regarded as eternal, that is as having existence, but being eternal.

According to the Naiyāyikas, God is the efficient cause of the world and is also the directive cause of actions (*prayojaka kartā*) of all living beings. According to the Nyāya view, man is the efficient instrumental cause of his actions; God is their efficient directive cause. Thus God is the moral governor of the world of living beings including ourselves, the impartial dispenser of the fruits of our actions (*karmaphala dātā*) and the supreme arbiter of our joys and sorrows (*Nyāyabhāṣya* 4.1.21).

The important question is how does the end or result matter to these philosophers? From the analysis of *vidhivākya* it is quite clear that according to the Naiyāyikas that consciousness of desirable consequence or good, i.e. *iṣṭasādhanatā jñāna* is one of the prerequisites for any volitional activity and old Naiyāyikas assume *vidhi-pratyaya* to make reference to knowledge of *iṣṭasādhanatā*. But the Prābhākara Mīmāṁsakas do not agree with the Naiyāyikas in their analysis of *vidhivākya*. The chief role of the import of an injunctive suffix is to prompt *niyojya* to perform an activity. Our analysis brings out clearly that excepting the Prābhākaras all other views discussed here broadly agree in accepting that knowledge that the act to be performed leads to desirable consequence, i.e. *iṣṭasādhanatā jñāna* is the prompting factor to volition. The Prābhākaras have argued that it is realization on the part of the person concerned that it is duty to be accomplished by him, i.e. *kāryatā* that prompts the person to undertake the activity. According to the Naiyāyikas an injunctive suffix has to convey

a. that the act leads to the desirable consequence, i.e. *iṣṭasādhanatva*,

b. the act is performable by the capacity of the person concerned, i.e. *kṛtisādhyatva*, and

c. the act does not lead to any adverse effect, i.e. *balavadaniṣṭhānubandhitva*.

The Naiyāyikas however, do not unanimously include these three states in the scope of the meaning of the injunctive suffix.

The purpose of this complex of three is to lead to incitement (*pravartana*) to activity. Thus, we find that apart from the Naiyāyikas, Vaiyākaraṇas and Bhāṭṭa Mīmāṁsakas accept knowledge of leading to desirable end or consequence, i.e. *iṣṭasādhanatva* as the source of motivation. Here we would like to point out that the Prābhākaras do not deny that in the case of so-called desirable act, i.e. *kāmya-karma,* some desirable end or result motivates the individual self to action. However, just by looking at such instances of *kāmya-karma,* if by generalizing, it is maintained that in all cases of motivation as a cause there must be consciousness of desirable consequence, that cannot be accepted as a legitimate theory by the Prābhākaras. The Prābhākaras, as we have seen, have drawn our attention to the fact that there are other than *kāmya-karma*s some unconditional duties (*nitya* and *naimittika karma*s) and individual selves that are motivated to perform such actions. If knowledge of desirable consequence is regarded as one of the necessary causes for volition, then in the absence of knowledge of desirable consequence in the context of *nitya* and *naimittika-karma,* there should not have been any volition towards such actions. The Prābhākaras, we have already discussed, proposed *niyoga* as the meaning of *vidhipratyaya.* According to the Prābhākaras, in moral prompting the real motive is not the consciousness of good but imperative itself as qualifying or specifying the self. In the opinion of the Prābhākaras, it is *kāryatā jñāna* (knowledge about the action) as ought to be done. They argue that the Naiyāyikas are wrong in conceiving an end or *phala* as a necessary accompaniment of *vidhi.*

What is the position of the Bhāṭṭa Mīmāṁsakas with regard to the status of end in motivating our will to action? For the Bhāṭṭa Mīmāṁsakas, the extraneous end is required to awaken the psychological motive, but not the moral authority of the duty. According to the Bhāṭṭa Mīmāṁsakas, the object of the imperative is *iṣṭa.* The command necessarily refers to this end to be accomplished, an end being logically implied in the command as well as required for psychological motivation in the execution of it. The moral authority of the command is independent of this end which is only a psychological and logical implication of it. This is evident from their admitting *śābdibhāvanā*, which resides in the word as a causal efficiency to produce *ārthibhāvanā*, another causal efficiency, inherent in the individual, prompts the will of the individual person towards the goal of heaven. For the Prābhākaras the extraneous ends may sometimes be implied but never consciously present to the agent. According to the Nyāya viewpoint, the imperative presents the duty as conducive to the end. But even to a Naiyāyika, if the agent's desire is awakened thereby, then only the duty acts on the agent's will as being conducive to the desired end.

Thus, the very perspective here is to trace the mode of operation of the imperative on the agent's consciousness and psychological reaction elicited by those agents. The different interpretations of the *vidhivākya*s that we are discussing are not to be viewed as merely difference in the methodology of interpretation. The Dharma-Ethics as the root has branched out into different sub-branches from certain deeper philosophical theoretical differences among the schools of Indian philosophy. The Dharma-Ethics may be interpreted as deontological or teleological depending upon the nature of interpretation of the Vedic imperative statements that is accepted to be more plausible. Dharma-Ethics would always remain elusive if we attempt to cover all these diversified branches of Dharma-Ethics under one cover to develop a unified view of Dharma-Ethics. Instead, we may talk about ethics of the Nyāya, ethics of the Advaita Vedānta, ethics of the Viśiṣṭādvaita Vedānta, ethics of the Sāṁkhya, ethics of the Yoga and so on without uprooting or severing these branches from their common source of origin.

7

Mitigating Qualms about Dharma-Ethics

THE Vaidika Dharma-Ethics takes into cognizance two aspects of a man: (a) the natural (including physical, vital and mental) aspect of man, and (b) spiritual-cum-liberated aspect of man as the highest end of life and looks upon ethics as the integrating intermediary between the two that provides "training" to man both objectively and subjectively for reaching the highest goal. Man himself is not a product of matter and eternally subject to physical nature, but man is a spirit that gets through all sorts of hurdles to fulfil its purpose. The conscientious endeavour of man is channelized through his performance of such actions that advances meritorious results (*dharma*) over unworthy results (*adharma*) and further through performance of actions accompanied with reversal of motives and desires and thus facilitating man's progress towards liberation (*mokṣa*). "Man in the Indian idea is a spirit veiled in the works of energy, moving to self-discovery, capable of godhead."[1]

This in brief is the kernel of Dharma-Ethics. The sceptics who are always suspicious about the possibility of Dharma-Ethics may first consider the idea of moral elevation quite absurd, second, the highest goal itself for which moral elevation has been sought is ridiculous, and finally would consider the belief in non-intervention of God in religious ethics like Dharma-Ethics is farcical. The sceptics would conjecture that the best possible response would be critical. To answer the critiques we may separate the issues to be decided. Most generally stated questions to be reconsidered are as follows:

1. How may an individual attain moral elevation or acclivity?

---

[1] Sri Aurobindo, 1998, *The Foundations of Indian Culture*, p. 104.

2. What for does an individual endeavour to attain moral elevation or growth?
3. Does God intervene into the domain of morality?

How May an Individual Attain Moral Elevation or Acclivity?

"By *cittaśuddhi* (purification of the mind)" is the spontaneous answer coming forth from the Vaidika Dharma-Ethics perspective. The deeper reflection, however, suggests that the answer to this question has both (1) theoretical aspect, and (2) practical aspect. The practical aspect of Dharma-Ethics is none the less of great consequence but in the present meta-ethical investigation my concern is with its underlying theoretical speculations. As per demand of the present study, bracketing the details about the practice of *cittaśuddhi*, to make the notion of *cittaśuddhi* clear we may concentrate upon the apparently simple answer which rests upon many philosophical presuppositions. In this connection the following matters are to be addressed:

a. Whose *cittaśuddhi* is being spoken of.
b. Why the question of *cittaśuddhi* does arise?
c. Why the performances of duties, both relative and absolute, were not sufficient?
d. How *cittaśuddhi* may be accomplished?

One of the important aspects of Dharma-Ethics is to deal with the nature and function of the moral agent. Dharma-Ethics when discussing about which action is obligatory, which action ought to be performed, is not discussing these things in vacuum. From the point of view of Dharma-Ethics, to have any idea about the nature of volitional activity, we need to have some idea about the nature of the agent. In fact, in the whole scheme of Dharma-Ethics, the nature of the agent is very important. All Indian thinkers admit *puruṣa* (embodied individual) as the agent of moral action. Even the Cārvākas speak about an individual as embodied, though for them nothing is left after a particular embodiment is dismantled.

The minimum requirement for being a moral agent is a sentient being. The psychology of this agent is important. The codes of duties that are generally discussed as *sādhāraṇa-dharma* (general duties) and *asādhāraṇa-dharma* (specific duties) are concerned with external codes of conduct and behaviour. If we just look at *sādhāraṇa-dharma* and *asādhāraṇa-dharma* – these would seem to be nothing more than certain code of external actions. But that would not be a true and complete account of duty from the perspective of Dharma-Ethics. The objective morality of the Hindus is not sufficient by itself, for just upholding only external codes of conduct and behaviour, the true goal of morality is not attainable. In Vaidika Dharma-Ethics, truly speaking, a sort of hierarchy of moral levels has been advocated. Sushil Kumar Maitra[2] introduced the nomenclature of objective morality and subjective morality to bring to focus the distinction between these two aspects of the Hindu ethics: according to him objective morality as represented through external code of duties required outward conformity to such codes of duties. The objective morality, however, lacks adequacy to cover total sphere of morality as projected through Dharma-Ethics. The objective morality is necessary no doubt but it is not sufficient. An individual disciplined in objective morality has still a long way to travel. The individual must try to look within himself/herself and attempt to purify internally. We have already discussed about the distinction between *sakāma-karma* and *niṣkāma-karma* and this distinction does not introduce another set of new duties and actions. This distinction works on the same set of actions prescribed as *sādhāraṇa-dharma*, *varṇa-dharma* or *āśrama-dharma*. The act of *yuddha* may be taken as an example to find out how does implication of the same act varies from context to context. In *Gītā* the act of *yuddha* (waging war) as a kind of act that Arjuna was advised to perform by Kr̥ṣṇa has some special implication. The act of *yuddha* ordinarily understood is one in which a king or a representative of power fights with another country just to get possession of land and treasury of that country. Thus interpreted, the act of *yuddha* is hardly considered as a *dharma* (obligatory act).

---

2 Sushil Kumar Maitra, 1963, *The Ethics of the Hindus*, p. 4.

The act of *yuddha* guided by certain ulterior motives of gaining fame, or extending land or territory of one's country at the cost of lives, property and security of millions of people a grossly violent act and is among the most heinous offences. In the *varṇa-dharma* model, when the act of *yuddha* has been prescribed as duty for kṣatriya it is a much morally loaded concept. Among the duties of kṣatriya are to look after his subjects and to give protection from the hands of enemies to his subjects. The situation of Arjuna is of the second type, for war was forced upon him by the adverse situation created by his relatives. Arjuna however had no option but to wage a war against his enemies for unlawfully Arjuna and his brothers had been deprived of their lawful possession over a kingdom. Arjuna as a kṣatriya is required to perform his *kṣātra-varṇa-dharma*, i.e. duties assigned to his class.

In the Dharmaśāstra it has been quite categorically stated that if required for the protection of his subjects, the kṣatriya king should wage wars against his enemies whether of inferior position, superior position or of the same position. A kṣatriya king should never run away from wars in such situations. Hence we find that the act of *yuddha* (act of waging war) in this sort of context has received the recognition of *dharma*. Translated into the ideology of *Gītā*, the act of *yuddha* in such situations is a duty none the less but is by feature a *sakāma-karma*. But in *Gītā* the same act of *yuddha* has been interpreted as *niṣkāma-karma* (desireless action) when it has been qualified as *dharma-yuddha* (just war). In *Gītā* the way the act of *yuddha* that Arjuna was advised to perform by Kṛṣṇa was a *niṣkāma-karma*, i.e. an act done without any consequence or end in view. Arjuna was asked to perform the act of *yuddha* only for the sake of duty without taking into consideration either victory or defeat, joy or sorrow. Rather Arjuna was advised to fight for the sake of the act alone. Kṛṣṇa says: *yuddhāya yujasva*.[3] The dialogue between Kṛṣṇa and Arjuna in this context brings out very clearly that the act of *yuddha*, when it is obligatory (*dharma*) can as well

3 *Śrīmadbhagavadgīta* II.38.

Indrani Sanyal, 2002, *The Just War or the Dharmayuddha*, pp. 22-23.

be viewed from two different perspectives: either as *sakāma-karma*, i.e. act done with certain end in view or as *niṣkāma-karma*. What has been shown to be true about the act of waging war is equally true about all *karmas*. It should not be supposed that doing a *sakāma-karma* is necessarily bad or leads to undesirable consequences. This is not the teaching of *Gītā* or of the Vaidika Dharma-Ethics in general. A *kāmya-karma* that produces good consequences and enables the agent to enjoy its results happily is not to be deplored. But the insufficiency of the performance of *sakāma-karmas* lies in dooming the prospect of release from the cycle of birth and death. But we have already discussed the objective of Dharma-Ethics is not to be satisfied with happy moral life in this world for happiness is viewed as temporary and may at any point of time be dismayed by sorrows and pain. For the Vaidika Ethics performance of duties is important but finally what matters is the performance of duties with an altogether changed attitude. This Dharma-Ethics tries to reach also to the very core of human action by penetrating within the psychology of the moral agent. How to distinguish between the performance of an action as *sakāma-karma*, that is with an end in view and the performance of the same action as desireless action is an important question. The answer depends on the will of the person concerned. The analysis of will (*pravṛtti*) which is the source for volition has been elaborated and analysed from the perspective of Dharma-Ethics. In this regard all sub-groups of Dharma-Ethics, whether Vedic, or Buddhists or Jainas broadly agree with one another. But the question still lingers as to why will sometimes leads to volition resulting in bad consequences and sometimes to volition resulting in good consequences? The other very important question is that if will always leads to actions which result in good or bad consequences how to obtain release from rebirth? To answer this, the very notion of the performance of action with a total changed attitude of mind or will has been presumed. This is the level of subjective morality, wherein the psychological ethics of the Hindus thrive. The basic assumption is that purification of the mind (*cittaśuddhi*) is the indispensable requisite at the subjective stage of morality. But without explaining why purification of mind is called for the matter remains unexplained. The natural man has always received its due recognition no doubt, but the natural man should be purified to ascend to the transcendental stage – the stage of spirit which is a moral stage of being.[4] Speaking of purification of mind or of will suggests some presence of impurity within mind, will. The Dharma-Ethics very much admits the important contribution of code of external acts and external conformations to certain norm. But these are considered as stepping stones to higher stages of morality. The individual must learn to imbibe in himself the true spirit of being free, to have the genuine taste of freedom is not to be whimsical and to run after whatever his mind seeks for. The right use of freedom which makes a moral agent true agent is also something that has to be acquired. In *Gītā*, we get the highest ideal of a moral being as a *sthitaprajña*. If we once again try to recapitulate what are the marks of a *sthitaprajña*, we will be able to have some idea about a genuine moral individual from the perspective of Dharma-Ethics. The sixth chapter of *Bhagavadgītā*, Ātmasaṁyama-yoga, is really one of the important chapters of the text, where most of the discussion about *yoga* in the sense of self-restraint has been discussed. The chapter opens with a clear-cut idea of who is a *yogī*:

> *anāśritaḥ karma-phalaṁ kāryaṁ karma karoti yaḥ* |[5]

> One who does the prescribed work without any desire for the consequence.

In *Gīta* VI.9 it is said:

> *sādhuṣvapi ca pāpeṣu sama-buddhirviśiṣyate* |

> A *yogī* is one who maintains equanimity among his friends and foes.

---

[4] Sushil Kumar Maitra calls the transcendental stage or the stage of absolute spirit as the third stage of morality. I do not consider this transcendental stage as a stage of morality. Hence I would like to accept, broadly speaking, two stages of morality – objective morality and subjective morality, and no third stage of morality.

[5] *Bhagavadgīta* VI.1.

In this *śloka* also the emphasis is upon equanimity, i.e. *sama-buddhi*. When Śrī Kṛṣṇa tells Arjuna to be a *yogī* at the close of this chapter, this is the sense in which Śrī Kṛṣṇa tells:

tasmād yogī bhavo 'rjuna ।

In *Gītā,* the expression *yoga* has been used in various senses, but one of the senses of the term *yoga* is *niṣkāma-karma*. The theory of *niṣkāma-karma* is really a very difficult theory to practise, but in *Gītā* it has also been discussed as *karma-yoga. Yoga* has been described to be a skilful action (*yogaḥ karmasu kauśalam*)[6] and has also been described as equanimity (*samatvam yoga uccyate*).[7]

Sri Aurobindo explains the notion of *karma-yoga* as follows:

> But what is the essence of this self-control, what is meant by action done as *yoga, karma-yoga*? It is non-attachment, it is to do works without clinging with the mind to the objects of sense and the fruits of the works. Not complete inaction, which is an error, a confusion, a self-delusion, an impossibility, but action full and free done without subjection to sense and passion, *desireless* and unattached works, are the first secret of perfection.[8]

In Dharma-Ethics purification of *citta* or cleansing of *ātmā,* these are frequently heard and used ideas. A demand for purification of the natural to a spiritual man is inherent in such ethics. These discussions make it clear why we need to have some idea about the psychology of the agent. This makes room for bringing in the concept of *doṣa* (faults) in the Vaidika ethics. This explains the utility of the discussion about the so-called flaws or faults that draw back or hinder a natural man to his progress towards the spiritual. Hence all the schools of Indian philosophy devote chapters in discussing about springs of actions. The Vaiśeṣikas, Naiyāyikas, Sāṁkhyas, as well as Vedānta schools – all have discussed the springs of action in detail. The Dharma-Ethics is not found to be satisfied by analysing the nature of springs of

---

6 *Bhagavadgītā* II.0.

7 Ibid. II.48.

8 Sri Aurobindo, 1970, *Essays on the Gita*, pp. 236-46.

actions and their classification, but it is more interested in the practice of removal of obstacles on the path to purification. There are also elaborate schemes of practical ethics as embodied in various practical schemes of *cittaśuddhi. Gītā* also prescribes practice (*abhyāsa*) and non-attachment (*vairāgya*) as means to control the fickle and fugitive mind. It seems that natural man left to itself without any *abhyāsa* and practice of *vairāgya* will have to suffer more and more.

A brief overview of Buddhist and Jaina viewpoints may be added before proceeding further with the explanation of the Vedic position. To grasp the idea of volition from the perspective of Buddhist Dharma-Ethics, we need to have some idea about the concept of *tṛṣṇā* (thirst) towards enjoyment. In *Dhammapada*, we find some account about the nature of craving (*tṛṣṇā*). This craving has a natural propensity to increase in volume. In *Dhammapada* the increase of *tṛṣṇā* or craving is compared with that of a creeper. To indicate the bad effect of *tṛṣṇā* it is compared with poison. A person guided by *tṛṣṇā* is like a person who has been poisoned. The Buddha teaches to eradicate this *tṛṣṇā*, which is *vardhananiṣṭha* (predisposed to increase) and *duratikramya* (difficult to overcome). To draw our attention to this peculiarity, the Buddha brought in various analogies to explain it. A man who is *pramatta* (one who is thirsty for enjoyment), his thirst goes on increasing like a fast-growing creeper. This thirst is very much looked down upon. It is described as *hīna* (mean) and *viṣākta* (poisonous). The thirst for enjoyment always downgrades a person, hence in that sense it is said to be *hīna*. It is also said to be poisonous. Hence it has been urged that one should try to remove the very root of *tṛṣṇā*. If anybody is bound by a rope or wood or iron, he can free himself from that bondage. But it is very different in the case of bondage created by affection. In the twelve wheels as maintained by the Buddha, *tṛṣṇā* occupies a middle position. The very existence of *tṛṣṇā* is accounted for in terms of *vedanā* (feeling). In the Buddhist metaphysics depending upon *nāmarūpa* (mind–body) complex six sense-organs arise namely, *cakkhu* (eye), *sota* (ear), *ghāṇa* (nose), *jihvā* (tongue), *kāya* (body) and *mana* (mind), and depending on these sixfold bases arise six types of contact. Being dependent on contact arises *vedanā*. Feeling (*vedanā*) is sixfold: feeling born of visual contact; feeling born of sound contact; feeling born of smell contact; feeling born of taste contact; feeling born of body contact and feeling born of mental contact. Dependent on *vedanā* arises *tanhā* (craving). And *tṛṣṇā* is regarded as the cause of *upādānā* which is often characterized as a strong *tṛṣṇā* (clinging). Thus, these are related as follows:

vedanā (feeling and sensation) > *tṛṣṇā* > *upādānā.*

The Buddhist literatures abound with description of the nature of *tanhā* or *tṛṣṇā* and about its varieties. There are many types of *tanhā* or *tṛṣṇā* depending upon six types of sources of sense-object contacts, namely, *rūpa-tṛṣṇā, śabda-tṛṣṇā, gandha-tṛṣṇā, rasa-tṛṣṇā, sparśa-tṛṣṇā* and *dharma-tṛṣṇā* (craving for mind-objects). These cravings are aroused by colours (forms or appearance), sounds, smells, tastes, contacts and ideas. Each *tṛṣṇā* can be divided into three kinds: *kāma-tṛṣṇā, bhāva-tṛṣṇā* and *vibhāva-tṛṣṇā*. *Tṛṣṇā* is called *kāma-tṛṣṇā* (sensuous desire) when it creates a taste for the objects say, *rūpa, rasa, śabda,* etc. In *bhāva-tṛṣṇā* (desire for eternality), *tṛṣṇā* is associated with the belief that world is eternal and *bhāva-tṛṣṇā* produces an attachment for future existence. Lastly, *vibhāva-tṛṣṇā* (desire for nihilism) is associated with the belief that there is no afterlife (*ucccheda*) and one becomes regardless of this life. This *vibhāva-tṛṣṇā* produces rebirth (*punarjanma*). These cravings arise from the sense of I-ness which leads to self-centredness. Craving is the chief cause of suffering. The concept of *māra* recurs in *Dhammapada*. *Māra* is generally associated with certain evil force. It has been advised that one should be cautious so that ill of craving does not destroy one. A lotus which is broken is carried away by the current. It is desirable that the condition of a person under the spell of craving be not such that he is carried away by the force of craving. The very root of craving has to be eradicated. A tree which has fallen again grows if its root is intact. Similarly *tṛṣṇā* has as its cause *vedanā* (feeling); this *vedanā* has to be removed and then *tṛṣṇā* as the cause of sorrow would cease to exist. Men are comparable to the hare caught in net and they run to free themselves from the net. Apparently, to men the life of enjoyment is pleasant, but people who are always indulging in pleasure are the victim of rebirths. For a *bhikṣu* it is desirable to shun the path of cravings and practise detachment. To be finally free, one has to cut the root of all cravings. If one reaches high in the ladder of *sādhanā*, one must continue the process; otherwise he will have a fall. If a *bhikṣu*, while having reached the peak of meditation, is under the spell of cravings then he will not be liberated.

People who are *paṇḍit*s understand the differences between two sorts of bondages. The bondage that is derived from attachment towards daughters, sons and other blood relation is stronger than bondages due to iron, wood and other materials. Like a spider a man is caught in the net of craving spun by him. One who gives in too much to cravings and indulges too much in pleasure his cravings go on increasing continuously. In the whole of Buddhist Dharma-Ethics how should a man as a moral agent act and behave to purge out *tanhā* and passion and be good in conduct are discussed.

In Jaina Dharma-Ethics also it has been maintained that a person to attain liberation and to free himself from the karmic bondage practises right conduct. In Jaina Dharma-Ethics also stress is upon controlling demands of the senses and passions. In Jaina philosophy, of the five causes of bondage, *kaṣāya* (passion) and *yoga* meaning acts of *manas*, speech or body are important among causes of bondage. The passions are considered to be special because passions are only responsible for producing long-term bondage. To quote from Umāsvāti's *Tattvārthasūtra* 8.2:[9]

> The karmic particles, attracted by the soul through actions motivated by passions, are assimilated and firmly bound to the soul.

---

9 *sakaṣāyatvājjīvaḥ karmaṇo yogyān pudgalānādatte* | – tr. Umāsvati, 1994, Tattvārthasūtra.

Vratas, from Sanskrit *vṛ* (to fence in) provides ways whereby the karmic influx can be prevented. *Ahiṁsā* (non-violence), *satya* (truth), *asteya* (non-stealing), *brahma* (refraining from illicit sexual activities) and *aparigraha* (non-possession) are five vows admitted in the Jaina ethics. The role of ethics is not just to direct human beings towards certain activity, but also to achieve by such direction some other objectives. In Hindu ethics, Buddhist ethics or Jaina ethics, it is assumed that the purification of mind is of utmost importance to ascend to the higher stages of life.

In the Vaidika Dharma-Ethics also we find that the role of morality lies in paving the way for liberation by controlling passions. Vaidika Dharma-Ethics is not represented by only a particular school but for the sake of convenience, the views of all other schools are not discussed. In *Nyāyasūtra* 1.1.18, "urge to volition" or cause of volition, i.e. *pravartanā* is attributed to *doṣa* (flaws/faults). Thus, Maharṣi Gautama has defined *doṣa* as the cause of volition (*pravartanālakṣaṇa doṣāḥ*). These flaws (*doṣa*s) are enumerated to be three: *rāga* (affection/attachment), *dveṣa* (aversion) and *moha* (delusion). According to *Nyāyasūtra* as these are all categorized as faults, it is expected that the definition of faults as proposed by *Nyāyasūtra* must be equally applicable to all major divisions of *doṣa* and to all instances of each of these categories. The question, however, has arisen as to if all these instances of faults are subsumable under the same definition what is the point of introducing *Nyāyasūtra* 4.1.3[10] stating that there are three sorts of faults? According to Maharṣi Gautama, though the general definition of faults is as the cause of volition, there are qualitative differences among desire, aversion and bewilderment as faults, hence these three sorts of categorization of *doṣa*s are advocated by the *nyāyasūtrakāra* and are mentioned separately. These three *doṣa*s, viz. affection, aversion and delusion, incite *jīvātmā* to perform actions that produce good results or bad (*pāpa*) results. The opponents who are not willing to admit any distinction

---

10 *tat trairāśyam rāgadveṣamohārthāntarabhāvāt* |

among these faults may point out that all these flaws, namely, *rāga, dveṣa* and *moha* are contradicted by true belief (*tattva jñāna*), hence it is established that *rāga, dveṣa* and *moha* are destroyed by one and the same destroyer, in this case true belief (*tattva jñāna*), hence these share the property of being liable to be destroyed or removed by the same *tattva jñāna* (*eka tattvajñāna nāśyatva*). The intention of the argument is to convey that the things which are contradicted by the same object are the same. Thus the proposed ground for establishing that *rāga, dveṣa* and *moha* are not to be viewed as three separate categories since these three faults share the property of being opposed or contradicted (*pratyānīka*) by one and the same thing or to put it in other words, *rāga, dveṣa* and *moha* have *ekapratyanīkabhāvavattā*. The literal translation of *pratyānīka* is contradictory or opposite. Whatever is opposite or contradictory to one and the same thing may be said to have the feature of being *ekapratyānīkabhāva*. But this argument has not been accepted by the Naiyāyikas.[11] All *jīva*s (embodied selves) having internal perception of themselves being affected, or being averse or being deluded are motivated to actions. Here the expression *pratyātmāvedanīya* (perceptible to each individual self) is the clause which explains the source of knowledge of these flaws. The man who is affected (*rakta*) performs these voluntary actions and experiences pleasure or pain. The man who has aversion (*dviṣṭa*) to something performs voluntary actions and experiences pleasure or pain. It can be explained in a similar way with regard to a person who is deluded (*muda*). Vātsyāyana argues that flaws arise from false beliefs (*mithyā jñāna*) about the nature of different kinds of reality. For the Naiyāyikas, *tattva jñāna* (true knowledge) leads to liberation but in order to acquire true knowledge purification of *citta* is essential.

Now, the definition of faults as proposed by *Nyāyasūtra*[12] is applicable to all those subclasses which come under the above-mentioned three faults. It has been pointed out that desire (*kāma*),

---

[11] *naikapratyanīkabhāvāt* – *Nyāyasūtra* 4.1.4

[12] *Nyāyasūtra* 1.1.18.

jealousy (*mātsarya*), eager desire/covetousness (*spṛhā*), craving (*tṛṣṇā*), greed (*lobha*), anger (*krodha*), indignation especially at the merit or happiness of another (*asūyā*), envy (*īrṣyā*), treachery (*droha*), non-endurance/intolerance (*amarṣa*), false belief (*mithyā jñāna*), uncertainty (*vicikitsā*), pride (*māna*) and pleasure/intoxication (*pramāda*) are all to be covered under faults. Uddyotakara in his explanation elaborated all these faults more elaborately.[13] *Kāma* has been described as the desire for women. The *vṛttikāra* Viśvanātha has added that desire for man is also *kāma*, hence just the desire for woman is not *kāma*. He has pointed out that *kāma* is the desire for sexual intercourse (*maithunecchā kāma*).[14] But the expression *kāma* when conjoined with word like *svarga*, the compound word *svargakāma* means desire for heaven. If something is not of any utility for someone, but the person concerned desires to prevent anybody else from getting it, that is called *mātsarya*. *Spṛhā* is the desire to acquire someone else's possession. *Tṛṣṇā* is the desire on account of which a person is reborn. Sometimes desire to hold wealth in a close-fisted way without spending for the required necessity is also called *tṛṣṇā*. *Lobha* signifies the desire to possess someone else's wealth illegally. These are all various instances of attachment or desire (or *rāga*). The *vṛttikāra* Viśvanātha has included some more instances of desire namely *māyā* and *dambha* to the list.[15] The desire to deceive anybody has been called *māyā* and the desire to show off oneself as virtuous is *dambha*. Praśastapāda in his *Padārthadharmasaṁgraha* has used the expression *icchā* (desire) instead of *rāga* (attachment/desire) and his classification of desire (*icchā*) included *kāma, abhilāṣā, rāga, saṅkalpa, kāruṇya, vairāgya, upadhā, bhāva*, as different instances of *icchā*.

Coming to the second main type of faults, i.e. *dveṣa*, or broadly speaking, aversion or hatred, we come across its different varieties, though it has to be admitted that the line of demarcation between

---

13 *Nyāyadarśana*, vol. 4, pp. 8-9.

14 Ibid.

15 Ibid., p. 9.

each variety is quite fuzzy. *Asūyā* is in literal translation envy: it expresses enviousness towards the possession of somebody. *Droha* stands for malicious disposition. *Krodha* has been mentioned among faults; *krodha* or anger has often been personified as the child of death. *Īrṣyā* is a type of enviousness. The frustration to bring harm to one who has harmed the person concerned is referred to as *amarṣa*. Again the author of *Nyāyavṛtti* has also included *abhimāna* as one of the instances of aversion (*dveṣa*). *Abhimāna* as a sort of *dveṣa* denotes an insidious disposition.

Among the category of *moha* (bewilderment/delusion) is included *mithyā jñāna* or false belief. Mistaking anything to be the reverse of what it is (*viparyaya*) is an instance of misapprehension. The expression *vicikitsā* stands for doubt (*saṁśaya*). The ascription of some quality to oneself on the false belief that one is superior to other is called *māna*. *Pramāda* signifies a sort of wrong reading – a confused perception failing to distinguish between what is duty and what and what is not duty. Viśvanātha has included some other varieties within the category of *moha* which are as follows: *tarka, bhaya* and *śoka*. *Tarka* has been called *mithyā* belief. The expression *bhaya* signifies also another instance of false belief giving rise to incapability to handle an adverse situation. The expression *śoka* stands for another false belief generating incapability to reverse the loss of a desirable object. *Moha* has been regarded as the most inferior among all these flaws. According to the Naiyāyikas *moha* is the cause of *rāga* and *dveṣa*. *Jīva* who is free from *moha* does not fall prey to flaws like attachment and aversion. *Rāga* and *dveṣa* are said to be born out of false belief (*mohayoni*).[16] According to Nyāyabhāṣyakāra, *jīva*s qualified by delusion or distraction are subjected to *rāga* and *dveṣa* in the form of *saṅkalpa*. This *saṅkalpa* is of two sorts, i.e. *rañjanīya* (delightful) or *kopanīya* (wrathful).[17] Thus, *saṅkalpa* is a sort of will that takes either the form of delightful will or wrathful will. The notion of *saṅkalpa* is a very important notion for the understanding

16 *Nyāyadarśana*, vol. 4, p. 14.

17 Ibid.

of Dharma-Ethics as well. It has been maintained that *rāga* and *dveṣa* are due to *saṅkalpa*, hence these are also defined as caused by *saṅkalpa* (*saṅkalpanimittaka*).[18] What actually is meant by *saṅkalpa* and how does it originate? Uddyotakara writes: *anubhūtaviṣaya prārthanā saṅkalpa ityuktam*. Thus, *saṅkalpa* is a sort of *prārthanā* for an object which has been experienced earlier. The commentators like Vātsyāyana, Vācaspati Miśra all admitted that *saṅkalpa* gives rise to attachment, aversion and delusion. Vācaspati Miśra explained the origin of *saṅkalpa* as follows: the continuous remembering[19] of any previously experienced object[20] is known as *anucintana* (after-thought). This *anucintana* gives rise to *prārthanārūpa saṅkalpa*, deliberation of the form of desire in the case of *jīvas*. The Nyāya commentator Viśvanātha has explained *saṅkalpa* as *iṣṭasādhanatā jñāna*, i.e. knowledge that something is conducive to achieve a desirable end. The underlying argument here is to ascertain the following: unless something is understood as conducive to a desirable consequence, nobody can have any desire for that object. From the very attraction of a newborn child towards some object it has been inferred that the child must have previous knowledge about that object as conducive to desirable result, i.e. *iṣṭasādhana*. In the case of a child, if that object has not been experienced to be conducive to desirable consequence in child's present life, then it has to be presumed that the child must have that experience in child's previous birth. The Buddhist philosophers also admit that *saṅkalpa*, i.e. deliberation, is the cause of *rāga, dveṣa* and *moha*.[21]

To get rid of all these obstacles the purification of self is considered to be most indispensable. The concept of *ātma-saṁskāra* (purification of the self) plays an important role in Dharma-Ethics. Gautama states in 4.2.46:

---

18 *Nyāyadarśana*, vol. 4, p. 14.

19 *dhāravāhika smaraṇaparamparā* । – Ibid., pp. 14-1

20 *pūrvānubhūta viṣaya* ।

21 *saṅkalpa prabhavo rāgo dveṣo mohāśca kathyate* – *Mādhyamikakārikā*, cited in *Nyāyadarśana*, vol. 3, p. 106

tadartham yamaniyamābhyām
ātmasaṁskāroyogāccādhyātmavidhyupāyaiḥ ।

With a view to obtain liberation, whether direct or indirect the purification of the self must be done by following *yama* and *niyama* and by following *adhyātmavidhi* and *yogācāravidhāna* as prescribed in the Yoga Darśana. The final *puruṣārtha mokṣa* presupposes *ātmasaṁskāra*. In the *bhāṣya* of the above-mentioned *sūtra*, the phrase *ātmasaṁskāra* (purification of the self) has been explained as *ātmasaṁskāraḥ punaradharmahānam dharmopacayaśca*. To translate the above line, it stands as follows:

> The self-purification is destruction of *adharma* and increase of *dharma*.

In Indian ethics whenever we are discussing all these concepts, these are in relation to the actual situation. It has some definite prescriptions regarding the fulfilment of requisites for *ātma-saṁskāra* by pursuance of *yama* and *niyama*, and *ādhyātmavidhi* and *upāya* according to *Yogasūtra*. There are some differences of opinion in the interpretation of the terms *yama* and *niyama* among the commentators of *Nyāyasūtra*.[22]

1. Vātsyāyana in his commentary explains *yama* to signify performance of duties which are common to all men (*sādhāraṇa dharmasādhana*). The *niyama* stands for the performance of specific duties in relation to one's stage of life (*āśrama*). Thus understood, *yama* represents common duties and *niyama* stands for specific duties.
2. Some ancient commentaries take the expression *yama* to stand for the non-performance of forbidden acts (*anācāraṇam niṣiddhakarma*) and the expression *niyama* stands for the performance of duties relative to different stages in life (*āśrama-dharma*). The *vr̥tttikāra* Viśvanātha refers to this usage.

Basically, this way of putting the meaning of *yama* and *niyama* does not come into conflict with Vātsyāyana's way of expressing

[22] *Nyāyasūtra* 4.2.46.

the difference. Negatively, putting non-performance of forbidden act is duty for everybody, i.e. *sādhāraṇa-dharma*. This would prevent increase of *adharma* and the performance of *āśrama-dharma* would lead to the increase of *dharma*. Thus the whole procedure would lead to what is referred to *ātma-saṁskāra*. *Ātmasaṁskāra* renders *ātmā* capable of obtaining release from the bondage.

The expressions *yama* and *niyama* are much in use in different ancient literatures. In the lexicography *Amarakośa*, the lexicographer Amarasiṁha interprets *yama* as duties performance of which is obligatory for the individual throughout his life and *niyama* as duties performance of which is dependent on the occasion. Thus in this view *yama* signifies necessary duties and *niyama* signifies contingent duties. In *Manu Saṁhitā*, it has been stated:

> *yamān sevet śatatam na nityam niyamān budaḥ* ।
> *yamān patatyakurvāno niymān kevalan bhajan* ।। – 4.204

In interpreting these *śloka*s of Manu, Medhātithi in his commentary has remarked that *pratiṣedharūpāyamāḥ*. That is *yama*s are prohibitory injunctions (*niṣedhavidhi*) like *brāhmāṇo na hantavya* (Do not kill a brāhmaṇa), *surā na peyā* (Do not drink wine), etc. By contrast *niyama*s are *anuṣṭheyarūpa vidhi* (performatory obligations).

Viśvanātha in his *Nyāyavṛtti* explains *yama* and *niyama* after Patañjali's Yoga philosophy.[23] Yoga philosophy of Patañjali has mentioned and explained eightfold constituents of *yoga* as follows:

1. *Yama* (abstentions)
2. *Niyama* (observances)
3. *Āsana* (adoption of steady and comfortable postures)
4. *Prāṇāyāma* (regulation of breath)
5. *Pratyāhāra* (sense-control)
6. *Dhāraṇā* (contemplation)
7. *Dhyāna* (meditation)
8. *Samādhi* (concentration).

---

[23] Patañjali, 1938, *Pātañjala Yogadarśana*.

Of these eightfold aids to *yoga*, known as *yogāṅga*, only the first two, known as *yama* and *niyama*, lay stress on the ethical preparations required for the practice of *yoga*. The Nyāyasūtrakāra of these eightfold *yogāṅga*s accepted *yama* and *niyama* as conducive to liberation. Now let us explain briefly, what are these *yama*s and *niyama*s according to the Yoga philosophy of Patañjali:

> *ahiṁsā-satyāsteyabrahmacaryāparigrahā yamāḥ* I – 2.30
> *śaucasantoṣatapaḥsvādhyāyeśvarapraṇidhānāni niyamāḥ* II
> –2.32

Thus we find that according to the Yoga philosophy of Patañjali, the following are *yama*s:

a. *ahiṁsā* (non-violence)

b. *satya* (truth)

c. *asteya* (non-stealing)

d. *brahmacarya* (continence)

e. *aparigraha* (non-acceptance).

The practice of non-violence has been regarded as a duty by all means, at all times and towards all beings. A person has been instructed to avoid causing injury or malicious assault to anybody. The practice of this duty has been encouraged to prevent all kinds of hatred, spitefulness or malevolence. In *Pātañjalabhāṣya* it has been stated: *tatrāhiṁsā sarvathā sarvadā sarvabhūtanāmānbhidrohaḥ*. . . .[24] The other duties like truthfulness are regarded as means for establishing non-violence as a virtue. In fact, in Dharma-Ethics also we find lots of discussions about non-violence. In Śruti, it has also been said that, "Do not cause violence to any beings" (*mā hiṁsyāt sarvabhūtāni*). In *Vyāsabhāṣya* of Patañjali attempts are made to clarify the notion of non-violence. In the first place, it has been attempted to project non-violence as a complete virtue, with a positive and a negative aspect. Generally, non-violence is understood negatively as only desisting from inflicting suffering

---

[24] Sādhanapāda, *sūtra* 30, p. 16.

and anguish to all beings, but it has also a positive aspect for spreading compassion towards everybody by maintaining a harmonious, non-hostile relationship with others. There is no doubt that selfish desire to satisfy oneself and to nourish oneself is one of the reasons for leading to violence. If one seeks pleasure from external sources, that necessarily inflicts suffering to others. To frighten someone or to hurt someone with harsh or discourteous speeches are also instances of causing violence. According to the Yoga philosophy non-violence is the root and with the aid of truth and other virtues spoken of they think that pure non-violence, in its unmixed state, can be attained. Thus, according to the Yoga philosophy, truth, non-stealing, continence and non-acceptance are means (*sādhana*) for attaining pure *ahiṁsā* (*śuddha ahiṁsā*) and so these are accepted or adored as virtues (*upādeya*). However, it has frequently been asked, how is it possible to practise non-violence when, to maintain one's life, killing or destroying others is inevitable? This is not the question that bothers us only, but this question was also raised so *many* years back: the author of *Yogabhāṣya* has admitted that without killing of animals, it is not possible to maintain one's embodied existence (*nanupahatya bhūtānyupabhoga sambhavati*). The crux of the Yoga philosophy is to emphasis upon three important *sādhanas* for attaining non-violence: people who practise *yoga* knowing all these things, practise *yoga* in such a way

a. to avoid re-embodiment,

b. to avoid as far as practicable causing harm to any movable and immovable beings, and

c. to avoid causing suffering as far as practicable to higher animals.

According to Yoga philosophy, violence (*hiṁsā*) which is variously described in Dharma-Ethics literatures as cruelty (*krūratā*), *jighāṅsā* (desire to kill), or hostility (*dveṣa*) are basically born out of polluted mind, hence pollution of mind has to be checked. Among different instances of violence some sort of gradations are advocated in Yoga philosophy. From Yoga account of violence, it seems quite comprehensible that injunctions such as "Do not cause violence to anybody" needs to be practised gradually, step-by-step because practical living situations of the world cannot be absolutely ignored off-hand. The Yoga theory of different levels of violence, from that perspective, seems to be quite logical. It has been maintained that killing of parents and killing of enemies are instances of violence no doubt, but these two instances of violence are not considered to be of the same level. The degree or level of violence, they sought to determine depending on the extent of pollution of mind. To kill a person and to unpluck a grassroot are not instances of violence of the same level. To kill a person and to hurt a person with rude remark are not cases of violence of the same level. A common man by killing his enemies or by destroying trees does not pollute much himself. They ask how far it is possible to stain with ink a piece of soiled cloth stained already with dark spots? But for the *yogīs*, they prescribe practice of non-violence stringently. In Yoga philosophy, we find more emphasis has been laid on freeing mind from the influence of violence. Some of the cases of violence, on the basis of levels, seemed to be permissible for ordinary lay persons. But for the *yogīs*, these are all to be avoided. But still, they admit some necessary violence may not be avoidable altogether, but for such violence the *yogī* must be able to cultivate determination that would enable to curtail violence by means of *yoga*. In Yoga philosophy for a *yogī* achieving non-violence is said to be *mahāvrata*; for him non-violence would mean absolute non-violence which is not relative to any class (*jāti*), place (*deśa*) and time (*kāla*). Thus *mahāvratas* are said to be *sārvabhauma* (universalistic).[25] In Yoga philosophy, ultimately the purpose of all these *aṅgas* of *yoga* is the purification of mind.

The practice of truth has also been encouraged. By truth is meant that which has already been proved to be true, and to cultivate one's mind and speech according to the requirement of

---

[25] *jātideśakālasamayānavacchinnāḥ sārvabhaumā mahāvratam* | – Sādhanapāda, *sūtra* 31

truth. The practice of non-stealing implies negation of stealing (*steya*). By stealing is meant acquisition of such objects which are neither given (*adatta*) nor obtained through proper means (*aprāpya dharmatā*). Hence non-stealing implies not only physically non-acceptance of these sorts of objects but also preventing arousal of any desire (*spṛhā*) in the mind for such acquisition. The Śruti statement enjoining *mā gṛdha kasyasviddhanam* (Do not steal anybody's property), is the guiding dictum here. Similarly, continence as a virtue implies not only physically preventing sense-organs or motor-organs from getting connected with their respective objects but also to achieve mental control over all the sense-organs and finally over sexual organ. Finally, the other duty that is to be performed, as has already been pointed out, is *aparigraha* (non-acceptance). Here by non-acceptance of objects has been meant primarily material objects which are very much required for the maintenance of embodied existence. The very nature of material objects is such that it is difficult, often painful to procure objects according to one's requirement. Even if such objects are acquired it is troublesome to retain those objects. The destruction of such objects causes sorrow and also possession of such objects leads to violence and because of such violence one suffers. Hence the person who desires to be liberated from suffering and sorrow gives up possession of all such things and practises non-acceptance of all such objects.

Regarding *niyama*, the following *sūtra* of *Yogabhāṣya* is relevant:

śauca santoṣa tapaḥ svādhyāyeśvarapraṇidhāṇāni niyamāḥ |[26]

Thus according to this *sūtra* the following are the *niyama*s:

a. *śauca* (purity),

b. *santoṣa* (contentment),

c. *tapaḥ* (austere endeavour),

d. *svādhyāya* (study of Mokṣaśāstra), and

e. *īśvarapraṇidhāna* (surrender to God).

---

[26] Sādhanapāda, *sūtra* 32.

Purity that is spoken of is taken to imply both external purities and internal purities. One is required to maintain bodily purity by regular bathing and by avoiding taking of intoxicating food which disturbs stability of the mind. Apart from these external impurities, one is required to keep his mind pure. Prevention of vanity, pride and jealousy is regarded as a means for internal purity (*ābhyanatarika śauca*). The other quality *santoṣa* is a state of mind revealed through satisfactoriness or contentedness with whatever one possesses. Thus, not to have any desire to acquire more than what is already in possession for carrying on one's daily life is *santoṣa. Tapa* indicates acquisition of quality of forbearance both bodily and mentally. Thus to acquire capability to stand physically and mentally the pangs of hunger and thirst, summer and winter is austerity. The study of Mokṣaśāstra and surrender to God are also two requisites specified in Yoga philosophy.

All these *yama*s and *niyama*s are brought into our discussion in relation to the Nyāya position regarding the purification of mind. Further it has also been noticed, according Gautama, the process of purification of mind does not end here. Gautama has also mentioned that further means, as established in Yoga philosophy, are to be pursued to purify *citta*. In this connection by the expression *adhyātmavidhi*, he is referring to other five *yogāṅga*s as advocated by Patañjali. Thus we are led more into the process of practising self-purification. Thus come processes of *prāṇāyāma* (regulation of breath), *pratyāhāra* (sense-control), *dhāraṇā* (contemplation), *dhyāna* (meditation) and *samādhi* (concentration).

From all these observations we find here that importance has been laid upon subjective morality which consists of subjective purity and the inner excellence of mind. This purification of mind also comes within the purview of Dharma-Ethics. The same actions, duties if performed externally are indicative of objective morality and if performed internally from within the fold of will, characterize the level of subjective morality. In the process of sequencing grades or levels of morality the *bhikkhu* (monk) and the laity (ordinary person) are not ranked at the same level. The

Jainas also make distinction between *mahāvratas* and *anuvratas* depending upon the maturity of the moral agent. In the case of Vaidika Dharma-Ethics the distinction between an ordinary moral person and a *yogī* or *mahāvratin* has also been drawn on the basis of their moral maturity. The domain of normal moral person and the domain of *karmayogī* do not necessarily imply two rigid demarcated domains. The same ordinary moral person when turns into a *yogī*, the objective morality coalesce with subjective morality and the individual concerned attains acclivity or moral elevation. Dharma-Ethics is a discourse that is unambiguous in its treatment of both theory and practice. Truly speaking abstraction of theory from practice or vice versa does not convey the true spirit of Dharma-Ethics. In recent times specially we hear about practical ethics or applied ethics in the Western ethical discourse where generally attempts are made to solve some practical moral situation by the application of existing ethical theories, namely, virtue theory or utilitarianism or de-ontology. In all these cases ethical codes are applied to external realities. But in the case of Dharma-Ethics when it is treated as practical ethics its approach is completely reversed from the object to the subject – from the external to the internal. The practical ethical perspective of Dharma-Ethics for that reason may as well be called psychological ethics.

What for Does an Individual Endeavour to Attain Moral Elevation or Growth?

"Why should one be moral" is no doubt an important question across traditions. Among Indian philosophers in general, whether Āstika or Nāstika, except the Cārvākas, morality is always considered as means towards a higher and deeper objective. That deeper and higher state of being was not a chimera for Indian philosophers, rather it was truer than the truth that we encounter and believe in. That state has been called the state of *mukti*. Different schools of Indian philosophers are unanimous in accepting *mokṣa, mukti* or *apavarga* as the highest goal. These schools of Indian philosophers do not offer however, any unanimous description about the nature of this state of existence. In the present discussion we need not enter into any detailed analysis about the nature of the state of liberation. Considerable debates are there as to whether the state of liberation is a state of bliss, or the state of absolute cessation of pain, or it is both a state of bliss and the state of absolute cessation of pain. Two characteristic features of liberation are commonly assumed to be the following: in the first place sorrow-stricken existence of an empirical being who necessarily goes through the pangs of old age, disease and death has the possibility of final release in the state of *mokṣa*; second, the state of *mokṣa* is a state of absolute negation of pain and suffering. The question, however, still remains as to how that state of *mokṣa* is to be attained? An answer to this question again distinguishes one school of thinkers from that of the other accordingly as it emphasizes the importance of the path of knowledge, the path of action or the path of devotion. No schools of thinkers have denied the importance of *karma* in the overall life of a man. There may be difference between a school of thinker and another regarding the issue of primacy to be accorded to *karma* in its tending to liberation. Thus we may find one school of thinkers assuming the path of action (*karma-mārga*) to be crucial in attaining the state of liberation, but another school of thinkers may not accord primary importance to *karma-mārga*. Thus we see that the importance of action has always been ascertained in the Indian philosophical literatures. Our discussion, so far, has already must have succeeded in convincing that ethical discussions rotate round the imperatives of actions. Actions, performed as per norms, are predisposed to purify minds (*cittaśuddhi*). All these discussions, all these presuppositions, all these imperatives of actions would be reduced to nothing, if it is established that the so-called aspired state of liberation does not exist at all. If no such state of liberation is possible, that overrules the possibility of Indian ethics as such. Indian ethics never claims to be an end in itself; rather, it is always viewed as a means to an end, and things that are thus implicated by means-and-end relationship, have to depend upon each of the relata to make intelligible the sense of the relational complex. It requires to be reiterated that the nature and goal of Indian ethics is inseparably tagged with the idea of liberation and its very possibility for the idea of means becomes a misnomer in the absence of the other, i.e. the end.

Hence, it would not be wholly out of place endeavour to discuss about the objections that are raised against the possibility of *mokṣa* as such. In this connection I would like to dwell upon some of the observations derived from the Apavarga-Parīkṣā-Prakaraṇam of *Nyāyasūtra*. *Nyāyasūtra* 4.1.58: *r̥ṇa-kleśa-pravr̥ttyanubandhādapavargābhāvaḥ* states the perspective of an objector who may argue that liberation is impossible by showing how do the following three factors hinder liberation:

1. The inseparable relation between debt and human existence is an obstacle (*r̥ṇānubandha*),
2. the inseparable relation between human suffering and human existence is an obstacle (*kleśānubandha*), and
3. the close relation between human motivation and human existence is an obstacle (*pravr̥ttyanubandha*).

Thus, it amounts to saying that liberation is a chimera.

In the first place let us try to understand what is meant by *ṛṇānubandha* (inseparability with debts). The *bhāṣyakāra* begins by quoting a line from Śruti which maintains:

> *jāyamāno ho vai brāhmaṇastribhirr̥ṇavā jāyate brahmacaryeṇa r̥ṣibhyo yajñena devebhyoḥ prajāyapitr̥bhyoḥ . . . .*[27]

The above-quoted Śruti, thus introduces three types of debts, namely, *r̥ṣi-r̥ṇa, deva r̥ṇa* and *pitr̥-r̥ṇa*. The main contention of this *śruti* statement is that all brāhmaṇas are born with threefold debts and each of these debts are to be paid off: the debt to teachers (*r̥ṣi-r̥ṇa*) is to be paid off by the study of the Vedas in the first stage of life as an unmarried student in a state of continence and

[27] *Nyāyadarśana*, vol. 4, pp. 331-32.
Kulluka Bhaṭṭa cited a similar *śrutivākya* in the explanation of the *śloka* 36, in the sixth chapter of *Manu Saṁhitā*.

chastity (*brahmacaryeṇaṛṣibhyoḥ*), the debt to gods is to be paid off by the performance of sacrificial rites (*yajñenadevebhyoḥ*) and finally the third debt to the ancestors (*pitṛ-ṛṇa*) is to be paid off by giving birth to sons (*prajāya*). The implication of this statement would be clearer if we have some understanding about the concept of *ṛṇa*, which is an important concept of Dharma-Ethics. In the tradition of Dharma-Ethics for any person to be in debt is not considered to be morally desirable. In order to free oneself from such debts as mentioned in the Śrutis, there are also some injunctions in the Śruti (*śruti-vākyas*) that tell about the performance of some actions throughout the life to get rid of such debts. Hence in order to free oneself from all these debts, the actions that are prescribed by Śruti as obligatory for the individuals are such actions with which individuals bear inseparable relation (*anubandha*). The expression *anubandha* signifies inseparable relation (*aparihārya sambandha*). Uddyotakara also explains the expression *anubandha* as *sadākaraṇīyatā*, i.e. ought to be performed for ever. The Śruti has clear-cut instructions about actions which are obligatory for individuals under debt in certain circumstances. To free oneself from *ṛṣi-ṛṇa* one will have to observe *brahmacarya* as per the instruction of Śāstra; second, to be free from debts to father and forefathers one must marry and have children; third, to free oneself from debts to God, i.e. *deva-ṛṇa*, one has been enjoined to perform *yajñas* like Agnihotra and Darśapaurṇamāsa throughout one's life. Vātsyāyana, the author of *Bhāṣya*, refers to *śrutivākya*: *jarāmāryam va etat satram*[28] (these actions ought to be performed till old age or death).[29] It has been said that due to old age, if it becomes impossible to carry on that action any further, then the performance of that action has to be abandoned. Otherwise, the injunction directs to carry on the action till death. Hence it has been pointed out that in order to free oneself from debts one ought to perform enjoined actions throughout his life. So if one

---

[28] *jarāmaryam vā etat satram yadāgnihotram darśapūrṇamāsau ca* |

[29] *jarayā ha vā eṣa tasmātsatrādvimucyate mṛtyunā ha va* |
These statements of Śruti are cited in *Nyāyadarśana*, vol. 4.

has to spend all his time to free oneself from debts, one will have no time left for performing any actions for liberation. Therefore, the opponents argue that *mokṣa* is an illusion, so the question of attainability of liberation also does not arise. Nobody can do any action for attaining liberation unless one has cleared off all his debts. In *Manu Saṁhitā* it has been said that if one attempts for *mokṣa* without clearing off his debts, then he would go downwards, i.e. he will incur demerits. To quote from *Manu Saṁhitā*:[30]

> *ṛṇāṇi triṇyapākṛtya mano mokṣe niveśayet* |
> *anapākṛtya mokṣatu sevamāno vrajatyadhaḥ* ||

The expression *apākaraṇa* implies *pariśodha* (repayment). Thus here it has been said that to concentrate on *mokṣa* without repaying debts leads to (moral) degradation. Now it is quite possible that with the completion of *brahmacaryāśrama* and giving birth to children one's debts to teacher and parents are repaid. But still one's debt to God has not been repaid and its repayment covers the whole life. Therefore, the obligation towards the performance of such Agnihotra and other rituals are obstacles towards obtaining *mokṣa*. These are obligatory for people belonging to brāhmaṇa, kṣatriya and vaiśya *varṇa*s. For people belonging to the śūdra *varṇa* there are many such life-long obligatory actions to perform. These considerations prompt opponents to think that liberation is an impossibility.

The second objection is stated as *kleśānubandha*. The crux of this objection is that men are born and die as inseparably related with suffering, and men are never found to be free from *kleśa*. Here *kleśa* signifies three main flaws (*doṣa*s), namely, *rāga*, *dveṣa* and *moha* which taken together account for mortal existence. The mortal beings have inseparable relation with these miseries (*kleśa*s) or three sorts of *doṣa*s. But the question is: if *jīva*s are inseparably related with these *kleśa*s, how can they get release from these *kleśa*s? The expression *kleśa* may be variously interpreted. The interpretation in terms of *doṣa* is given by Gautama.[31] Patañjali in

---

30 *Manu Saṁhitā*, chap. 6, *śloka* 35.

31 *Nyāydarśana* vol. 4, p. 336. Also *Nyāyasūtra* 4.1.63.

his *Yoga Darśana* in 3rd *sūtra* of Sādhanapāda speaks of *avidyā,* etc. as five types of *kleśas*.[32]

The third objection is that embodied individuals are inseparably related to volitional activities (*pravṛttyanubandha*); so *mokṣa* is impossible to achieve. According to *sūtra* 1.1.17, volitional activity (*pravṛtti*) stands for oral (*vācika*), mental (*mānasika*) and physical (*śārīrika*) actions,[33] and also for virtue and vices (*dharma* and *adharma*) as arising out of those *karma*. Man from his birth till death is engaged in these sorts of *karma*s and it is not possible for him not to be engaged in *karma*s. Man has an inseparable relation with volitional activity, and because of this inseparable relation with the performance of action, results of action cannot be avoided. As consequences of these actions *dharma* and *adharma* arise and bind men to the world. Hence according to the infallible law of *karma*, man will again have to be reborn to enjoy the fruits of these actions and the process of rebirth and death would continue for *ad infinitum*. Thus the promise of liberation becomes abortive. Volitional activity (*pravṛtti*) as caused by faults (*doṣa*) is the cause of *saṁsāra* (world cycle of births and deaths). Thus the occurrence of *pravṛtti* has to be inhibited to prevent the occurrence of world cycle. But it is not possible to stop the occurrence of *pravṛtti*. Therefore, it has been argued that *mokṣa* is impossible. Gautama however, has said:[34]

> Of suffering (*duḥkha*), birth (*janma*), activity (*pravṛtti*), evil (*doṣa*) and false knowledge (*mithyā jñāna*) – when each previous one (in the series) is removed as a consequence of the removal of the one immediately following it (in this series), liberation (*apavarga*) is attained.[35]

---

32 *avidyā 'smitārāgadveṣābhiniveśāḥ pañcakleśāḥ* | 2.3
– *Pātañjala Yogadarśana*, 1938

33 *pravṛttirvāgbuddhisarīrārambhaḥ* – *Nyāyasūtra* 1.1.17

34 *Nyāyasūtra* 1.1.2: *duḥkha-janmā-pravṛtti-doṣa-mithyājñānāmuttarottarāpāye tadantarāpāyād apavargaḥ* – *Nyāyadarśana*, vol. 1, p. 63.

35 D.P. Chattopadhyaya and M.K. Gangopadhyaya, 1975, *Nyāya Philosophy*, part I: *Indian Studies: Past and Present*, p. 29.

Thus from the above *sūtra* we find that removal of *mithyā jñāna* would lead to the removal of *doṣa*s. Again removal of faults would make it possible to put a halt upon volitional activity. With the elimination of volitional activity, the cycle of *janma* can be done away with. The elimination of *janma* would lead to the eradication of *duḥkha* – and this finally results in *apavarga*. Thus in this series, volitional activity or *pravr̥tti* has important role to play in the process of attaining *apavarga*. The volitional activities performed by an embodied individual through speech (*vāk*), thought (*manas*) and body (*śarīra*) – all need to be stopped to prevent the cycle of births from taking place at all. The main objection here is that a man has to free himself from three debts and on account of which he will have to spend his whole life for doing those duties, he will have no time for *śravaṇa* and *manana* which are important preliminaries for obtaining right knowledge (*tattva jñāna*): hence his false knowledge, i.e. *mithyā jñāna* cannot be eradicated; so *doṣa*s which are the products of *mithyā jñāna* cannot be eradicated. Again *karma*s (*pravr̥tti*) that are due to *doṣa*s cannot be eradicated and so also *dharma* and *adharma*, i.e. which have resulted from volitional activity (*pravr̥ttijanya dharmādharma*) cannot be stopped. So *apavarga* is not possible.

In answer to these objections against the possibility of *mokṣa* or *apavarga*, the author of *Nyāyasūtra* Gautama and the commentator Vātsyāyana have given their reply. The charge of non-existence of *apavarga*, its impossibility or illusory nature have been urged because of the *śruti-vākya*:

> *jāyamāno ho vai brāhmaṇastribhirr̥ṇavā jāyate brahmacaryeṇa r̥ṣibhyo yajñena devebhyoḥ prajayā pitr̥bhyoḥ. . . . .*

One important issue has cropped up regarding the interpretation of the expression *r̥na* in the *sūtra* mentioned above. The Bhāṣyakāra in this instance draws attention to the fact that an expression may be treated as a primary expression or as a secondary expression (*pradhāna śabda* or *gauṇa śabda*). The proposed distinction between treating an expression as *pradhāna śabda* and *gauṇa śabda* may as well be applicable in the case of the expression *r̥ṇa*. An expression when used in its primary sense (*mukhyārtha*), it is treated as a *pradhāna śabda*. When will it be said that the expression *ṛṇa* has been treated as *apradhāna śabda*? When a person *x* gives an object *o* to *y*, not, however, any and every sort of object given by someone to somebody, but where a person *x* gives an object *o* to *y*, which is to be received back, i.e. *pratyādeya*, and the second person *y* accepts that object *o*, then with regard to that object which is to be received back, i.e. *pratyādeya dravya*, the expression *ṛṇa* is treated as the primary word. But in the *śruti-vākya* mentioned above the expression *ṛṇa* has not been used as the primary word. In this *śruti-vākya*, the expression *ṛna* is used in the sense *ṛṇairva*, i.e. in the sense of being "similar to debt" (*ṛṇasadṛśa*). As in the sentence, *agnirmāṇavaka*, i.e. a new *brahmacārī* (*mānavaka*) is said to be *agni* (fire) in the sense of his being similar to *agni* (*agnisadṛśa*), so in this case when Śruti speaks about three types of *ṛṇa* towards preceptor, parents and God, these are said to be debts not in the primary sense of the expression *ṛṇa* but in the sense of being similar to debt (*ṛṇavat* or *ṛṇasadṛśa*). In the original statement though actually no word expressing similarity has been used, similarity or likeness is the intended sense of the expression. Now, the question may be raised as to why the expression *ṛṇa* has been used here, even in secondary sense? If one gives something to somebody on the ground that the object will be returned, and the person returns it then he is praised and if he does not return it then he is criticized: in the similar vein if one does something for his preceptor who introduced him to the vast domain of knowledge, for his parents who brought him to this enormous world of existence and for God who provides all round sustenance, then in recognition of his service he is praised, otherwise he is blamed. Just as a person in debt, if he does not repay the borrowed money, is censured by people so also a brāhmaṇa if he fails in his duties, viz. the observance of celibacy, the performance of the Agnihotra sacrificial rite, etc. and the production of offspring, is criticized. Just like a person in debts, if he repays the borrowed money, he is praised by people, a brāhmaṇa, if he rightly performs his duties, he is praised. And this is the underlying similarity between the two.

Second, the Bhāṣyakāra Vātsyāyana elaborated further the *sūtra* 4.1.59 after Gautama to bring out some other implication of the quoted *śruti-vākya*: *jayamāno ha vai*. . . . It has been suggested that sense of the expression *jāyamāna* occurring in *śruti-vākya*, has the literal meaning of being "a just-born baby", but that primary meaning is not the intended meaning of the expression in *śruti-vākya*. If the primary meaning of *jāyamāna* is retained here, then the injunction of duties with regard to the newborn baby would become meaningless. The baby, when comes out of mother's womb, is not entitled to any action like Agnihotra and others. The newborn baby does not have any entitlement to any such sacrificial rites at the moment of his/her birth. The entitlement (*adhikāra*) to any *karma* (duty) depends on whether the person concerned is desirous of the action (*arthī*) and has the requisite capacity (*sāmarthya*) for performing the duty. The Bhāṣyakāra writes quite clearly: *arthinaḥ śaktasya cādhikārāt*. Hence a person's entitlement to a duty is conditional, provided the person is *arthī*, i.e. desirous of performing the action and has the requisite ability to carry out the action. Thus the Bhāṣyakāra observes that if the primary sense of the expression *jāyamāna* is considered, we find that it is deficient on both of these grounds. The newly-born baby lacks the characteristic features of being entitled for performing these sacrificial actions for neither he has desire nor he has capability for performing.

The scriptural statements (Vedic *vākya*) are not essentially different from the statements in ordinary discourse (*laukika vākya*). Even an ordinary person does not enjoin a just-born baby to study the Vedas or perform sacrificial rites, by uttering imperatives, viz. "study the scriptures", "perform sacrificial rites", etc. The Vedic *vākya*s are uttered by the seers with the intention to advise living beings, and a seer who always speaks the truth cannot provide absurd advice to a newly-born baby to perform sacrificial rites. Again the objective of advice requires to be conveyed to only such person who can comprehend the sense of the advice. A newly-born baby cannot comprehend the sense of the advice as it is beyond the baby's capacity. Thus *śruti-vākya* quoted by the opponent which speaks of the performance of certain duties can be rightly interpreted if the word *jāyamāna* is taken in its secondary sense.

This prescriptive statement occurs in the Mantra-Brāhmaṇa portion concerning actions, the performance of which relates to wife (*patnī*), hence these are defined as actions whose defining mark is the quality of being a householder (*gārhasthyaliṅga-karma*). The mark of a household is defined by a wife, for without wife the duty of a householder cannot be performed. Without the assistance of wife, the Agnihotra *yajña-karma,* which consists in offering oblation to fire (*agni*), cannot be performed. In the secondary sense of the term *jāyamāna* it has been taken to signify *gr̥hastha* (family person), i.e. one who after the completion of *brahmacarya* has entered into family life, has been referred to as *jāyamāna*. The *gr̥hastha* is advised to free himself from debts towards parents by producing offsprings and debts towards gods by performing Agnihotra and similar other rites.

Śruti-vākya, viz. "one is to perform sacrificial rites until one is rendered incapable by old age or death" – is apt for a *gr̥hastha* so long his beseeching for a meritorious *gr̥hastha* life has not been outweighed by other considerations. As a *gr̥hī,* he has to perform constantly the prescribed duties. But it is not the correct reading of *śruti-vākya* to jump from it to the conclusion that one must constantly perform those rites till old age or death. If a person in a proper time shuns the life of a householder or adopts prior to that the life of a *saṁnyāsī* then Agnihotra rites are no longer his duties. During that time he being desirous of attaining liberation only, may go through the process of acquiring knowledge by hearing, thoughtful reflection, and profound and repetitive meditation (*śravaṇa, manana* and *nididhyāsana*). Hence, for attaining liberation nobody will have time is not a logical argument.

It has been further stated that if one insists on retaining the sense of the expression *jāyamāna* in its primary sense then it has to be said that newly-born babies are also enjoined to perform sacrificial rites. But then such a *śruti-vākya* turns out to be meaningless like the statement, "one is sprinkling water by fire" (*vahnināsiñcati*). For a newly-born or a very young brāhmaṇa boy has no agency concerning sacrificial rites (*yajñakartṛtva*), hence the injunction pertaining to sacrificial rites (*yajña*) does not apply to him. If the meaning of expression, *jāyamāna* is accepted in the secondary sense then only verbal competency (*yogyatā*) of the *śruti-vākya* can be ascertained.

The second objection to the possibility of *apavarga* rests on the argument from *kleśānubandha* (inseparability of a *jīva* from sufferings). Gautama, however, does not accept this argument to disprove the possibility of *mokṣa*. *Śruti* 4.1.62 is Gautama's rejoinder to the critique of *mokṣa*. According to Gautama, there is no such principle claiming that *kleśa*, i.e. *rāga*, *dveṣa* and *moha* (*mithyā jñāna*) can never be eradicated. The state of dreamless sleep (*suṣupti*) has been cited as a state when a person's entire connections with attachment as well as pleasure and pain are stopped. Hence it is admissible that during the state of *suṣupti* all connections with attachment, aversion, pain and pleasure are severed or annulled. As in the waking state, so also in the state of dream, attachment, suffering, pleasure and pain do arise. When a person is asleep and does not have dreams, which is the state of *suṣupti*, where no knowledge, attachment, pleasure or pain originate. The people who know the true nature of *Brahman* cite this state of dreamless sleep as an exemplar for explaining the nature of the liberated self.

Gautama also cites this example to explain the instance of cessation of sufferings. One thing, however, is to be borne in mind carefully, for though in the present *sūtra* the state of liberation is compared with the state of dreamless sleep but one is never to be confused with the other. Vācaspati Miśra points out that in both of these instances, of dreamless sleep and liberation, there is cessation of affliction, but in the former case the absence of suffering lasts for a particular period, and seeds (*saṁskāra*) of future suffering are not prevented, but in the latter case the seeds of suffering are absolutely destroyed. The liberated person, unlike the person waking up from the state of dream, does not experience suffering ever in future.

To the third objection, Gautama provides an answer by *sūtra* 4.1.63: *na pravr̥tti pratisandhānāya hīnakleśasya*: meaning thereby that the volitional activity of a person, who is without *kleśa*, i.e. devoid of attachment, aversion and delusion (*rāga*, *dveṣa* and *moha*), does not bind him to the cycle of rebirth. This answer of the Nyāya does not lead to any rejection of the theory of Karmavāda. It does not imply any sort of rejection of the view that fruits of *karma* are to be enjoyed. Generally, from birth to death all men perform some action or other, by his speech, mind and body, which are good or bad thus acquire merit and demerit; on account of this merit or demerit, they have to take rebirth to enjoy their fruits. From this the opponents tried to arrive at the conclusion that *mokṣa* is not attainable. But in reply to the opponents, Gautama points out that this argument is not tenable. If a person frees himself from *rāga*, *dveṣa* and *moha*, then that person may be characterized as *rāgadveṣādiśūnya*. Under that circumstance, his volitional activity may not cause his *punarjanma*. According to Gautama, without the acquisition of *tattva jñāna*, no one can be liberated. Hence one who wills to be liberated must have true knowledge (*tattva jñāna*). With the origination of *tattva jñāna* the false knowledge, i.e. *mithyā jñāna* or *moha* will be eliminated, and so he will no longer fall victim to *rāga* or *dveṣa*. When the person concerned thus frees himself from *moha*, *rāga* and *dveṣa*, then his performance of actions may not in any way lead to rebirth. Thus having no new birth implies absence of transition, and is known as the state of *apratisandhāna*, or literally speaking, absence of putting together again. This is nothing other than the state of *apavarga*. In the Sūtra, we come across the notion of *pratisandhāna*, which requires some elucidation to avoid any misunderstanding. In the *sūtra* quoted above the expression, *pratisandhāna* literally speaking means joining together, thus signifies rebirth. *Mithyā jñāna* or *avidyā* is the root cause for the origination of this worldly existence (*saṁsāra*). This is the standard viewpoint of all Indian philosophers, whether Āstika or Nāstika except the Cārvākas. With the dispersal of *mithyā jñāna* or *avidyā*, the root of empirical existence gets dissipated, hence rebirth becomes impossible. The same truth may be recapitulated after Patañjali's statement:[36]

> *kleśamūlaḥ karmāśayo dṛṣṭādṛṣṭajanmavedanīyaḥ* ।
> *sati mūle tadvipāko jātyāyurbhogāḥ* ॥

A précis of Patañjali's statement is as follows: According to *karmas* (actions) performed by an agent wrapped up in *kleśas* or afflictions like that of ignorance, egotism, desire, aversion and tenacity of human existence, he has to go through their consequences determining life-span (*āyu*), birth (*jāti*) and enjoyment (*bhoga*) in the present birth (*dṛṣṭajanma*) or through their fruition in some unseen birth (*adṛṣṭajanma*).

Belief in the law of *karma* or the so-called Karmavāda is one of the pillars on which Dharma-Ethics thrives. Hence Indian philosophers seriously deal with any objection relating to the violation of Karmavāda. The opponents, on the other hand, to embarrass the proponents of Karmavāda here, may further raise the question as to whether this sort of explanation, that we have presented on behalf of the Naiyāyikas or the Yoga philosophers would lead to embrace the failure of the fruition (*karmavaiphalya*) with regard to the previously done action (*pūrvakṛtakarma*). The reason behind this sort of apprehension is not difficult to identify. It is maintained that with the origination of *tattva jñāna*, *mithyā jñāna*, *rāga* and *dveṣa* are dissolved; and once released from the clutches of false knowledge, attachment and aversion the knower of truth who is devoid of attachment and aversion (*rāgadveṣaśūnyatattvajñānī*) does not have *punarjanma*. But it may be asked what about the enjoyment of fruits of actions that he has not yet enjoyed? Since the possibility for that person to enjoy the fruits of actions has been closed, should we say that he has no scope for the enjoyment of fruits of his previously done actions,

---

36 *Pātañjala Yogadarśana*, Sādhanapāda, 12 and 13.

so he would not have to enjoy those fruits? The Bhāṣyakāra, however, quite clearly rules out any such possibility. Restricting themselves to the Karmavāda framework, the Naiyāyikas, however, cannot support any sort of running away without enjoyment of the fruits of the action already performed. It has been maintained that a person who is a *tattva jñānī* does not have rebirth. But this possibility of the absence of rebirth for a person who has acquired proper knowledge (*tattva jñāna*) has given rise to some queries. It may be asked unless this person, who is a *tattva jñānī*, has another rebirth, how could he enjoy fruits of his previously done actions? In this connection, to avoid any such misunderstanding, it has been said that a person who has true knowledge (*tattva jñānī*) enjoys fruits of all his *prārabdha karma*s in his final life. If all the consequences resulting out of his performance of actions (*karmaphala*) have not been enjoyed by him, he continues to live in physical body till all the fruits of his previously done actions are consumed. That is why in spite of being a *tattva jñānī*, he has to suffer till the consequences of his previously performed actions (*karmaphala*s) are exhausted through enjoyment. In the literature, often references are given to the formation of *kāyavyūha* bodily aggregate, by entering into which *yogī puruṣa*s try to consume fruits of their action within a short time. The sum and substance of this is that a person who has acquired *tattva jñāna* remains alive so long all results of his previously performed *karma*s are not exhausted through their enjoyment. Here a distinction has been drawn between a *prārabdha-karma* and a *sañcita-karma.* Regarding *sañcita-karma*, it has been assumed that such *karma*s are extinguished by *tattva jñāna*. But so far *prārabdha-karma*s are concerned, these are not extinguishable by *tattva jñāna* for *prārabdha-karma*s are eliminated only through their *bhoga* (enjoyment). *Śāstra-vākya* like *nābhuktam kṣīyate karmakalpakoṭiśatairapi* maintains that in spite of *tattva jñāna*, no *karma*s are extinguishable without enjoyment, implying by the expression '*karma*' *prārabdha-karma*s.

Nyāyasūtra (*na kleśasantateḥ svabhāvikatvāt*)[37] has been posed from

[37] *Nyāyasūtra* 4.1.64.

the voice of an opponent to clarify further doubts regarding the possibility of liberation. The *pūrvapakṣin* (opponent) may raise an objection regarding the very possibility of absolute annihilation of *kleśa*s (sufferings). The objection may take the following form: Since the stream (*pravāha*) of *kleśa*s is natural it can never be absolutely destroyed. Here the expression *svābhāvika* is taken to mean *anādi* (beginningless). The contention of the opponent is to urge that liberation would not be possible, for liberation to be possible requires connection with affliction be brought to an end. That is, in other words, liberation would have been possible had the connection between *pravṛtti* and afflictions could have been severed. The opponent urges that a living being can be free from afflictions temporarily and not absolutely. The continuous production of three afflictions – attachment, aversion and *moha* – represents a process which is beginningless or going on from time immemorial without any permanent break. Consequently, it can never come to an end and must go on forever. A living being can, therefore, never be liberated.

It may be argued, further, if the natural property of an object is supposed to be annihilated absolutely then that would lead to the annihilation of the object as such. If coolness (*śītalatva*) of water or warmth (*uṣṇatva*) of fire are absolutely annihilated then how could water or fire exist? But when the state of liberation will be attained by a self (*ātmā*) then self is never supposed to be absolutely annihilated. Hence if *ātmā* exists, how can it be urged that its natural properties like afflictions are absolutely annihilated? This may also be the ground for the rejection of the possibility of *apavarga* by the opponents. However, in this argument the sense of the expression *svābhāvika* has been taken to imply a natural or an essential property. The Nyāya Bhāṣyakāra has interpreted *svābhāvika* to mean *anādi*.

The *sūtra* 4.1.64 brings to notice another objection which may be brought against the view that speaks of liberation as a possibility supposing the absolute destruction of afflictions; the possibility of liberation may be questioned on the ground that the flow of afflictions (*kleśasantatipravāha*) is beginningless (*anādi*), and can never be absolutely destroyed. The Nyāya reply to this objection consists in addressing the misperception about necessary connection between two concepts, viz. being beginningless (*anādi*) and being endless (*ananta*). The *prāgbhāva*, which is an instance of prior non-existence of an object, is said to be beginningless (*anādi*) but when that object comes into being, *abhāva* ceases to exist. Hence *prāgbhāva* is *anādi* but *śānta*, i.e. it has an end. Just like that the external flow of afflictions, though natural, can be non-eternal.

There are some differences of opinion about the nature of *prāgbhāva* (prior non-existence) as a negative entity which has been cited as an example in this argument. Some have attempted to draw an analogy between the black colour of an earthly atom and stream of afflictions (*kleśasantatipravāha*) for both of these are beginningless but non-eternal for as the black colour of the earthly atom in conjunction with fire is destroyed, so by true knowledge the stream of affliction is destroyed. However, none of these arguments found much favour with the Naiyāyikas. The *sūtra* 4.1.67 of Gautama: *na saṅkalpanimittatvāccarāgādinām*[38] is the final Nyāya response to the objection raised by the opponents against the possibility of liberation (*mokṣa*) on the charge of *pravṛttyanubandha*.

In *sūtra* 4.1.67, Gautama admits that attachment, aversion and ignorance have for their cause deliberation also. The addition of *ca*, i.e. also in the *sūtra* is quite suggestive. The concept of deliberation has been variously interpreted by the Nyāya philosophers. The Bhāṣyakāra Vātsyāyana has attempted to define *saṅkalpa* as born out of the recollection of the objects previously perceived: *saṅkalpaśca pūrvānubhūta viṣayānucintanayoniḥ*. From this it is inferred that the desire of the just-born baby also originates

[38] No [i.e. the objection given in *sūtra* 64 above does not stand], because attachment, etc. [i.e. the three afflictions, viz. attachment, aversion and ignorance] have for their cause deliberation also (*ca*). 4.1.67 – *Nyāya Philosophy*, Part IV: Fourth *Adhyāya*, First *Āhṇika*, Mrinal Kanti Gangopadhyaya, Indian Studies, R.D. Press, Kolkata, 1973.

from the recollection of objects previously perceived. Vātsyāyana upholds this fact to be established by common observation. It has been proposed by Vātsyāyana to apply the concept of *saṅkalpa* by extension also to the case of just-born baby. Uddyotakara says that by *saṅkalpa* is to be understood the craving for the object previously experienced. Vācaspati elucidates this further: An experience of an object results in a continuous stream of recollections about it, which produces a craving for it and this finally results in the desire for the object. The author of the commentary *Tātparyaṭīkā* Vācaspati Miśra realized that there was some sort of vacillation about the exact connotation of *saṅkalpa* among the interpreters of *Nyāyasūtra*. He accommodates *saṅkalpa* to account for (a) wish for the previously experienced object, and (b) and also its prior experience (*pūrvānubhāva*).[39]

According to Viśvanātha, *saṅkalpa* here means knowledge as conducive to one's own welfare. Such an instance of knowledge is the source of the desire for the object. Phanibhūṣaṇa concludes that whatever may be the exact meaning of the word, *saṅkalpa*, the main point is that it is the cause of the desire for an object. According to the Bhāṣyakāra, *saṅkalpa* (determination) assuming three sorts of forms, viz. *rañjanīya* (tends to produce rejoice), *kopanīya* (tends to produce anger) and *mohanīya* (tends to produce delusion or error) as false (*mithyā*) determination, which are the producers of *rāga, dveṣa* and *moha*. In *sūtra* 4.1.67 explicitly the reference is only to *saṅkalpa* or determination as the cause of worldly afflictions. But we must not overlook the occurrence of the expression *ca* as suggestive of some other causes to account for *kleśa*s. Two *nimittaka*s or *kāraṇa*s have been admitted to account for afflictions (*kleśa*s). One is *saṅkalpa* and the other is *adṛṣṭa* or *karma*. That is why *rāga, dveṣa* and *moha* which are taken together stand for *kleśa*s, and are said to be caused by *saṅkalpa* and unforeseen traces of past deeds (*adṛṣṭa*).

---

39 *yadyapyanubhūtaviṣayaprārthanā saṅkalpaḥ tathāpi tasyapūrvabhāgo 'nubhavo grāhyaḥ, prārthanāya rāgatvāt* | *tena mithyānubhāvaḥsaṅkalpa ityarthaḥ* | *mohaniyasaṅkalpamithajñānasaṁskāraḥ* |

– *Tātparyaṭīkā*. See *Nyāyadarśana*, vol. 4, p. 411

Second, *karma* in the sense of *adṛṣṭa* of a living being, as an efficient cause for its birth, produces living beings endowed with various distribution and measure of *rāga, dveṣa* and *moha*. Among living beings it is quite obvious to observe that living beings of some species are predisposed towards *rāga* in greater measure, some are inclined towards *dveṣa* in greater extent and some are prone to ignorance in greater extent. Thus we find *saṅkalpa* in the sense of *mithyā jñāna* is the cause of all sorts of afflictions, viz. *rāga, dveṣa* and *moha* in general. Without the assumption of determination (*saṅkalpa*), origination of *rāga, dveṣa* and *moha* cannot be accounted for. Further the roles of specific *adṛṣṭa* in the origination of a specific species (*nikāya*) is also worthy of consideration. The particular species – specific body is due to specific *adṛṣṭa*, and that *adṛṣṭa* is also the efficient cause in determining sorts of afflictions to have effect upon those living beings. The word *nikāya* has been used to signify *jāti* (class).[40]

Third, it has been pointed out that attachment, aversion and ignorance because of their mutual affection, one sort of affliction gives rise to another sort. Thus, one under ignorance becomes attached, one under ignorance gets angry, i.e. characterized by aversion, one who gets attached becomes ignorant and one who gets angry becomes ignorant. From this, we come to find that *rāga, dveṣa* and *moha* each of which causes the coming into being of the other. Thus the Bhāṣyakāra writes: *itaretaranimitta ca rāgadināmutpattiḥ*. To put it in other words, attachment, aversion and delusion are begotten by mutual causation. This is also referred to as *parasparanimittakatva* (mutual efficient causality).

The author of the commentary *Nyāyabhāṣya* has instantiated his contention by saying further, "The ignorant is pleased" (*mūḍharajyati*), "The ignorant is angry" (*mūḍhakupyati*) and "The passionate is ignorant" (*raktomuhyati*). Indian philosophers who

40 *nikāyenajātirūpalakṣyate* | – *Tātparyaṭīkā*

Nyāyavārtikakāra writes: *dṛṣṭo hi kaścit sattvanikāyo rāgavahulo yathā pārāvatādiḥ* | *kaścit krodha vahulo yathāsarpadiḥ* | *kaścinmohavahulo yathājagaradiḥ* || –*Nyāyadarśana*, vol. 4, p. 413

are protagonists of *mokṣa* urge that if all these faults (*doṣas*) are absolutely eliminated then only the state of *mokṣa* ensues. The opponents would urge that the root cause of afflictions is false belief (*mithyā jñāna*) for the absolute annihilation (*atyanta uccheda*) of which no cause does exist; it is impossible to have absolute annihilation of afflictions, hence *mokṣa* is impossible. To meet this allegation of the opponents, Vātsyāyana in his *Bhāṣya* states, that because of true beliefs all false beliefs become non-productive (*anutpatti*).

With the origination of *tattva jñāna* all sorts of *mithyā jñāna* can no longer originate. The continuous series or flow of afflictions (*kleśasantati*) which is beginningless (*anādi*) ceases to originate for with the arising of *tattva jñāna*, *mithyā jñāna* is annihilated and with the absence of *mithyā jñāna* its effect *kleśa* is absolutely annihilated.

One of the points of argument for the opponent is that the continuum of *kleśasantati* is *anādi* and how can there be annihilation of such a continuous series. But this objection as we have already discussed, is based on a false logic for what is said to be *anādi* need not be necessarily non-eliminable. Also what are said to be bodies, these are also as series *anādi*. It has been maintained that from a time beginningless due to beginningless false belief various sorts of bodies of living beings are originating. None of the living beings can be said to possess body which did not have a previous origination, i.e. not *anutpannapūrva* (devoid of any previously unproduced body). But what is said to be *tattva jñāna* is definitely different from all these beginningless (*anādipadārtha*), for *tattva jñāna* is only *anutpannapūrva*. The Naiyāyikas tried to prove the existence of *apavarga* with the example of inference and *śruti-pramāṇa*. The argument offered by the Naiyāyikas is that one instance of suffering comes after another instance of suffering, again comes another instance of suffering and so on from beginningless time an uninterrupted series or flow of sufferings is originating. The absolute annihilation is a necessary event for this uninterrupted series or flow of suffering to terminate. The continuum of afflictions is comparable with the continuous flame of a lamp. As one flame of a lamp succeeds another flame of lamp, and so on and so forth the flame of a lamp persists until this continuous flow of flames gets absolutely annihilated. When the final flame of the lamp is destroyed then that lamp is extinguished, no longer that continuous flow of flame originates. On the analogy of succession of flames (*pradīpasantati*) and its final blowing out, the succession of afflictions (*kleśasantati*) and its final elimination have been explained.[41]

Does God Need to Intervene in the Context of Morality?

Do we need God to assist us in any way or other in the context of morality? How do Indian philosophers react to this question?

The individuals engage themselves in various sorts of *karma*s with a view to achieve some results. But generally in all the cases, the individuals do not get the result expecting which they worked. It is not a rule that on every occasion, the *jīva* will get the result that he aims to achieve by performing a *karma*. The aberrations in the cause–effect relationship between the performance of an action and its outcome are noticed even in cases where in spite of the performance of a morally good action, the outcome or result of the action is distressing. Exactly, in the opposite way the irregularity between the performance of an action and its expected result is noticed where the performance of a morally heinous action produces a delightful result. In this connection, it would be quite relevant to refer to *Nyāyasūtra* 4.1.19 – *īśvaraḥ kāraṇam puruṣakarmāphalyadarśanāt*[42] (God is the cause, because it has been observed that an individual's performance of an action does not necessarily produce the desired result (of his action). If an action produces the result desired by the performer of the action, then that action is considered to be a successful action; on the other hand, if an action fails to produce the result desired by the agent, that action is considered to be unsuccessful.

---

41 *kiṁ punoratrapramāṇam? duḥkhasantatiratāntam ucchidyate santatittvāt pradīpasantativadityācāryāḥ* – Kiraṇāvalī, cited in *Nyāyadarśana*, vol. 4, p. 417.

42 *Nyāyadarśana*, vol. 4, p. 42.

This quoted *sūtra* represents the viewpoint of the proponents of *kevaleśvarakāraṇatāvāda* (the thesis proclaiming God alone is the cause). Thus further analysed, *kevaleśvarakāraṇatāvāda* maintains that God alone is the cause, and neither *jīva*s nor their *karma*s cause the resulting consequences of the action for no necessary connection has been observed between the performance of an action (by an individual) and its being successful. Thus the ground of inference is as follows: *puruṣakarmāphalyadarśanāt*. The Nyāya-vṛttikāra Viśvanātha also argues in the same vein to point out how in many cases in spite of agent's *puruṣakāra* (human effort), *karma* does not turn out to be successful (*saphala*). Why does it happen like that? It has been suggested that because of the absence of a particular unforeseen factor (*adṛṣṭa viśeṣa*) which is one of the causes for obtaining the requisite result from the performance of an action, hence the performed action becomes useless (*viphala*).

From this observation some have concluded that the result of *karma* is not determined by the will of the agent. This establishes that on many occasions *karma*s do not lead to the end desired by the agent. It has been presumed, if all *karma*s are successful in producing the desired result, then there should not have been any *karma* that fails. All these observations led them to maintain that what will be the result of an action is determined by the will of God and not by the will of the individual. If individual *jīva*s could have enjoyed results of action as they have desired, then results of action would have been subordinate to their own selves, *svādhīna*. Further if the results of *karma* were determined by the agents themselves (*svādhīna*), then there would not have been pain, suffering or sorrow. For who would like to suffer and bear pain? If every individual had the power to manipulate events in such a way to maximize his own pleasure everybody would have done this. But since the actual case is not like that, it has been maintained that results of action are determined by something else other than *jīva*s themselves. Hence it has been admitted that there must be some highest being (*parama puruṣa*) whose *ichā* determines the results of the actions that are performed by *jīva*s. Hence there must be a God, who controls all the results – good or bad, of actions performed by *jīvas*. *Īśvara* does not determine the results of *karma* according to the nature of *karma* of *jīvas*. Rather *Īśvara* is supposed to determine the results of *karma* according to its own desire. From this angle, it may be argued that God independently of the actions performed by *jīvas* is the cause of the world. The view that God alone is the cause of the world, and nothing else, is known as *kevaleśvarakāraṇatāvāda*. Thus *Īśvara*, independently of *karmas* performed by *jīvas* (*jīvakarma nirapekṣa*) and not depending on *karma* of *jīvas* (*jīvakarma sāpekṣa*) is the creator of the world and created beings and their joy, happiness everything.

But this viewpoint does not find support from the Naiyāyikas who are being considered as one of the spokespersons for Dharma-ethical perspective. In *Nyāyasūtra* 4.1.20 maintaining *na puruṣakarmabhāve phalaniṣpatteḥ* (in the absence of actions performed by the individuals, no consequences are produced), we derive the main rejoinder to the upholder of the thesis that God alone is the cause of the creation. This *sūtra* emphasizes the importance of the action of *jīvas*. If *jīvas* do not perform any action then no consequences are produced. This is the argument of Gautama to show that God alone is not the cause of the world.[43] If God only by his own wish gives someone pleasure and some other person pain, then God will be accused of being cruel and partial. If any individual is said to have been assigned with consequences as willed by God, then question will arise as to why does God give some individual painful consequences and some others pleasant consequences? If his will only determines who will be happy and who will be unhappy, then God turns out to be a whimsical being. Under these considerations God would be blamed for the defect of partiality (*vaiṣamya doṣa*).

In *sūtra* 4.1.21 we find a definite response from the perspective of the Naiyāyikas. The point of the Naiyāyikas is not to establish that *Īśvara* or God is not the cause (*kāraṇa*), but to establish that

---

[43] There are some differences of opinion regarding the interpretation of *Nyāyasūtra* 4.1.19 among the Nyāya commentators. For details vide *Nyāyadarśana*, vol. 4.

God as dependent on *karma* of *jīva*s, is the cause[44] of the world. What sorts of *karma* has been performed by a *jīva*, and what sort of fruits are to be borne by those *karma*s – all these are known to God and accordingly God arranges the world order. From the standpoint of the Naiyāyikas following two opposite views are to be refuted:

1. The view God alone is the only cause.
2. *Karma* of the individual alone is the cause.

The Mīmāṁsakas maintain that *karma* itself is the cause of consequences of *karma*. According to Jaimini, *karma* independently of God is the cause of *karamaphala* (consequences of *karma*). The same view has been maintained by Bādarāyaṇa in *Vedāntasūtra*. This also establishes the difference between the position of the Naiyāyikas from that of the Mīmāṁsakas and the Vedāntins. According to the Naiyāyikas, God arranges for the result to be enjoyed by *jīva*s depending upon the nature of *karma*. Even though it is admitted that in the absence of actions performed by the individuals, no results or consequences are produced, that does not ensure that whenever actions are performed, that would produce the result (desired). In many instances in spite of performing an action by an individual, that action is said to be unproductive (*niṣphala*), of course not in the sense of producing no consequences but in the sense of not producing desired consequences. The Naiyāyikas maintain that not only performance of an action is the only cause that produces the consequence that has been desired by the individual, but also something else has also to be admitted. Uddyotakara maintains God's grace/favour (*anugraha*) is what very much required for the successful fruition of an *karma*. To grasp the full sense of the expression, *īśvarānugraha* (God's favour), we need to take into account the following sentence as stated in *Nyāyabhāṣyavārttika*: *api tu puruṣakarma īśvarānugṛhṇāti*[45]

---

[44] Here by *kāraṇa* (cause) has been meant *nimitta kāraṇa* (efficient cause) by the Naiyāyikas.

[45] Anantalal Thakur, 1997b, *Nyāyabhāṣyavārttika of Bhardvāja Uddyotakara*, p. 432.

(but yet God favours actions of the individuals). We have already discussed as one of the presuppositions of Dharma-Ethics its belief in the law of *karma* or Karmavāda. In the context of Dharma-Ethics, no Indian philosophers are able to overlook the role of *karma* in the form of unforeseen cause or *adr̥ṣṭa*. In this case Uddyotakara also makes it clear that in getting the desired result or consequence by the performance of an action, the unforeseen merit and demerit, or *adr̥ṣṭa* plays crucial role. God as the dispenser of the consequences of the action (*viniyoga* of *karma*) takes into cognizance the nature of the *karma* performed by the individual (*jīva*), unforeseen merits and demerits (*adr̥ṣṭa*) stored for the individual and time when it will bear its fruits, if a *karma* is set to bear fruits. To quote from Uddyotakara's *Nyāyabhāṣyavārttika*:

> *ko 'nugrahārthaḥ? yad yathābhūtam yasya ca yadā paripākakālaḥ, tat tathā tadā ca viniyukta iti*।[46]

In this connection, an objection would arise about the very possibility of individual's freedom. If it is said that God favours individuals by providing them results for their actions, then how can individuals be said to be free? According to the viewpoint analysed here, it may seem to imply that individual's actions to be effective depends upon God. If God propels individuals to perform good actions and sometimes bad actions, then how can individuals are held responsible for the performance of any bad actions? A distinction has been introduced between two sorts of agency (*kartr̥tva*), calling one *prāyojya kartā*, one who has been commissioned or employed to perform some action and *prayojaka kartā* who is the commissioner or employer of the individual who has been commissioned to perform the action. It has been argued that individuals are actually performing the actions, hence individuals are *prayojya kartā*s but God has caused or made the individual perform the action, hence God is *prayojaka kartā*. Individuals when they are performing actions they are thus under the influence of *doṣa* as *rāga*, *dveṣa* and *moha* are proceeding to

---

[46] Anantalal Thakur, 1997b, op. cit.

perform those actions. If individuals are the agents of actions, they are also to be admitted as the enjoyer (*bhoktā*) of the consequences of actions. Thus the agency of individuals is subservient to God, but there is no denial that individuals are doing actions (*karma*s). Since individuals are agents, all the imperative statements of Śāstra enjoining performance of some *karma*s and non-performance of some *karma*s become relevant for the individuals who are desirous of obtaining the good and avoiding the bad.

Vṛttikāra Viśvanātha has further explained that if *karma* of *jīva* or his *puruṣakāra* enables *jīva* to have their consequences, then always his *karma* should have been successful. But that is not the case. In many case, in spite of agent's *puruṣakāra, karma* does not produce the requisite result. Why does it happen so? It has been said that in spite of agent's *puruṣakāra,* it does not bear the requisite result, because of the absence of *adṛṣṭa viśeṣa,* which is the other cause for obtaining the requisite result.

The main contention of the author is to rule out the possibility of bringing any accusation on God on the ground of *vaiṣamya* (partiality) and *naighṛṇya* (impudency). God cannot by his sheer whim create some as men, some as animals and some as insects. God cannot be supposed to be that sort of partial being. In *Gītā,* God himself says (IX.29) *samo 'haṁ sarvabhūteṣu na me dveṣyo 'sti na priyah*। (I am fair to all creatures, nobody is despised or favoured by me). In *Śārīrakabhāṣya,* Śaṅkarācārya recapitulating the distinction admitted between two sorts of causes, viz. *sādhāraṇa kāraṇa* (common cause) and *asādhāraṇa kāraṇa* (special cause) for the origination of crops like paddy, barley and others proposed the similar understanding of this distinction to account for the creation of human beings, beasts and other entities accepting God as the common cause and unforeseen forces or *adṛṣṭa* located in *jīva*s as their *asādhāraṇa kāraṇa*. Hence whatever differences are there in the creation of men, animals and insects that is due to earlier done action of the agent, the charge of impartiality does not arise. God cannot act like ordinary men out of his own attraction or repulsion. Śaṅkarācārya maintained that God has created the world of diversities and dissimilarities by depending upon the merits and demerits of the individuals.[47] There is no question of bringing the charge of impartiality towards God for all inequalities and differences are the result of *karma*s of the individuals. In support of this viewpoint, Indian philosophers refer to the Śruti and propound arguments to establish their viewpoint. Thus, God is *kāraṇa* of the universe depending on *karma* of the individual. It may be objected, if *Īśvara* creates the world depending on *karma* of the individual, then God does not have control over everything. Then it may be said that God is not the caretaker of the entire world. This way of arguing has been supposed to deprive God from being the creator of everything (*sarvakartṛtva*) and controller of everything (*sarveśvaratva*). There are also various debates and discussions on this objection, to which I do not want to focus here. It may be said that to account for God as the cause of the world without any partiality towards anyone, enjoining results according to *karma* of each individual does not invalidate the qualification of God as Sarveśvara, i.e. creator of all nor does it deprive God of the power to create.

In this discussion to ascertain the role of God in the context of the Vaidika Dharma-Ethics, I have just sketchily presented the viewpoints of those Indian philosophers who assign importance to God apart from the performance of *karma*s by the individuals in making those actions successful. It has already been pointed out that there are some Mīmāṁsaka philosophers who do not admit God as the efficient cause of the world or as the distributor of fruits of actions. In their view, *karma* does not require any assistance to bear its consequences. Pūrva-Mīmāṁsakas admit the doctrine of *apūrva*, an unseen force or potency which relates fruits of action to the agent. The Mīmāṁsakas put more emphasis on the performance of *yajña-karma* (sacrificial rites), the performance of which creates a positive potency or force, i.e. called *apūrva*

[47] *sāpekṣo hī śvaro viṣamām sṛṣṭim nirmimīte kimapekṣata iti cet? dharmādharmāvapekṣata iti vadamaḥ* || – cited in *Nyāyadarśana*, vol. 4, p. 59

(unprecedented, unique) by virtue of which *svarga* is attained. According to the Mīmāṁsakas, *svarga* (heaven) is not a place but *svarga* denotes happiness. In their opinion the postulation of God as one whose causal efficacy is dependent on the merit and demerit (*adr̥ṣṭa*) of individuals, would be deflating for any such being called God. Kumārila Bhaṭṭa does not accept the concept of creator or God. In this system *karma* has been treated as primary cause. In Sāṁkhya philosophy also the existence of God as an efficient cause has been disproved. In Sāṁkhya *karma* has been given a primary role. *Sāṁkhyapravacanasūtra* 5.2 says: *na īśvarādhiṣṭhite phala niṣpattiḥ karmaṇā tatsiddheḥ*: the effectuation of results (*phala*) is not done under the supervision of God, but done by *karma*. Again in *sūtra* 6.67, *karma* has been presumed as the efficient cause (*nimitta kāraṇa*) of the relationship between *puruṣa* and *prakr̥ti*. The Buddhist Dharma-Ethics or Jaina Dharma-Ethics does not admit God or Creator. Hence from the perspective of those who do not admit God or Creator, no arguments are required to disprove God's partiality in the distribution of fruits of actions to individual beings. Though in Indian philosophy there are lots of debates and discussions about God, His nature and roles, it is neither possible nor judicious to incorporate all these discussions in the present chapter. However, in course of elucidation to find an answer to the question regarding God's intervention in the realm of morality from the perspective of Vaidika Dharma-Ethics, it may be summed up as follows:

First, among the proponents of Vaidika Dharma-Ethics, there is no unanimity regarding the role of God in morality. The Vaidika Dharma-Ethics is not to be clubbed with theistic ethics. If we look into the history of ethics, it is not difficult to find different ways of relating God and morality. The one that has been much discussed in the Western ethics is known as the Divine Command theory according to which ethics is based on compulsion emanating from God. The Vaidika Dharma-Ethics is not to be read as another interpretation of the Divine Command theory of Western ethics.

Second, even those who accept God's intervention in the

domain of morality are never ignoring the role of the individual, his deeds (*karma*) and effort (*puruṣakāra*) in ascertaining his moral worthiness. It may seem for some of them in the domain of morality, an individual and his actions are primary.

Third, those who do not admit God or place God to a less important position or to an ambiguous position, had no vacillation in according importance to actions (*karma*s) of the individuals and their results. Thus, whether God has been accepted as the creator of the moral world where individuals enjoy or suffer according to the merits or demerits of their actions, or God has been relegated to a dubious position, individuals (*jīva*s), their *karma* and their *pāpa* or *puṇya*, *dharma* and *adharma* matter most. This also evinces the importance of *karma* and Karmavāda as the inalienable aspect of Vaidika Dharma-Ethics in particular and all systems of Dharma-Ethics in general. It is impossible to purge the doctrine of *karma* from Dharma-Ethics as such and sustain it in its essentiality.

To delineate unambiguously the scope of Vaidika Dharma-Ethics in all its details by covering all its aspects is really a Herculean task. The main communiqué of Vaidika Dharma-Ethics, as a prototype of Dharma-Ethics, is to dwell on the necessity for being morally good is to earn reward points for a better life in this birth or in future birth. This is the normal, mundane and partial fulfilment or expectancy of such fulfilment obtained from being moral. A deeper commitment of Dharma-Ethics lies in ensuring being moral to transcend the limits of morality. This pseudo-paradoxical aspect of Vaidika Ethics necessitates not only performance of morally good actions but also performance of actions with a drastic change in the psychology of the agent. This is the reason for making a provision for the performance of *sakāma-karma* with good intention and *niṣkāma-karma*, i.e. actions without any desire for consequence. This also necessitates the purification of self (*ātma-saṁskāra*). Hence for the Vaidika Dharma-Ethics postulation of self in its purity is a distinctive step from its embodied existence. A critique of disembodied existence failing to find supportive arguments finds no match between the ideals and ideology of Vaidika Dharma-Ethics and his perspective. Indian philosophical schools that fall within the purview of Vaidika Dharma-Ethics never required to straighten out their differences of opinion about the nature of self, its function and number to be a member of the close-knit family of the Vaidika Dharma-Ethics. This ethics speaks of stages of self development, stages of elevation of self through *abhyudaya* and *mokṣa,* the highest end of life. If morality is presumed to lead to transcendence and if such an idea of transcendence is a hoax, the complete scaffolding of Dharma-Ethics would fall to the ground. This consideration led to a full-fledged discussion both for and against the very possibility of attaining *apavarga*. The belief in the possibility of *mokṣa* is also another distinctive aspect of Dharma-Ethics in general and Vaidika Dharma-Ethics in particular. There is no dearth of theory in this discourse if one is not prejudiced by any previously held theory of "theory". The individual through his actions – physical, mental and verbal – through his moral merits and demerits, through his *puruṣakāra,* humanly effort may be able to elevate self. Instead of predicting horrors of the doomsday, it leaves open the possibility of going beyond the doomsday.

8

Conclusion

FROM the meta-ethical perspective the Vaidika Dharma-Ethics – a paradigm of Dharma-Ethics has been elaborated and explained in the present volume taking into consideration its generic aspects and its specific aspects. The Vaidika Ethics as a prototype of Dharma-Ethics shares some common features with other prototypes namely the Jaina ethics and Buddhist ethics. But there are also some differentiating features of Vaidika Ethics that mark its significant difference from the other prototypes. The primary subject of concern is the Vaidika Ethics which is one of the ideal representatives of Dharma-Ethics, though sometimes in this volume I have simply referred to that primary subject of discourse as Dharma-Ethics. This clarification, I thought, would be helpful lest there be some confusion or doubt regarding my use of the expressions "Dharma-Ethics" and "Vaidika Dharma-Ethics" and "Vaidika Ethics" interchangeably. This sort of ambiguity has been cherished quite consciously and is obvious from the very title of the volume *Through the Lens of Dharma-Ethics*. Strictly speaking it is an articulation of a standpoint through the lens of an archetype of Dharma-Ethics. Thus when it has been stated that the essence of Dharma-Ethics is to be reclaimed on its own terms, the referent of "Dharma-Ethics" in the present discussion is none other than the Vaidika Dharma-Ethics.

The Vaidika Dharma-Ethics is a treasure trove of many oral and written literary resources which are accumulating since nearly 4,000 years; of which only some are sustained, and most of the ancient texts are reportedly fragmented, extrapolated, misplaced, lost in time or are forgotten. Most of the details relating to ancient texts about their legitimate and authentic authorship, number of author/s, place and time of writing, frame of reference are shrouded in mystery. Researches on Dharma-Ethics are not confined to the study of one or two well-defined single-authored texts along with at most say, ten-fifteen commentaries. It is an endeavour to unearth the history of an ideology of a continuing tradition through its periods of ups and downs. Notwithstanding the intricacies of Western ethical discourse, the Western ethical discourse may seem to be Lilliputian compared to the wide-ranging panorama of Dharma-Ethical discourse. The perception behind this disproportionate difference in extent and depth between Dharma-Ethics and Western ethics is not far to seek. The major reason, of course, is the difference in the method generally pursued for the study of the subject: in the case of Dharma-Ethics the meta-ethical enquiry concentrates upon an all-encompassing generic domain, whereas in the case of meta-ethical enquiry of the Western ethics the trend is to forsake this sort of non-specific approach and to follow more specific domains of investigation. Broadly speaking, the three dominant trends of Western ethics are Aristotelian virtue ethics, Mill's utilitarianism and Kant's deontology. In recent times, discussions on post-modern ethics, hermeneutical ethics or feminist ethics are frequently heard of. These studies are all confined to single authored text/texts. In spite of there being much difficulties in fathoming all the implications of a theory and settling all its issues by responding to newer challenges, allegations and providing justifications for and against these theories, the domain of Western ethics seems to be manageable. But from this to jump to the conclusion that Western ethics is shallow, Dharma-Ethics is profound, Western ethics is easier and Dharma-Ethics is more difficult, Western ethics is simpler, Dharma-Ethics is more complex is unwarranted. The trend to judge Dharma-Ethics as the exotic other of the Western ethics, which has been identified with reason, freedom and consistency, and identifying Dharma-Ethics with irrationality, dogmatism and anomaly is also not an encouraging move while investigating into the spirit of Dharma-Ethics. In the case of Western ethics, the similar mode of generic meta-ethical enquiry would demand a beginning from the pre-historical Western tradition till recent date. On the other hand, the approach to Dharma-Ethics needs not be bound by this sort of prevalent general approach only. In this volume, commonly pursued generic approach to Dharma-Ethics has been followed, but that does not validate the claim that this is the only befitting approach to Dharma-Ethics. One should guard oneself from towing the mistaken idea that the only way for studying Vaidika Dharma-Ethics is by delineating a grand master plan of one universal viewpoint which may be characterized as the Vaidika view about morality.

The meta-ethical study concerning the Vaidika Dharma-Ethics can be specifically oriented towards some text or similar types of texts or towards texts of the same period or of different periods and so on and so forth. Nobody has any reason to be oblivious of various schools of thought in Indian philosophy nor has any reason to be doubtful about the varieties of perspectives from which issues relating to metaphysics, epistemology or logic have been relentlessly pursued. Even if by Indian philosophy is taken to mean only those philosophers who owe their allegiance to the Vedas, or in other words, the Vaidika philosophy, in spite of their similarities in outline, their dissimilarities in detail do not escape a discerning mind. If various schools of philosophy born out of classical Vedic tradition are hardly replicas of one another in the domain of metaphysics, epistemology and logic how could then they be the votaries of one rigidly defined uniform viewpoint in the domain of ethics? Our habit of speaking in singular as the Vaidika view about the nature of ethics should not allow us to forget how much diversities and differences are also contained in its bosom.

We may as well talk about the ethics of Nyāya, Advaita Vedānta, Viśiṣṭādvaita Vedānta, Bhāṭṭa Mīmāṁsā, Prābhākara Mīmāṁsā, Sāṁkhya, Yoga, and so on without uprooting from the soil or severing these studies from their common source of origin. It is not uncommon to talk about the Nyāya theory of *pramāṇa* as distinct from the Vaiśeṣika theory of *pramāṇa* or from the Advaita

Vedānta theory of *pramāṇa*. Talks about the Mīmāṁsā metaphysics of *sāmānya* as distinguished from the Vaiśeṣika metaphysics of *sāmānya* are not unheard of. This is also one of the possible methodologies for dealing with Dharma-Ethics and in that case study of each branch of Vaidika Ethics will be more specific. The discourse of Dharma-Ethics, specifically the Vaidika Dharma-Ethics, presented in its generality, is as old as the history of the land of its origin. To trace the domain of Dharma-Ethics is to trace the domain of history of Indian thought. Hence, if any comparison is to be drawn between the Vaidika Dharma-Ethics and Western ethics two must be viewed either in their generality or in their speciality to decide between their shallowness or profundity and other issues.

There are some characteristic opposition between Indian standpoint and Western standpoint but that should not be the ground either for ignoring Western ethics or for demeaning Dharma-Ethics. Because one standpoint is different from the other does not necessarily imply that one is better and the other is worse, or that one should be worshipped and the other should be despised. There is no doubt some major conspicuous differences exist between the Dharma-Ethical perspective and the Western ethical perspective. But before entering into discussion about the differences in these two perspectives, let us once again recapitulate the major characteristics of Dharma-Ethics. The Dharma-Ethics undoubtedly is an inalienable part of Indian philosophy and is teleological in its orientation. In Indian philosophical discourse, especially in the Vedic tradition, most of the texts present a well-knit holistic approach to philosophy as such. Darśana as a discipline includes metaphysics, epistemology, ethics or logic as inseparable in its final pursuit. It is really hard to earmark any particular text in classical Vedic philosophy solely as a text either in metaphysics or in epistemology or ethics. From this it would be wrong to draw the conclusion, as it had been reportedly done by some, that there is no ethics at all. In fact, compartmentalizing or branching different areas of Darśana into watertight domains must have been carried out under the influence of Western philosophy. In order to understand the nature of morality and conditions of being moral from the perspective of different schools of Indian philosophy cannot be dissociated from their respective metaphysical and psychological presuppositions. There is no doubt that ethics in India is impregnated with metaphysics and psychology for here ethics is never a dry intellectual enterprise consisting only of abstract conceptual analysis. The most distinguishing aspect of Dharma-Ethics is its concern for the psychology of the moral agent. This has often given an edge to the critics to say that Dharma-Ethics is loaded with metaphysics. It is, however, believed that any ethical theory must be grounded in a philosophical conception of the relation between human conduct and the ultimate reality. To put it in the nutshell, the objective of Dharma-Ethics is to prepare the ground for the transcendence of birth and terrestrial existence and realization of self in its true essence. The jittery reactionaries to Dharma-Ethics from their ignorance about what Dharma-Ethics claims, teaches and preaches complain against it for glorifying rampant asceticism and maligning vital instincts and life.

When we are talking about Dharma-Ethics in this volume, it has already been made clear that we are dealing with the Vaidika Dharma-Ethics. The very urgency of calling it as Vaidika Dharma-Ethics is not unclear for here an attempt is being made to outline the core content, if any, of the Dharma-Ethics that had its root in the Vedas. The Vedas are, in one sense, nothing but collections of sentences; hence the source of Dharma-Ethics is being traced to sentences, no doubt, of very special sort. To all *āstika* thinkers sentences are sources of true belief (knowledge), though according to the Vaiśeṣikas, sentences are not independent sources of true belief. Sentences, however, are required to be comprehended (*śābdabodha*) to derive knowledge from sentences. The explanations as to how through the Vedic imperative sentences the sense of duty is channelized to finite human consciousness are very interesting and fascinating aspects of Vaidika Dharma-Ethics. The discussions on *śabda-pramāṇa*, in some of their aspects, are considered similar to deliberations on philosophy of language. Hence we have to admit another important characteristic of Vaidika Dharma-Ethics is its close interrelation with philosophy of language. It is never possible to have pristine pure Vaidika Dharma-Ethics dismantled from all these aspects.

At the very beginning it has already been pointed out that *dharma* is the subject matter of all Dharma-Ethics. In the Vaidika Dharma-Ethics four expressions, namely *dharma*, *satya*, *ṛta* and *yajña*, are considered as defining the range of Dharma-Ethics. This is the very distinguishing feature of Dharma-Ethics. The semantics of *dharma*, *ṛta* and *yajña* never remained rigidly tied to one domain. From the lexicographical analysis of the concept of *dharma*, first, the idea of static *dharma* which upholds everything is being derived. In this sense *dharma* is synonymous with *Brahman*, truth (*satya*). This sense of *dharma* has already been nicknamed as the transcendental sense of *dharma*. The manifestation of the absolute is called as cosmic manifestation. The movements of sun and moon, movements of day and night, cycles of seasons all these dynamicity are representative of the dynamic aspect of *ṛta*. *Ṛta* is also *dharma*, it may be conceived as the dynamic aspect of *dharma*. We thus arrive at the cosmic sense of *dharma* as its second sense of *dharma*. In the third sense, *dharma* stands for volitional activities of embodied agents. The expression *yajña* is also taken to imply sometimes *sakāma-karma* and also sometimes to mean *niṣkāma-karma*. These have already been discussed in one of the previous chapters. In an extended sense of the term *dharma* also stands for merit as resulting from the performance of *karmas* (actions) which ought to be performed. There are lots of deliberations among Indian philosophers about the ontological status of *dharma* or *adharma* as a result accruing from the performance of volitional activities. In Dharma-Ethics our primary concern is with *dharma* at the individual level covering free actions and their results thereof. An action which is *sakāma* is obligatory or duty because its performance results in merit (*dharma*) and not demerit (*adharma*) and an action, which is *niṣkāma*, is duty or obligatory because it produces result which does not bind the doer in the cycle of birth and death. In this sense in the domain of Dharma-Ethics we may accept *dharma* and *yajña* as equivalent expressions. Actions are not blind actions. These are goal-oriented actions. Neither the Vaidika Dharma-Ethics, nor the Buddhist Dharma-Ethics nor the Jaina Dharma-Ethics make any sense if these are segregated from their basic presuppositions regarding Karmavāda, rebirth and conscious agency. Since this volume concentrates on the Vaidika Dharma-Ethics, mainly as sources of moral knowledge, such sources have been discussed that are relevant in the context of the Vaidika Dharma-Ethics. The Buddhist Dharma-Ethics and the Jaina Dharma-Ethics are none the less weighty and valuable with their rich literary and philosophical resources.

In the Western ethics it is quite convincing to draw the boundary between action-oriented ethics and virtue ethics. Deontology or deontological ethics is an approach to ethics that focuses on the rightness or wrongness of actions themselves, as opposed to the rightness or wrongness of the consequences of those actions (Consequentialism) or to the character and habits of the actor (Virtue ethics). Thus both deontological ethics and consequentialism in the Western ethical tradition attach primary moral value to actions. The second sort of ethics that deals with the character or conduct of the agent is known as virtue ethics. In fact to look into Dharma-Ethics which aspect of it is related to action and which part of it is related to character is an absurd endeavour. In this connection a quotation from *Bṛhadāraṇyaka Upaniṣad* IV.4.5, stating the observation of the Sage Yājñavalkya, may be noticed:

> *. . . yathākārī yathācārī tathā bhavati sādhukārī sādhur bhavati, pāpakārī papo bhavati . . .*

> As a man acts, as he behaves, so he becomes; one who does good becomes good, one who commits sin, becomes evil.

In this context, it would not be out of place to draw our attention to the most discussed Western ethical legacy of teleological vs deontological distinction prevailing between one viewpoint that upholds moral duty or obligation stemming from what is good or desirable as an end or consequence and the other that insists upon the independence of moral rightness of an action from the good result or desirable consequence generated. Broadly speaking, each of these theories, irrespective of their multifarious interpretations and formulations, is against one another on the issue as to whether moral worthiness is inherent in actions themselves or it depends on certain external consequences. In the domain of Dharma-Ethics among its various proponents hardly any attempt has been observed to work out consciously by weighing pros and cons of actions to arrive at any full-fledged theories like what we come across in Western ethical discourse. If we take into consideration the vast expanse of Dharma-Ethics along with its intricate and inseparable objective, subjective, transcendental and semantical aspects, then we need to find out what will be our method for defining a theory to be teleological or deontological, in other words, by depending on which aspect of the theory the issue is to be resolved. Since we derive these terminologies from the Western ethics, we need to carefully find out how these nomenclatures have been used in the history of Western ethical theories and then try to apply these nomenclatures to Dharma-Ethics perspective. This is no doubt a very extensive work and it is not possible to enter into any such discussion off-hand. The other way may be to work out some family resemblance concept from teleological vs deontological debate and try their suitability to Dharma-Ethics. These are all interesting works to be achieved no doubt but these discussions are not within the purview of the present volume.

However, I would just like to draw attention to some features of Dharma-Ethics that have been covered in this volume wherefrom some hints may be obtained. In the present volume while discussing on "Human Agency and Motivation" in Chap. 5 and "On Decoding Moral Prescriptions" in Chap. 6 among many other things, our reference to the Nyāya and the Prābhākara perspectives about the nature of moral motivation and the nature of duty is difficult to overlook. Among the Indian philosophers, the Naiyāyika's standpoint often seems to come quite closer to that of the teleological theorists. The most obvious reason for drawing such analogy between the Naiyāyikas and the teleological theorists of morality derives from the Nyāya emphasis on cognition of desirable consequence, i.e. *iṣṭasādhanatā jñāna*, along with other conditioning factors, in explanation of the origin of motivation (*pravṛtti*). The Prābhākara Mīmāṁsakas, however, do not leave unnoticed in some cases, especially with regard to empirical actions some awareness about desirable consequences is not to be undone. But the Prābhākaras, as we have already discussed, did not pin down any cognition of desirable consequence or *iṣṭasādhanatājñāna* as the universally acceptable conditioning principle for psychological motivation. The Prābhākaras have pointed out that the agent is motivated to perform an action on the basis of cognition of something to be done as provided by his grasping himself as qualified by the capability to perform that action which is fit for being performed. Apart from this discussion, some traces of teleological–deontological distinction may be discovered in Chap. 6, while trying to unearth the meaning of *vidhi pratyaya*. We have already discussed viewpoints of different Indian philosophers and have found even the old Naiyāyikas and the Neo-Naiyāyikas are differing from one another, what to say about their difference from the Prābhākaras. The old Naiyāyikas accept cognition of desirable consequence along with other causal factors as determining semantics of *vidhi pratyaya* but the neo-Naiyāyikas with elaborate arguments try to expose short fallings of the Old Nyāya position and introduce their analysis of the meaning of *vidhi pratyaya* in terms of intention (*abhiprāya*). The Prābhākaras decoded moral prescriptions as revealing *niyoga, kārya* (duty) to the self of the acting agent. The position of the Bhāṭṭa Mīmāṁsakas is also very important in this connection. If we demarcate zones of Dharma ethical content, this is also one of the very important one where semantics of *vidhi pratyaya* is being discussed. Through these discussions on the semantics of moral language an attempt has been made to define the notion of duty, obligation by identifying its source of origin. But still one had to be cautious in trying to understand semantics of duty from the perspectives of Dharma-Ethics by the application of Western nomenclatures of teleological ethics and deontological ethics. Some interpreters may propose a deontological reading of Prābhākara ethics and suggest similarities between Prābhākara concept of *niyoga* and Kant's dictum of duty for duty's sake. How far such characterization of Prābhākara viewpoint as Kantian would be legitimate is also a matter of debate. There is also transcendental direction of Dharma-Ethics wherein the notion of end or consequence is important. According all *āstika* thinkers morality is not an end itself and while in Chap. 4 discussing on "The Fourfold Scheme of Puruṣārthas", it has been found that all of them clinch to *mokṣa* as the final goal. The position of the Bhāṭṭa Mīmāṁsakas has often seemed difficult to be fitted within the fold of such straitjacket. In the chapter on *Tattvāloka* of *Prakaraṇapañcikā* of the Prābhākara Mīmāṁsakas, there are discussions about whether *mokṣa* is to be considered as the final goal.[1] To describe the state of liberation, one may maintain that annihilation of all worldly sorrows is *mokṣa*. All living beings try to get release from sorrows hence in that sense as absence of all sorrows, *mokṣa* may be described. But if all sorrows are removed and according to very common understanding sorrows and happiness (*sukha*) are inseparably related, so with the annihilation of sorrows can any happiness be left? Or should we subscribe to the position that *mokṣa* (liberation) is not one of the *puruṣārtha*s (object for human seeking). The Prābhākaras maintain *mokṣastu sāṁsārikaduḥkhapaśamāt puruṣārtha iti puṣkalaṁ*. In other words, according to them *mokṣa* is a *puruṣārtha*, i.e. object of human seeking because it destroys all worldly sorrows. From this observation, it will be not correct to maintain that the Prābhākaras do not have any focus on *pariṇāma* (desirable consequence). It has also been discussed whether liberation is to be treated as gaining something not previously found or it is just getting what has been already with us. This is indeed one of the issues that has introduced

1 Indrani Sanyal, in *Dharmanīti O Śruti*, pp. 99-100.

divisions among Indian philosophers. We are to ponder over whether this aspect of Dharma-Ethics is to be taken into consideration in formulating the distinction between a deontological viewpoint and a teleological one. In this volume, I do not propose any straight-cut similarity or dissimilarity in our understanding of perspectives of Western ethics and Dharma-Ethics regarding the distinction between a teleological frame of morality or deontological one and their feasibility. I only try to draw attention to different aspects of psychology, metaphysics and semantics which may be taken into consideration in the case of Dharma-Ethics to find any positive suggestion in this connection.

The other quite current distinction between theory and practice is also a futile distinction to bring into the sphere of Dharma-Ethics. There is also another distinction which has become very popular after Western ethics, the distinction between applied ethics and theoretical ethics. Within the fold of Dharma-Ethics, these sorts of divisions are irrelevant divisions. Whatever be the theories, whatever be the strength of theories, varieties of theories, ultimately melt into practice (*sādhanā*). No ethics is able to sustain without any agent and Dharma-Ethics as ethics is also thriving upon its subject. Dharma-Ethics from the very start deals with the agent in its full-blooded sense. The practical aspect of Dharma-Ethics depends upon the psychology of the agent. Hence when we are talking about practical ethics in the context of Dharma-Ethics we are meaning thereby the practical aspect of the application of ethics. We may again refer to what Yājñavalkya further observes:

> *. . . kāmamaya eva ayaṁ puruṣa iti sa yathākāmo bhavati, tat kratur bhavati, yat kratur bhavati, tat karma kurute, yat karma kurute, tat abhisaṁpadyate* ।[2]

A person is of the nature of desires. As he desires, so becomes his will: As is his will, so is the action (*karma*) that he does; and whatever actions he performs, so he becomes.

---

2 *Bṛhadāraṇyaka Upaniṣad* IV.4.5.

What we find that not only relation has been shown between action and conduct, but something deeper has been highlighted by showing intimate relation between desire, will and actions of men as constituting his character.

Indian conception of man is altogether different from the Western conception of man. All men are in their inmost self an infinite being. All men in their inmost self are equal. But men in their state of embodiment are not equal, each has his type of nature and accordingly each man his own type of actions to be performed. This presupposition is very conspicuously present at the back of the Vaidika Dharma-Ethics. This rules out the possibility of admitting that all men perform actions by following one common and invariable code of action. According to the differences in human nature in the state of embodiment, according to the difference in position in the stage of life, actions which are to be performed by which individuals are determined by the demand of such actions. For the Western ethics man is a static being. But in Dharma-Ethics in general, a man has been perceived as a dynamic being. As an embodied being man is not stuck with a particular nature or particular potency for work or particular action which are worthy of his performance. Men are continually growing but the growth chart is not uniform; rather there are many obstacles and relapses. Dharma-Ethics does not advise to put all men under one uniform law as the law of their growth. In this connection a few lines from Sri Aurobindo is worthy of quoting:

> All ought not to be put under the same tables of the law; for that would be a senseless geometric rigidity that would spoil plastic truth of life.[3]
>
> No man can be "permanently bound in any system of ideas or frame of living".[4]

Dharma-Ethics lays down the grand architecture of growth and development to the highest level of truth (*dharma*), and it is for

[3] Sri Aurobindo, 1998, *The Foundations of Indian Culture*, p. 103.

[4] Ibid.

the moral agent in the guise of a builder to implement the architectural plan to its detail for elevation through the performance of *dharma* and avoidance of *adharma*. In the process of elevation, the individual does not disregard *abhyudaya* (well-being). Its goals are *abhyudaya, niḥśreyas* or in Sri Aurobindo's idiom the divine life. The ideology of divine life in a sense is a wonderful homogenization of *abhyudaya* (acclivity), *niḥśreyas* (liberation) and something else. What is the actual connotation of the expression *abhyudaya*? *Abhyudaya*, i.e. elevation that is spoken of as the consequence of *dharma*, has some ambiguities accordingly as it is taken to be inclusive of Brahma, or *brahmaprāpti* (attainment of *Brahman*) or as exclusive of *brahmaprāpti* indicating some advancement, but other than the attainment of Brahma, or *brahmaprāpti*. The interpretation of the meaning of *abhyudaya* in the latter sense finds support in the Upaniṣads also. In *Kaṭhopaniṣad*, the distinction between *śreya* and *preya*, i.e. the most excellent, the bliss of final emancipation and more desirable has been elaborated. On the basis of that analysis *brahmaprāpti* is comparable with *śreya* (bliss) of final emancipation and *abhyudaya* is comparable with *preya*, the more desirable.

The distinction between *niḥśreyas* and *abhyudaya* also suggests taking *abhyudaya* as synonymous with acclivity or flourishing rather than *brahmaprāpti*, i.e. realization of *Brahman*. Śaṅkarācārya does not believe in the synthesis between *jñāna* and *karma* and according to him *mokṣa* (liberation) can be attained by *jñāna* and not by *karma* for *mokṣa* according to him is *akārya* (not the product of any activity). According to him the performance of Śrauta *karma* founded on or conformed to the Vedas (Vedic rites) and Smārta *karma* and *karma* prescribed or sanctioned by Smr̥ti, i.e. traditional usage, enables people to attain *abhyudaya* (prosperity). According to Śaṅkarācārya goals of *karma* and *jñāna* are different, Śrauta *karma* enables one to attain the world of gods called *svargaloka*; but only *jñāna* enables him to realize eternal self. Sri Aurobindo, however, does not whole-heartedly support the viewpoint of Śaṅkarācārya and has shown that *Gītā* speaks of superiority of *karma-yoga* over renunciation of *karma* (*karma-saṁnyāsa*). The *Gītā* view is that to obtain liberation, purification of mind is essential, which is obtainable through *karma*. The Vaidika Dharma-Ethics with its commitment to spirituality as the ultimate highest – though the definition of spirituality may vary from system to system – projects man's nature as bifurcated into natural and psychological and the relation between the natural and psychological to the ultimate spiritual. To effect this transformation men are provided with *karma*-like tools by utilizing which the doer of action may free himself "from the mastery of senses".[5] The whole of Dharma-Ethics is the discipline (*sādhanā*) to inculcate the feeling

> that there is a soul within us which is other than the mutations of mind in its reception of the touches of outward things, a soul in its depths goes back to something self-existent, master of itself and unaffected by the eager runnings of our external nature.[6]

The other related imperative of the Vaidika Dharma-Ethics is equally undeniable:

> And since we have still to live and act in the world and our nature in works is to seek for the fruits of our works, we must change that nature and do works without attachment to their fruits, otherwise desire and all its results remain.[7]

[5] Sri Aurobindo, 1970, *Essays on the Gītā*, p. 244.

[6] Ibid.

[7] Ibid.

Bibliography

Ādidevānanda, Swāmi, 2007, *The Puruṣārtha Explanation of Indian Ethics.*

Avasthī, Bramhamitra (Hindi tr.), Śālikanātha's, *Vākyārthamātr̥kāvr̥tti* with *Dīpikā*, Delhi: Indu Publishers.

Aurobindo, Sri, 1970, *Essays on the Gita*, Pondicherry: Sri Aurobindo Ashram Trust.

———, 1997, *The Human Cycle: The Ideal of Human Unity, War and Self-Determination*, Pondicherry: Sri Aurobindo Ashram, 1962, 7th impression.

———, 1998, *The Foundations of Indian Culture*, Pondicherry: Sri Aurobindo Ashram, 4th edn.

———, 1999, *The Secret of the Veda*, Pondicherry: Sri Aurobindo Ashram Trust.

———, 2001, *The Life Divine*, Pondicherry: Sri Aurobindo Ashram.

———, 2004a, *The Upanishads* I, *Isha Upanishad*, Pondicherry: Sri Aurobindo Ashram Trust.

———, 2004b, *The Upanishads* II, *Kena and Other Upanishads*, Pondicherry: Sri Aurobindo Ashram Trust.

Bandyopadhyaya, Jayanatanuja, 2007, *Class and Religion in Ancient India*, Delhi: Anthem Press.

Bandyopadhyaya, Suresh Chandra, 1999, *Manusaṁhitā*, with Bengali translation, Kolkata, Ananda.

Basu, Rajsekhar (tr.), 1394 BS, *Mahābhārata*, Kolkata: M.C. Sarkar & Sons.

Bhatta, V.P., 2001, *Navya-Nyāya Theory of Verbal Cognition*, Delhi: Eastern Book Linkers.

Bhattacharya, Viswanath (Nyāyapañcānan), 1982, *Kārikāvali: Explanation of Nyāyamuktāvalī Samvalita Dinakarī by Rāmarudrī*, Ātmārama Nārāyaṇ, Varanasi: Krișnadas Academy.

Bhattacharya, Haridas Siddhantavagish, 1400 BS, *Mahābhāratam*, Kolkata: Visvabani Prakasani.

Bhattacharya, Pañcānan, 1377 BS, *Muktāvli Saṁgraha: Bhāṣāpariccheda, Nyāya-Sidhāntamuktāvali Ṭīkā Saha*, Calcutta: Sanskrit Pustak Bhandar.

Bhattacharya, Phaṇibhūṣaṇa, 1981, *Nyāyadarśana* (in Bengali), Pratham Khaṇḍa, Calcutta: Paścimbaṅga Rājya Pustaka Pariṣad.

———, 1982, *Nyāyadarśana* (in Bengali), Tr̥tīya Khaṇḍa, Kolkata: Paścimbaṅga Rājya Pustaka Pariṣad.

———, 1984, *Nyāyadarśana* (in Bengali), Dvitīya Khaṇḍa, Kolkata: Paścimbaṅga Rājya Pustaka Pariṣad.

———, 1988, *Nyāyadarśana* (in Bengali), Caturtha Khaṇḍa, Kolkata: Paścimbaṅga Rājya Pustaka Pariṣad.

———, 1989, *Nyāyadarśana* (in Bengali), Pañcama Khaṇḍa, Kolkata: Paścimbaṅga Rājya Pustaka Pariṣad.

Bhattacharya, Sailaja Kumar, 2000, *The Vaidika Ethics: An Analytical Approach*, Delhi: Allied Publishers in collaboration with Department of Philosophy, Jadavpur University, Calcutta.

Bhutanath, Saptatirtha (tr.), 1345 (Baṅgābada), *Mīmāṁsā Darśanam*, vol. 1, Calcutta: Basumiti Sahitya Mandir.

Brahma, Nalinikanta (ed.), 1986, *Śrīmadbhagavadgītā*, Calcutta: Nababharata Publishers.

Cargail, James, 1998, "All Consequentialism", in *Ethical Theory*, ed. James Rachels, New York: Oxford University Press.

Chakraborty, Dhyanes Narayana (ed. & tr.), 1997, *Vālmiki Rāmāyaṇa*, Calcutta: Newlight.

Chakraborty, Śibapada, 1996, *Nītitattva*, vol. 2, Calcutta: Paścimbaṅga Rājya Pustak Pariṣad.

Chattopadhyaya, D.P. and M.K. Gangopadhyaya, 1975, *Nyāya Philosophy*, part I: *Indian Studies: Past and Present*, Calcutta: Firma KLM.

Coward, H.G. and O.K. Kunjunninraja, 1990, "The Philosophy of the Grammarians", in *Encyclopaedia of Indian Philosophy*, vol. V, New Delhi: Motilal Banarsidass.

Dandekar, R.N., 1987, "The Theory of Puruṣārthas: A Re-Thinking", *Annals, BORI*, 1(XVIII).

Das, Maya, 1413, *Ṣaḍdarśane Puruṣārtha Vicāra*, Bolpur: Sri Lakshmi Press.

Davis (Jr.), Donald R., 2010, *The Spirit of Hindu Law*, New York: Cambridge University Press.

Dhammapada, tr. Mihir Gupta, Kolkata: Haraph Prakasani, 1996.

Dikṣit, Srimat Bhaṭṭoji, 1996, *Vaiyākaraṇa Siddhānta Kaumudī*, Hindi tr., 1996, Sridharananda Bildiyal, Delhi: Motilal Banarsidass.

Dutta, Manmath Nath, 1978, *The Dharamśāstra*, English tr. and Text, vol. 1, New Delhi: Cosmo Publications.

Dutt, Manmath Nath, 1979a, *Hārīta Saṁhitā in the Dharamśāstra*, vol. 1, New Delhi: Cosmo Publications.

———, 1979b, *Atri Saṁhitā in the Dharamśastrā* (Hindu Religious Codes), vol. II, New Delhi: Cosmo Publications.

———, 1979c, *Vyāsa Saṁhitā, Śaṅkha Saṁhita, Vasiṣṭha Saṁhitā in the Dharmaśāstra*, vol. III, New Delhi: Cosmo Publications.

Dutta, Hirendranath, n.d., *Manur Varnasramadharma*, Calcutta: Jadavpur University.

Flood, Gavin S. (ed.), 2003, *The Blackwell Companion to Hinduism*, New York: Blackwell Publishing.

Gambhirananda (Swami) (ed.), 1348 (Baṅgābda), *Upaniṣad Granthāvalī*, vol. 1, Calcutta: Udbodhana Karyalaya.

———, 1358 (Baṅgābda), *Bṛhadāraṇyaka Upaniṣad, Śvetāśvatara Upaniṣad, Taittīriya Upaniṣad*, in *Upaniṣad Granthāvalī*, 3 vols., Calcutta: Udbodhana Karyālaya.

Gambhirananda (Swami) (ed.), 1962, *Upaniṣad Granthavālī*, vols. 1-3, Calcutta: Udbodhan Karyalaya.

Ganeri, Jonardan (ed.), 2002, "Elusiveness and Ambiguity in Dharma-Ethics", in *Ethics and Epics*, New Delhi: Oxford University Press.

Harshananda (Swami), 1999, *The Purusasukta: An Exigesis*, 3rd edn, Bangalore: Ramkrishna Math.

Hill, Tomas E., 2006, "Kantian Normative Ethics", in *The Oxford Handbook of Ethical Theory*, ed. David Coop, New York: Oxford University Press.

Hiltebeitel, Alf, 2011, *Dharma: Its Early History in Law, Religion and Narrative*, New Delhi: Oxford University Press.

Jitatmananda (Swami), 2004, "Ṛta-Satyam: Modern Relevance", in *Ṛta: The Cosmic Order*, ed. Madhu Khanna, New Delhi: D.K. Printworld and Indira Gandhi National Centre for Arts.

Kane, P.V., 1930 (1st edn), *History of Dharmaśāstra*, vol. 1, Pune: Bhandarkar Oriental Research Institute.

———, 1941 (1st edn), *History of Dharmaśāstra*, vol. 2, parts 1 & 2, Pune: Bhandarkar Oriental Research Institute.

———, 1946 (1st edn), *History of Dharmaśāstra*, vol. 3, Pune: Bhandarkar Oriental Research Institute.

———, 1953 (1st edn), *History of Dharmaśāstra*, vol. 4, Pune: Bhandarkar Oriental Research Institute.

———, 1958 (1st edn), *History of Dharmaśāstra*, vol. 5, part 1, Pune: Bhandarkar Oriental Research Institute.

———, 1962 (1st edn), *History of Dharmaśāstra*, vol. 5, part 2, Pune: Bhandarkar Oriental Research Institute.

Kauṇḍa Bhaṭṭa, 1988, a *Vaiyākaraṇābhūṣaṇasāra*, Savitri – Hindi tr. Ādyāprasad Miśra, Varanasi: Sampurnananda Sanskrit University.

Krishnan, Y., 1992, "The Meaning of the Puruṣārthas in the Mahābhārata", in *Moral Dilemmas in the Mahābhārata*, ed. Bimal Krishna Motilal, Shimla: IIAS, in association with Motilal Banarsidass, Delhi.

———, 1997, *The Doctrine of Karma*, Delhi: Motilal Banarsidass.

Laugākṣi Bhāskara, 1977, *Arthasaṁgraha*, "Arthaloka" Sanskrit Ṭīkā by Pattabhiram Shasri, Hindi Explanation by Bācaspati Upādhyāy, Bārāṇāsī: Chaukhambā Oriyanṭaliyā.

Madhusudan Saraswati (Sri), 1962, *Śrīmadbhagavadgītāa* (Ṭīkā), Varanasi: Chowkhamba Sanskrit Series.

———, 1986, *Śrīmad Bhagavadgītā* (Ṭīkā), tr. with explanation, Bhutanath Saptatirtha, Calcutta: Nababharata Publishers.

Maitra, Sushil Kumar, 1963, *The Ethics of the Hindus*, Calcutta: University of Calcutta.

Malvania, Dalsukh and Jayendra Soni, 2007, *Encyclopedia of Indian Philosophies*, vol. X: *Jain Philosophy*, part I, Delhi: Motilal Banarsidass.

Matilal, Bimal K., 1990, *The Word and the World*, Delhi: Oxford University Press.

———, 1992, "Moral Dilemmas: Insights from Indian Epics", in *Moral Dilemmas in the Mahābhārata*, ed. Bimal K. Matilal, Shimla: IIAS, in association with Motilal Banarsidass, Delhi (first repr.).

———, 2002, "Elusiveness and Ambiguity in Dharma-Ethics", in *Ethics and Epics*, ed. J. Ganeri, New Delhi: Oxford University Press.

Mishra, (Acharya) Mandan, 1982, *Vidhiviveka*, with *Nyāyakaṇikā Ṭīkāsahit*, by Vacaspati Misra, tr. Sri Srimohan Bhattacharya, Calcutta: Sanskrit College.

Misra, R.S., 2002, *Philosophical Foundations of Hinduism*, New Delhi: Munshiram Manoharlal.

Miśra, Śālikanātha, 2004, *Prakaraṇapañcikā*, English tr. K.T. Pandurangi, New Delhi: Indian Council of Philosophical Research.

Misra, Vidya Niwas, 2004, "Ṛta in Veda", in *Ṛta: The Cosmic Order*, ed. Madhu Khanna, New Delhi: D.K. Printworld and Indira Gandhi National Centre for Arts.

Mohanty J.N., 2000, "Moral Philosophy", in *Classical Indian Philosophy*, New Delhi: Oxford University Press.

———, 2001, "Indian Thought: Between Tradition and Modernity", in *Explorations in Philosophy: Essays by J.N. Mohanty*, vol. 1, ed. Bina Gupta, New Delhi: Oxford University Press.

Monier-Williams, Monier, 1986, *A Sanskrit-English Dictionary*, Delhi: Motilal Banarsidass.

Olivelle, Patrick (ed.), 2009, *Dharma: Studies in Its Semantic, Cultural and Religious History*, Delhi: Motilal Banarsidass (enlarged Indian edn).

Pandey, R.C., 1963, *The Problem of Meaning in Indian Philosophy*, New Delhi: Motilal Banarsidass.

Pandurangi, K.T. (ed.), 2006, *Purvamimamsa from an Interdisciplinary Point of View*, PHISPC, Centre for Studies in Civilizations, vol. II, part 6, Delhi: Motilal Banarsidass.

Patañjali, 1938, *Pātañjala Yogadarśana*, Hariharananda Aranya, Calcutta: University of Calcutta.

Patra, Aditi, 2009, "Ayurveda śāstre svīkṛta karmavāda o kichu samasyā", in *Dharmaniti O Sruti*, ed. Indrani Sanyal and Ratna Datta Sharma, Kolkata: Mahabodhi Book Agency.

Potter, Karl H., 1996, *Encyclopedia of Indian Philosophies*, vol. VII: *Abhidharma Buddhism to 150 AD*, Delhi: Motilal Banarsidass.

Pramath Nath, Tarkabhusan and Laksana Sastri Dravid, 1843 (Śakābada), *Vedantadarsanam*, Kolkata: Kalika Press.

Praśastapada, 1969, *Praśastapādabhāṣyam*, Varanasi: Sampurnanand Sanskrit University.

Prasad, Rajendra, 1981, "Theory of Puruṣārthas: Revaluation and Reconstruction", *Journal of Indian Philosophy*, 9(1).

———,1989, *Karma, Causation and Retributive Morality*, New Delhi: ICPR in association with Munshiram Manoharlal.

———, 2008a, "Theorizing in Ethics: The Indian Way", in *A Conceptual–Analytic Study of Classical Indian Philosophy of Morals*, vol. XII, part I, PHISPC, New Delhi: Centre for Studies in Civilizations and Concept Publishing Co.

———, 2008b, *A Conceptual–Analytic Study of Classical Indian Philosophy of Morals*, vol. XII, part I, PHISPC, New Delhi: Concept Publishing Co.

Radhakrishnan, S., 1913, *Indian Philosophy*, vols. I & II, London: George Allen and Unwin.

———, 2005, *The Bhagavadgita*, New Delhi: HarperCollins.

Ranganathan, Shyam, 2007, *Ethics and the History of Indian Philosophy*, Delhi: Motilal Banarsidass.

Ranganathanada, Swami (ed.), 2005, *The Message of the Bṛhadāraṇyaka Upaniṣad*, Kolkata: Advaita Ashrama.

Ravindra, Ravi, 2004, "Ṛta, Yajña and Dharma", in *Ṛta: The Cosmic Order*, ed. Madhu Khanna, New Delhi: D.K. Printworld and Indira Gandhi National Centre for Arts.

Rodrigues, Valerian (ed.), 2007, *The Essential Writings of B.R. Ambedkar*, New Delhi: Oxford University Press.

Roy, Anilbaran, 2000, *Srimadbhagavatgita*, Kolkata: Sarvasevak Sangha.

Sanyal, Indrani, 1998, "Vidhir Artha Viṣaye Anunaitika Paryālocanā" in *Bhāratīya Dharmanīti*, ed. Amita Chatterjee, Calcutta: Allied Publishers and Jadavpur University.

———, 2002, "The Just War or the Dharmayuddha", in *Ethics: An Anthology*, ed. Madhumita Chattopadhyay and Tirthanath Bandyopadhyay, Kolkata: Jadavpur University and Allied Publishers.

———, 2003, "The Nature of Human Motivation", in *On Mind and Consciousness*, ed. Chhanda Chakraborti, Manas K. Mandal and Rimi B. Chatterjee, Shimla: IIAS and Department of Humanities and Social Sciences, IIT, Kharagpur.

———, 2009, "Prabhakarasammataniyogerdharana", in *Dharmaniti O Sruti*, ed. Indrani Sanyal and Ratna Datta Sharma, Kolkata: Mahabodhi Book Agency and Jadavpur University.

———, 2010, "Varṇa and Jāti", in *Ethics and Culture: Some Indian Reflections*, ed. Indrani Sanyal and Sashinungala, Delhi: Decent Books.

———, 2015, "Dārasanik Sri Aurobindo O tār Pūrṇādvaitavāda", in *Darsanviksa, Jadavpur Journal of Philosophy* (in Bengali), 24(II).

Sanyal, Indrani and Ratna Datta Sharma (eds.), 2009, *Dharmaniti O Sruti*, Kolkata: Mohabodhi Book Agency and Jadavpur University.

Saraswati, Madhusūdan, 1986, *Śrimadbhagavad Gītā*, tr. Bhūtanātha Saptatirtha, Kolkata: Nababharat Publishers.

Sarma, R.N., 1988, *Mīmāṁsā Theory of Meaning* (Based on the Vākyārthamātṛkā), Delhi: Sri Sadguru Publications.

Sarma, Rajendranath, 1990, *Verbal Knowledge in Prābhākara Mīmāṁsā*, Delhi: Sri Sadguru Publications.

Sastri, Dakshinaranjana, 1982, *Cārvāka Darśana*, Kolkata: Pascima Banga Rajya Pustaka Pariṣad.

Sinha, Kaliprasanna (tr.), 2001, *Mahābhārata*, vols. 1 & 2, Kolkata: Tulikalam.

Tarkabagisa, Phanibhusana, 1988, *Nyāya Darśana*, vols. 1-5, Calcutta: Paścima Baṅga Rājya Pustaka Pariṣad.

Tarkavagisa, Phanibhusana (ed.), 1984, *Nyayasutra, Nyayadarsana*, vol. 2, Kolkata: West Bengal Book Board.

Thakur, Anantalal (ed.), 1997a, *Gautamiya Nyāyadarśana with Bhāṣya of Vātsyāyana*, vol. I, New Delhi: Indian Council of Philosophical Research.

——— (ed.), 1997b, *Nyāyabhāṣyavārttika of Bhardvāja Uddyotakara*, vol. II, New Delhi: Indian Council of Philosophical Research.

———, 1996, *Nyāyavārttikatātparyaṭīkā of Vācaspati Miśrā*, vol. III, New Delhi: Indian Council of Philosophical Research.

———, 1996, *Nyāyavārttikatātparyapariśuddhi of Udayanācārya*, vol. IV, New Delhi: Indian Council of Philosophical Research.

Thapar, Romila, 2003, *Cultural Pasts*, New Delhi: Oxford University Press.

Udayanācārya, 1957, *Nyāyakusumāñjali: Bodhani, Prakāśa, Prakāśikā, Makaranda Vyākhyācatuṣṭyapeta*, ed. Nyāyācārya Padmaprasadapādhya o Nyāyācārya Dhundhirajśāstrī, Chaukhamba Sanskrit Serise.

———, 1962, *Nyāyakusumāñjali*, Sanskrit explanation by Haridas Bhattacharya, Kusumañjaliparimal Hindi explanation by Ācārya Viśveśwar Sidhānta Śiromaṇi, Varanasi: Chaukhamba Vidya Bhavan.

———, 1995, *Nyāyakusumājali (Gogyapadyātmaka)*, tr. Sri Sri Srimohan Bhattacharya, Calcutta: Paścim Baṅga Rājya Pustak Pariṣad.

Umāsvati, 2000, *Tattvārthasūtra*, Ahmedabad: L.D. Institute of Indology.

Umāsvāti/Umāswami, 1994, *Tattvārthasūtra*, tr. Nathmal Tatia, New Delhi: Motilal Banarsidass.

Vedavyasa, Śrīkr̥ṣṇadvaipāyana, *Mahabharatam*, Bengali tr. Haridas Siddhantavagisa, Calcutta: Visvabani Prakasani.

Vidyāraṇya, 1984, *Bauddhadarśana O Dharma*, Kolkata: Paścima Banga Rajya Pustaka Paṣad.

Vidyasagar, Ganga Charan Vedanta (tr.), 1313, *Kāmasūtra of Vātsyāyana*, Kolkata: Navapatra Prakasana.

Visvarupananda (Swami), 1988, *Vedāntadarśanam*, vol. I, tr. and Elucidation, ed. Cidghananda Puri and Ananda Jha, Calcutta: Udbodhan Karyalaya.

Wilson, H.H., 1961, *The Vishnu Purana: A System of Hindu Mythology and Tradition*, Calcutta: Punthi Pustak.

Witzel, Michael, 2003, "Vedas and Upanisads", in *The Blackwell Companion to Hinduism*, ed. Gavin Flood, Malden, MA: Blackwell.

Index